Learning to Fail

During a decade of relative prosperity from the mid-1990s onward, governments across the developed world failed to crack one major issue – youth unemployment. Even when economic growth was strong, one young person in 10 in the United Kingdom was neither working nor learning. As the boom ended, the number of young people dropping out after leaving school – already acknowledged to be too high – began to rise at an alarming rate. As governments face up to the prospect of a new generation on the dole, this book examines the root causes of the problem.

By holding a light to the lives and attitudes of eight young people, their families, their teachers and their potential employers, this book will challenge much of what has been said about educational success and failure in the past 20 years. For two decades, policymakers largely assumed schools were the key to ensuring young people got the best possible start in life. Yet for many children the path to failure began well before their first day at school.

Through the stories of these young people, this book reveals how marginalised young people are let down on every step of their journey. Growing up in areas where aspiration has died or barely ever existed, with parents who struggle to guide them on life in the twenty-first century, they are let down by schools where teachers underestimate them, by colleges and careers advisers who mislead them and by an employment market which has forgotten how to care or to nurture. *Learning to Fail* goes behind the headlines about anti-social behaviour, drugs and teenage pregnancy to paint a picture of real lives and how they are affected by outside forces. It gives a voice to ordinary parents and youngsters so they can speak for themselves about what Britain needs to do to turn its teenage failures into a success story.

Fran Abrams is an investigative journalist with 20 years' experience of observing and reporting on education in the United Kingdom. She works regularly for the UK broadsheet newspapers and for the BBC, and lives in Suffolk.

Learning to Fail

How society lets young people down

Fran Abrams

Routledge
Taylor & Francis Group

LONDON AND NEW YORK

First published 2010
by Routledge
2 Park Square, Milton Park, Abingdon, Oxon OX14 4RN

Simultaneously published in the USA and Canada
by Routledge
270 Madison Avenue, New York, NY 10016

Routledge is an imprint of the Taylor & Francis Group, an informa business

Typeset in Garamond
by Pindar NZ, Auckland, New Zealand
Printed and bound in Great Britain
by TJ International Ltd, Padstow, Cornwall

British Library Cataloguing in Publication Data
A catalogue record for this book is available from the British Library

Library of Congress Cataloging-in-Publication Data
Abrams, Fran, 1963-
Learning to fail : how society lets young people down / Fran Abrams.
    p. cm.
    Includes bibliographical references.
    1. Youth with social disabilities—Education—Great Britain—Case
studies. 2. School failure—Great Britain—Case studies. 3. Youth—
Employment—Great Britain—Case studies. 4. Youth—Great
Britain—Social conditions—Case studies. I. Title.
    LC4096.G7A37 2010
    373.1826'94—dc22   2009017720

ISBN 10: 0-415-48395-6 (hbk)
ISBN 10: 0-415-48396-4 (pbk)
ISBN 10: 0-203-86482-4 (ebk)

ISBN 13: 978-0-415-48395-7 (hbk)
ISBN 13: 978-0-415-48396-4 (pbk)
ISBN 13: 978-0-203-86482-1 (ebk)

Contents

Acknowledgements

The writing of this book was made possible by the generous award of a Journalist Fellowship from the Joseph Rowntree Foundation. I would particularly like to thank Julia Unwin, Julia Lewis, Janet McCulloch and Michelle Ong at the Foundation for their support and help during my research.

I am also grateful to the huge numbers of other people who agreed to help, giving up time to talk, to show me around their localities or workplaces. Because there were so many, I have decided to restrict my thanks to those who do not appear in the text – though many of those, too, were extremely generous with their resources.

In particular I received help and guidance from Professor John Bynner at the Institute of Education in London and Professor Howard Williamson at the University of Glamorgan – for which, many thanks.

I would also like to thank Tif Loehnis and all at Janklow and Nesbit for their ongoing support, and Philip Mudd at Routledge for agreeing to take the project on as publisher.

Inevitably I will have missed some people out – for which, apologies – but I would also like to thank the following: Doreen Gwilliam and her colleagues at Voluntary Action Barnsley; Jason Lever and Rebecca Palmer at the London Mayor's office; Richard Williams, Paul Fletcher, Peter Gibson and numerous other staff at Rathbone who helped with introductions to young people and with their expertise; Jools Townsend and Emma Greenwood at East Potential in Stratford; Anne Pinney and Jane Evans at Barnardo's; Angela Lomax at Nord Anglia Lifetime Development in Barnsley; Ruth Higgins; Lorraine Headen at Athersley Cares; Andrea Smith and all at Wombwell Community Partnership; Nick Whittingham; Ken Wilson at Tate and Lyle; Samantha Dunbar at the Greater Manchester Chamber of Commerce; Carl Emery at Manchester College; and Dr Tony Sewell at Generating Genius.

This book would never have been written without the sharp eyes of Samantha Fenwick, who spotted the JRF's advertisement about fellowships, or the support of my partner, Phil Solomon, and friends Isobel Howie and Bob Delbridge. But the most heartfelt thanks of all must go to my friend Angie Ruane, who read and gave detailed comments on every draft and proposal from start to finish, as well as offering enormous amounts of moral support and encouragement – as always, I am unable to express the full extent of my gratitude.

Preface

Educational success tends to be measured in round numbers: six in 10 young people getting five good GCSEs; 50 per cent slated to go to university; eight out of ten staying on at 16.

But those big figures leave too many behind: the four in ten who fail to leap that all-important GCSE target; the half who will never go to university, the quarter who embark on college courses but then drop out.

The high-flyers and the trouble-makers will always grab attention: in August the newspapers are full of tearful, joyful, exam candidates with strings of A's, while the transgressions of the knife-wielders and the drug-takers never cease to fascinate. But what of the rest? What of those who just fail quietly, without fuss?

In South Yorkshire recently I met a kindly, motherly college tutor who had taken just such a group of young people under her wing: "You're what I term 'Wallpaper Kids'," she told them. "You turn up every day of the year, you try hard, but you don't get much out of it."

At the time I thought this rather a generous description – some of them had wavered and drifted, seemingly unready to grasp any one of a series of opportunities that had been offered. But later it struck me as apposite: they were always with us, these exam-shy, drift-along kids. Thirty years ago, they would have been "set on" at their parents' workplaces as drivers' mates, brickies' labourers or factory floor assistants. Now they were left rootless in a changed world, pushed aside or ignored – so long as they weren't actually causing trouble. At school they sat in the library doing fill-in courses for those not taking GCSEs, or they were sent out to do hairdressing or riding for the disabled while their classmates took maths. Often at home no-one really understood the modern economy's voracious demand for qualifications, and conversations about the future tended to centre on parents' experiences in a world that was now long gone. Sensible, informed advice on jobs, opportunities or training was bafflingly hard to find. So every year a whole raft were pushed from school into easy-to-fill college courses: public services, performing arts, media studies – which many would fail to complete and from which most of the rest would emerge unfit for any job related to what they had learned.

Even in the midst of prosperity, when labour was in short supply, employers were rejecting Britain's youth and turning to Eastern Europe for staff. Left behind, these teenagers were labelled failures, drop-outs or misfits in an increasingly target-driven world. To put a round number on it, about one in 10 remained lost to the education system and to the labour market. Many, many more ended up drifting from dole queue to unskilled job and back again.

So in these times of economic crisis, with so many older, more experienced people looking for work, it might seem perverse to make a plea for these legions of the footloose and the uninitiated. Yet all too easily they could emerge, blinking, into the light of the next new economic dawn to find they have missed their chances – that younger, cheaper school leavers are ahead of them in the queue for jobs and training. All too easily, this already half-invisible multitude could become a lost generation – the workless, the long-term disabled, the single-parent benefit recipients of the future. In their turn, they will be the bearers of offspring who will go on to be labelled delinquent, lazy, overweight, undereducated.

Their numbers were growing fast as this book went to press, and new initiatives were being announced to help them, with promises of jobs or training places for all long-term unemployed under the age of 25. Yet such guarantees had been made before for teenagers, to little avail. Often hard to find and sometimes hard to help, they are easily overlooked and pushed aside. Yet politicians and policymakers will do so now at their peril.

The young people (*some names have been changed*)

Elvige: Came to England from Togo aged 10, missed a year of school through homelessness. Aged 18, living independently in East London.

Yasmin: Aged 17, left school in East London in 2007. Hoped to go to college to do business studies but missed enrolment because of a family visit to Bangladesh.

Will: Aged 20, moved from Ipswich to East London as a teenager. Took performing arts at college but dropped out; recently became a father.

Claire: Aged 16, living with her father and grandparents in Wombwell, Barnsley. Unsure what to do after leaving school.

Ashley: Aged 16, living with parents in Wombwell, Barnsley. Hoping to study childcare at college.

Tom: Aged 17, living with parents in Kendray, Barnsley. Left school in 2007 with good GCSEs but unable to find a placement as an apprentice plumber.

Ricky: Aged 17, dropped out of school in north Manchester before GCSEs. Taking an 'Entry to Employment' course with the Rathbone charity.

Rachel: Dropped out of school aged 15. Aged 18, with two children who are being looked after by their father and his family.

FACT BOX

About one in 10 young people in the UK aged between 16 and 24 are neither working or in education or training.

Four out of 10 teenagers fail to get five or more good GCSEs at age 16.

A quarter of all teenagers embarking on full-time courses in further education colleges in England drop out.

A young person leaving school and embarking on an apprenticeship in the retail trade in England has a 50/50 chance of qualifying.

The number of unemployed 18–24 year-olds in Great Britain rose by 70 per cent between February 2008 and February 2009.

Introduction

On a hot summer day just before the storm clouds burst over the economies of the Western world, I was talking to a group of teenage outreach workers at the London Mayor's office. What motivated them, I wanted to know? I suppose in a way I was looking for some sort of spark of optimism in a picture that seemed unremittingly gloomy. No-one ever seemed to have anything good or even hopeful to say about the young. At school they disrupted their lessons, had no focus, passed their exams only by dint of the fact that standards were falling. On the streets they drank, smoked too much and got embroiled in violence. When they were forced to look for a job they lacked direction, had no idea how to dress or behave and in any case rarely turned up because they couldn't get out of bed. Even if they were not lazy, feckless, drunk or violent, they were probably depressed, overweight and unfit: the United Nations' children's body UNICEF had reported young people in developed countries, particularly Britain and the US, were too often unhealthy and unhappy.

So Elvige, 18 and full of life, was a tonic. As she spoke she leaned forward in her chair, her thoughts keeping intermittent pace with her words. She just felt as if she had something in her, some personal strength that pulled her on, she said. "When you work and earn your own money, doesn't that make you feel like you've got more control of your own life? If you have the motivation to expand your horizons, it isn't like there are – what's the word? – shackles – holding you down." She paused, thinking: "If you stretch out your horizons, you go looking in different places."

Later I would learn Elvige had other role models to strengthen the inner light that seemed to burn in her. Yet while she and her young colleagues at the mayor's office had plenty to say about their inspirations – a mother who worked three jobs to give her children a better chance, friends who believed they would succeed, a youth worker who never switched off her mobile phone – in one way they were perplexing. If some other young people lacked the optimism, the sense of purpose this group had, could it be manufactured in some way, bottled up and prescribed? It was hard to see how.

By this time I was several months into an exploration, a journey into the darker places frequented by some of the nation's youth on which I hoped to find workable solutions to some of the problems they faced. If they drifted, why did that happen? If they were unhappy, what ailed them? How could a life of crime or inebriation seem more attractive than the other options open to them? Most of all, if employers had rejected them as unfit for purpose when there was a shortage of labour, what hope was there for them now?

Over the previous decade the position of young people between the ages of about 15 and 25 had posed something of a paradox. Britain's economy, like those of many countries in the developed world, had been strong. There had been full adult employment, by and large, leading to much talk of skills short-ages and how the needs of burgeoning industries could be met in the future. And yet at the same time there was also talk of how too many of the young were languishing, idle, indolent and irresponsible, outside the labour market.

The last time youth unemployment had been a major topic for discussion was a generation earlier, in the 1980s. Back then, there were millions on the dole and the industries which traditionally mopped up school leavers in their thousands were not hiring. Those that did take on apprentices increasingly laid them off again before they were qualified in trades. This was no longer the case. More often, employers could be heard bemoaning the fact that the young people they tried to recruit were simply not up to the job. So what had changed? If the parents and grandparents of today's teenagers were able to leave school and survive in the workplace, why could their offspring not do the same? They sprang, after all, from the same stock, with the same cultures, the same genes. From where, then, had their sickness sprung?

Over the previous decade the issue had been increasingly hotly debated but for the most part just one solution had been posited: education. Or, as the former Prime Minister Tony Blair had put it: "Education, Education, Education". Before he had even come to power, he had nailed his political colours to the mast of school reform as a sort of panacea for all society's ills. When I began my research the results of that reform could clearly be seen. Numbers of exam passes had risen, university entrance had grown, a major school building programme had been embarked upon. Yet there remained this apparently insoluble issue, which manifested itself annually in the official statistics on what happened to school leavers. Despite endless speeches, reforms, debates, initiatives and programmes about the importance of education, almost a quarter of those aged 17 or 18 were neither in education nor in training, a proportion that continued to rise while the economy boomed. Worse, that nagging figure of one in 10 – again, a higher proportion than a decade earlier – out of work as well. The official term was "NEET" – "Not in Education, Employment, or Training". The unofficial one was "drop-outs", or worse.

I had begun to wonder whether all this activity had somehow pointed in the wrong direction, and what Elvige said seemed to underline my unease: neither she nor her colleagues talked about how they were driven on by school, how they looked up to their teachers, though they could easily have done so. While there had been a great deal of talk about reforming education, there had been less about what actually inspired young people to learn and to succeed. The focus, instead, had been on goals and standards: more children in nursery schools, smaller classes, higher levels of attainment, particularly in English and maths. And there were good reasons for all that. Schools were places in which the state had a clear and legitimate locus, where easily definable goals could be set and progress towards them measured. But was this, I wondered, getting to the root of the problem? Could this supreme effort to push up standards for the average child simply have left those at the bottom of the heap more marginalised than ever?

That might be one possible explanation for this apparent malaise among the young, but it could not be the only one. There was plenty of evidence that schools could make a difference to young people's lives. Yet there was also evidence the extent of that difference was strictly limited. In 2007 academics from the London School of Economics reported secondary schools could add about 14 per cent to the statistical explanation of low achievement by pupils – that is, schools accounted for about one-seventh of the causes of failure. For the rest, it was necessary to look elsewhere. It seemed so much time had been spent debating how schools could shape young people's lives that the other 86 per cent of the picture had somehow been forgotten. The truth was that the biggest factor in determining whether children would succeed or fail at school, by some margin, was their family background. In particular, their life chances were shaped largely by whether their families were poor or whether they were well off. Gender also made a difference, with girls more likely to succeed at school than boys. White British children of either gender were more likely to persist in low achievement than those from other ethnic groups – if they started out at the bottom of the class, they were likely to stay there. So poor white boys made up the bulk of those who left school empty handed.

While there was a wealth of academic research which pointed to trends and statistical evidence, there were fewer places to which policymakers and concerned citizens could go in order to put a human face to the problem of educational failure. My aim was to provide such a human face for an often marginalised and vilified stratum of society. To that end I decided to seek out a group of young people who, with their families, would be prepared to open up their lives to me and who would let me follow their progress over the course of a year.

My focus was on the transition from school into the labour market – why did so many young people seem to slip through the net at this stage? So I looked for young people between the ages of 15 and 24 who either had dropped out or had been deemed at risk of doing so. I sought them in three locations. Young people in Barnsley, I reasoned, would be able to tell me how, in the second or even third generation since the pits closed, they were coping with life in a changed labour market. In Manchester I could examine the experience of growing up in a large and dynamic city where a myriad of different choices and opportunities seemed to be available to the young. In the East End of London, with its constantly shifting and changing population, I would meet teenagers whose parents had "got on their bikes", to borrow Norman Tebbit's phrase, to flee war or poverty or simply to try to build a better life for their children.

Eventually, after one or two false starts and abrupt endings, I found eight families, two in Manchester, three in Barnsley and three in London. Three teenagers – Rachel and Ricky in Manchester and Yasmin in London – I contacted through the Rathbone charity, which ran programmes for young people aged 16–18 who were disengaged from education and work. Two, Claire and Ashley, I met at a group for final-year pupils from Wombwell, near Barnsley, who were thought to be at risk of dropping out. A worker at that group then put me in touch with Tom, who had left school the previous summer hoping to be a plumber but who had not been able to find a job or a college place. At Focus E15, an accommodation centre for young people in East London, I met Will. And finally through the Mayor's office I met Elvige, who had not dropped out but who had faced real difficulties with such determination and insight that I could not resist including her.

The year that followed was one of great change and turbulence, starting as it did in a time of economic prosperity and ending in a recession. As I reached the end of my research the youth unemployment rate had risen by more than 70 per cent, year-on-year, and even the best-qualified university graduates were struggling to find work. Yet it seemed more important than ever that those young people who faltered when times were good should not now be lost in the fog of mass unemployment. Past evidence showed those with good qualifications would find it easier, as the economy recovered, to re-establish themselves. It would be all too easy for the most vulnerable to slip into an economic ravine from which they might never escape.

I wanted to know what tools the young people I met had at their disposal. Who were their families, their friends, their teachers? What schools and colleges did they attend, and who made a difference to their lives? Who helped them to make decisions, and how did the people they knew and the places they lived in shape their futures? If they struggled to make a smooth transition from school to work, what were the factors that caused them to falter? Were their barriers linked to things that happened at home – marital breakdown, housing problems, a general belief that they didn't have much going for them? Or did they set out full of hope, only to find themselves thwarted by external factors such as a lack of guidance, jobs or college places in the areas where they lived?

My aim, then, was to lay bare some of the root causes of failure, those which had persisted through the good times and into the bad. What issues did the less successful young people face as they grew up? Some of the key factors – poverty, gender, race – were clear, but how did those factors interact within an individual's life story to shape his or her chances? Did some children just start life with the word "failure" virtually stamped on their foreheads? Were there points at which they reached forks in their metaphorical roads, and at which the right guidance could be vital? What sort of intervention could lead them into more fulfilled and prosperous adult lives? It seemed to me, starting out, that it would be all too easy to apportion blame and nigh-on impossible to come up with a coherent solution. My aim, therefore, was merely to get under the skin of the problem a little, in the hope that a greater understanding would help those who were in a position to make a difference.

THE NUMBERS GAME

How many school leavers ended up with no full-time job, college or training place? There were many ways of adding up the numbers, but one thing was certain: there were far more than the official statistics suggested.

According to the figures, a little more than six per cent of 16 year-olds who left school in England in June 2007 were "not settled" five months later. That would put the number who remained unemployed at just under 40,000, which would be a cause for concern. But the real total could be not far short of twice that – at one in seven of the population.

First, the official statistics ignored those young people who had gone "missing" from school – the drop-outs, those excluded and not placed elsewhere, those who never even went to school at all. A look at the official population statistics suggested about 20,000 of the 670,000 who reached school leaving age in 2007 in England were not actually in school at all.

Then there were those who were in school, but who were missed by the annual Connexions survey on whether school leavers found jobs or college places. Its sample should have been exactly the same size as the school population – 650,000. But it wasn't. It was based on an even smaller number – around 635,000, leaving a total of 35,000 now unaccounted for. Because the Connexions workers were unable to trace a

Table 1 16 year-old school leavers in England – 2007

670,000 reached school leaving age in the year to August 2007
20,000 dropped out or went missing before reaching 16
40,000 were still seeking a placement in November
15,000 were not included in official surveys
15,000 were untraceable

Source: *ONS, Connexions*

further 15,000 of the pupils they were looking for, those too were left off the official figures – even though it was likely many of them would have been drop-outs. That meant that in addition to the 40,000 officially disengaged, a further 50,000 were unaccounted for.

A small part of the discrepancy might have been because some independently educated students were missed by the annual Connexions survey, but that still left a total figure nearer 12 per cent than the 6 per cent to which the government admitted.

Even the sample on which Connexions was supposed to base its figures was extremely narrow – just those who reached school leaving age in a given year. If you were 19 and unemployed you didn't count, by this measure. These statistics only included those aged 16–18. But figures obtained by the Conservatives via parliamentary questions showed far more people dropped out between the ages of 18 and 21 than between the ages of 16 and 18. The total unemployed aged 16–24 was 750,000 in the spring of 2008, an increase of 20 per cent since 2003. During those five years, major efforts had been made to reduce the numbers of school leavers who failed to find their niche. The figures suggested many of the young people who went to college at 16 merely dropped out later.

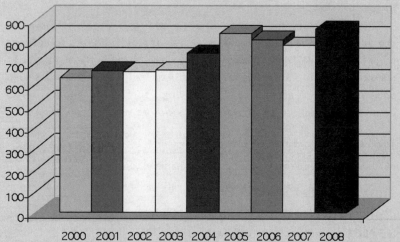

Figure 1 Growing rates of disengagement among the young.

Source: Parliamentary answer to David Willetts, April 2009.

There was one more worrying trend, too. While ministers talked vigorously of reducing numbers on incapacity benefits, their officials were actually signing off large numbers of young people as unfit for work. Of course if they were included in the disability statistics, they would not be in the unemployment statistics. While the total number of adults claiming Incapacity Benefit remained stable between 1995 and 2005 at around two and a half million, the number aged 18–24 rose by 50 per cent, from around 100,000 to 150,000.

In the last quarter of 2008, as recession took hold, the numbers of young people on unemployment benefits began to rise, too. The number of 18–24 year-olds claiming job-seekers' benefits rose 45 per cent from the same period the previous year, from 200,000 to 290,000.

The real numbers of 16–24 year-olds outside the labour market and not engaged in any form of education or training were far higher than the government wanted to admit, and they were rising fast.

YASMIN

Yasmin didn't like school dinners, she told me the first time we met, so she used to climb out over the gates to get to the Kentucky Fried Chicken. I could almost see her doing it, skinny and pretty in dark trousers and with thick liner under her eyes, cheerfully waving to the teachers as she hoiked her leg over the metal bars at the top.

"You just wanted to get out of school, you felt trapped in there," she said. "It was against the rules to go out. I would be telling the teachers: 'I'm coming back – don't worry!'"

Later, when I'd met Yasmin a few times – and failed to meet her a few times because she'd forgotten I was coming, or she'd lost her phone, or just wasn't answering it that day – I thought maybe that little story said a lot about her. She did like to escape sometimes. There was nothing really angry or defiant about her; she just liked to go walkabout, hang about with her friends, do nothing. And when I asked if she would have done things differently, given the time again, she just shrugged and said no she wouldn't have, because she had fun.

During her early years at Central Foundation Girls' School in Bow she struggled to live down her older sister's reputation. "She was in year 10 when I went there. She got into fights, bunking off all the time," Yasmin explained. "She's got a bit of a temper, and she was in a really bad gang. My mum just thought she was off the rails. She had a mentor and everything. I think it helped, but she got kicked out in year 11. I never used to mention she was my sister, because after they knew, people would say things."

For her own part, Yasmin rarely really fell out with anyone, though she gave the impression she may have driven some of her teachers mad sometimes.

"I'm calmer, I'm a very loveable person and I usually get on with everybody," she told me. "And the teachers were fine. We had one teacher who really loved us, but sometimes she would get really disappointed. She expected us to work hard and we used to feel really guilty when we didn't. She was really trying."

But in her last couple of years, things started to go a little awry for Yasmin and her work drifted off.

"I did bunk off in year 10, but then I started it on a regular basis, half a day and then a whole day, just hanging round with friends mostly. Do I regret it? No way! I don't regret it! Because I met a lot of new people and did a lot of things I wouldn't have done, getting to know people, forming relationships. When I'm stuck in school, I can't do that. But in my last year I really messed up and got influenced into a lot of things I shouldn't have done. Friends, family, everything just gets to you in the end. Exams coming up, and everyone's giving you stress."

We were chatting in the Whitechapel office of the Rathbone charity, where Yasmin was working on improving her maths in the hope of going to college the next year. She'd left school the previous summer – it was spring now – with four good GCSEs, two of them in English and the others in RE and sociology, but with only a D in maths because she didn't complete her coursework. Sitting with us was another young woman, Tasneem, whom I hoped to include in this book but who in the event proved even harder to pin down than Yasmin.

"After I left school I went back home to Bangladesh … That's originally where my parents are from," Yasmin was saying in response to a question about why she hadn't gone to college the previous autumn. "East London is my home, though – born and raised here. And we were in Bangladesh for four months …"

Tasneem cut in: "How did you manage?" And they both laughed.

When I asked why they were laughing, they laughed some more.

"The food!"

"The weather!"

"You don't get any privacy …"

"Grandma's really funny," Yasmin said. "Every time I go she's like: 'What are you doing over here? Go back to London!' She knows when I go there I complain a lot. I'd never adjust to living there.

"I used to go to the beauty parlour and get myself pampered up. And when I came back my mum would be like: 'Where've you been? I've been worried.' And it was only across the road. If I was a boy …" She tailed off for a minute. "Boys have more fun in Bangladesh because they can do whatever they like. Here I have more freedom now, because I'm getting older.

"My mum always tells me she's going to leave and go back to Bangladesh one day. She misses it a lot. She asked me if I wanted to go back this year, and I was like: 'Are you mad, woman?' Last year when I went I was really stressed out by a lot of things, relationships, friends, a lot of things. And I just cleared my head. I forgot all the old people, got on with the new. That's all done and dusted, fresh start, just concentrate on myself."

Yasmin was 17 when we met and she'd lived in three places in her relatively short life, all within a mile or so of one another; all in that part of the East End that had its face jammed up against the plate glass of the City.

"At first we lived in Globe Town, five minutes from Whitechapel," she explained. "But when I was in year 3 I moved to Bow, and then after a couple more years I moved to Poplar. At first we had a two-bedroom house and I have five siblings, three brothers and two sisters. So, too many people for a two-bedroomed flat! So we moved to Bow to get three bedrooms, and then finally we got a four-bedroomed house in Poplar.

"My mum and dad are separated, so I live with my mum. My oldest brother is 24, he's married with two kids and they live with us. My next brother's 22 and he's married with two kids too, but he lives in Harlow. His wife's mother moved to Harlow and he wanted to be close to her family. He tries to come back whenever he can. He works in Primark. Then my older sister is 20, she's married with a son. She lives two minutes away from us. Luckily she got a two-bedroomed flat one street away. My youngest brother is 10, going on 11. He'll start secondary school this year."

For Yasmin, this little area was where she belonged: "I feel comfortable in East London. I don't see myself anywhere apart from here. I don't know other places. You spend your childhood here, and you grow up here. I've been out of London but I found it too quiet."

Chapter 1

The importance of places

Just off the traffic-clogged East India Dock Road, through a concrete archway and across a bleak square surrounded by three-storey 1960s blocks, was a flight of stairs leading to the maisonette where Yasmin lived. Running down these one muggy August morning I came face-to-face with a striking piece of graffiti: on the painted breeze-block wall were a dozen sets of initials set out in two neatly sprayed columns, and next to them an inscription: "E14 4 LYF".

Halfway out into the pedestrianised square, with its moth-eaten shrubs and its air of decay, I found myself sufficiently intrigued to turn back for a second look. Something about the work said it was more than the mere defiant scribbling of some bored teenager. The care with which it had been placed there spoke of serious intent, almost of ceremony. What intent, I wondered? To express some lasting bond, some deep solidarity between these 12 unseen youths, certainly. But "E14 4 LYF"? Not "E14 Rules" or "E14 Rocks", not even "E14 for ever". For Life. It looked almost a statement of resignation, like some sort of sentence – a promise that this group would stick together and never leave, perhaps despite some perceived pressure to do so. Or maybe an affirmation that even if they did go, their little piece of this London postcode would go with them.

This little inscription struck me as symptomatic of something vital to understanding why so many young people failed to make a neat transition between the worlds of education and work: the centrality of place to their decision-making processes.

None of the young people I met on this journey had come from "London" or "Manchester" or "Barnsley". They came from Wombwell, or Kendray, or Collyhurst, or Cheetham Hill. When the spray-painters of Poplar did their work they were almost certainly not even referring to the whole of London East 14, which stretched from the smart gastropubs and converted warehouse dwellings of Limehouse in the north to the white working class enclaves around Island Gardens in the south. This tight little group would surely have seen its turf as extending merely to a few streets around this square. When I Googled "E14 4 LYF" I turned up a web page for East London Bengali rappers and the battle cry: "BuRdEtT E14 RuN Da EaSt BuRdEtT MaSsIvE 4 LyF E14" – a reference to a gang based on a thoroughfare that ran north from the East India Dock Road just opposite Yasmin's block. Places mattered to most of the young people I met, and many of them saw "their" places in quite precise, tightly drawn terms.

How do places affect life chances?

How much difference did this make, I wondered? Was this territoriality just another version of the tribalism long since associated with youth cultures and football teams? Or was it something deeper, more likely to narrow young people's horizons and restrict the choices they might make in the future? In short, having decided to stay rather than to go elsewhere, would those dozen spray-painters from Poplar be more or less likely to succeed in life as a result?

The first question, it seemed, was whether people in poorer areas were actually more or less geographically mobile than others. Were they, as some commentators had suggested, held back by their own inability or reluctance to move? Academic studies seemed to suggest the answer to this question was not simple.

Researchers from the University of Teesside, for instance, interviewed young people in post-industrial neighbourhoods in the late 1990s, and returned five years later to find out whether they had moved, and how far. While many had moved locally, only two had left the area. There was a similar pattern among the eight young people I chose to follow, too. One had lived in the same house all her life; the other seven had had a total of 25 moves between them. But only two had ever moved more than a few miles – one from West Africa to London and one from Ipswich to London. Five had been forced to move, sometimes several times, because of family problems. One had had a total of eight moves, largely prompted by poverty and homelessness.

It seemed the young people I met were suffering a kind of double whammy – they had to deal with frequent disruptions caused by house moves, which often forced them to go to a new school and make new friends even when they had only moved a short distance. Yet while their more affluent contemporaries might have suffered the same disruption it was likely to have been counterbalanced by them getting more space or going to a higher-achieving school – the moves of the young people I met were often to communities and housing no better than that they had left. While some of them *had* moved to get an extra bedroom or two, others had been on downward spirals in which family breakdown led to a move to a worse area, which then led to them making the "wrong" kind of new friends, which then led to further moves.

So, it seemed clear places did have a practical effect on the young people growing up in them. If they lived in areas where there were few jobs and the schools were struggling under the weight of social problems, they would have to work hard to overcome those problems. In some cases, families who had lived in previously quite prosperous – though solidly working class – areas had found themselves, without moving at all, in places that had become increasingly dysfunctional.

Barnsley

"I don't know if it's me being sensitive," Chris Sorby told me. "But Barnsley does seem to have an image problem with the rest of the country. It appears to be the butt of people's jokes."

The day before I met Sorby, the manager of a private-sector company that ran the contract to provide careers advice to teenagers in the town, Barnsley had beaten Liverpool in the FA cup and had won the chance to play Chelsea at home. I parked up on a freezing February day and wandered through a bustling, attractive town centre, a solidly built place that felt as if its long-dead architects had a real sense of civic pride. It was hard to tell whether the atmosphere had been boosted by the win, but the traders in the market hall did seem to have something of a spring in their step.

The BBC had been up to do a report, Sorby told me over a cup of tea in the warm offices of Nord Anglia Lifetime Development, but even through the haze of euphoria the coverage had been viewed locally with some suspicion: was Huw Edwards taking the mickey?

"They wheeled out Dickie Bird, that old Barnsley stereotype," Sorby said. "And a pub landlady who said, 'We're all hard up here, we can play anyone.' I think people here play up to it. It's almost as if we know what they want, and we give it to them. I wonder whether they would have bothered if it had been some place down south. There are some places that get treated differently, and Barnsley seems to be one of those."

If the people of Barnsley were a little chippy it was hardly surprising, for the town had taken some serious knocks in recent years. The closure of its pits, its sewing factories and its glassworks had left it struggling to re-establish a clear identity. A year or so before I arrived, that struggle manifested itself in hard statistics when Barnsley was officially declared as having the highest proportion of disengaged 16–18 year-olds in England. In late 2005 one in seven had been out of work and out of education.

Since then a co-ordinated effort had been made, and the figure had begun to drop. Barnsley, unlike Manchester or the London boroughs I visited, had a monthly "strategy group" to deal with the issue, chaired by its director of children's services and attended by key people working in relevant education and community organisations. Yet everyone agreed the history of the area made the job a tough one.

Almost everyone I spoke to in Barnsley talked about generation following unemployed generation, about a lack of aspiration that sprang historically from an abundance of well-paid manual work. Yet the authors of a classic 1950s study of a Yorkshire coalfield community – pseudonymously named Ashton – gave rather a different picture. It described a world in which at least a proportion of families had had high aspirations for their children, although in most cases it seemed they had led nowhere: "It is reliably learned the mining areas are the best areas in all Yorkshire for selling such publications as *The Children's Encyclopaedia* – publications which cost from £12 to £15 and which parents buy because they want to 'do something' for the child's education," they explained, before going on to describe how they asked a sample of residents whether they would encourage their sons to be miners. Two-thirds – about the same as the proportion of the adult male population that actually *were* miners – said they would not: "Indeed this question was only asked in order to confirm the statement heard many hundreds of times in the Yorkshire coalfields since 1945: 'I hope no son of mine ever works in the pit.'"

Many young men would find jobs as errand-boys, drivers' mates or builders' labourers, only to be drawn into mining by the wages, they said. Yet they also described a community in which the work ethic was not always strong, perhaps as a result of jobs being both easily available and often unpleasant:

> In Ashton the working men's clubs hold a weekly draw, and winnings can amount to £60. For a prizewinner in this draw to turn up with his workmates on Monday morning would occasion a great deal of surprised comment. It is thought natural to take the opportunity of not going to work when such a windfall occurs. 'Winning the pools' is the great vision of ending worries and giving a man the chance to decide his own destiny, to be no longer at the mercy of all that his job represents. Money gained in such ways holds out the possibility of breaking down barriers.

It was something of a paradox about Barnsley that when outsiders arrived, its people formed what seemed to be quite a tight little unit with a clear idea of who and what they were. Yet in fact it was nothing of the kind, and never had been. Within its own family, there were very clear divisions.

"Kendray is only about – what? – two miles from Barnsley centre, it's walkable. Yet it's a distinct community," Sorby told me. "And people there would present issues like travel to Barnsley as a barrier to working here." One of my interviewees, who lived in Wombwell, told me she was not local though she had lived there 20 years or so: she came from Jump, which was two miles further down the road. In the days of the pits, people lived and worked within their own small community. Very few people thought they came from Barnsley; each village had its own identity and the rivalries between them were intense.

"It does link back to the mining communities," Sorby said. "The vast majority of the villages probably exist because there was a pit there. There were a number of sewing firms too – SR Gent was very dependent on Marks and Spencer, with its 'Buy British' slogan that it used to have. They were industries that were reliable. The pit was a job for life. That whole thing's changed. You had sewing firms, you had M and S, and you just assumed that would always be there."

Everyone in Barnsley knew things were not what they used to be. Yet on one level, the town did seem sometimes to be in denial about the fact that its bedrock had been so radically changed.

"It goes back to that sort of pit village where all your employment needs and all your shopping needs and whatever are met within the community," said Sorby's colleague Angela Lomax. "You do still stumble across these attitudes, that education isn't that important, that it doesn't matter what you do, that you can leave school and get a job. I'm not sure what mythical job that is. There's a misunderstanding from parents' perspective about the nature of the economy. I think they saw grandparents maybe having certain things and there's an assumption they can too."

The type of job people expected to get had changed, though. "I was working at Willowgarth, near Grimethorpe, before Christmas," said Lomax. "I had one young lady who wanted to work in a hairdressers, but it had to be at Grimethorpe. I said, 'Tell me where the hairdresser's are in Grimethorpe'. Between us we came up with one. You try to unpick the reasons why, but sometimes they don't know, it's almost what they've been brought up with."

Parents' attitudes to their children's futures had changed little in recent decades, she said. "It's almost that they want to keep people here. You have instances of young people who have the potential to go to university, and our role is to encourage that. But then they go to the family and they say: 'What does someone like you want to do something like that for?'"

After I left the town centre I drove the couple of miles south-east to Kendray, a post-war estate on the side of a hill which formed part of Barnsley's urban sprawl. Not much further out, the borough became a series of villages with open countryside in between.

My first impression of Kendray was that it looked like a demolition site. Coming in at the bottom end of the estate there were piles of rubble, giving way further up to dilapidated houses and run-down shops. But the centre of the estate was a revelation. At its heart was a large, well-tended green area with modern play equipment. Further up the hill was a huge new health centre, a new primary school, a new police station. Across the green, a private-sector company was building new houses. Kendray was a place in transition.

The offices of the Kendray Initiative were just off the green in a former council house with no visible doorbell. Eventually I managed to attract someone's attention and the heavy steel security door was opened – the bell was hidden in a special place where local children could not find it, I was told – life here was still far from perfect. Over a cup of tea – Barnsley is a great place for tea-drinkers – the initiative's programme manager, Elaine Equeall, gave me some history.

"It had become – I hate the expression – a sink estate where people didn't want to live," she said. "High levels of crime, really poor quality roads and gardens. The initiative came from the ground up. There's a lot of people who live in this area who've been here a significant number of years and have seen it deteriorate, and they've said: 'Enough's enough.'"

The initiative started in 2001, with a group of residents laying the foundations. More than £3 million in public money was promised over seven years, with the environment and crime being the first issues to be tackled. And to a very large extent, it worked. At the start, there were 240 empty homes on the estate. By early 2007, there was a waiting list for housing in Kendray. The estate had seen a huge improvement, Equeall said, though some of the underlying problems were still there.

We had been joined by Karl Lyons, who worked part-time at the local referral unit for pupils excluded from school but who had also been knocking on doors in Kendray looking for disengaged youngsters.

"They were the forgotten army. But this year for the first time because of the pressure from central government, there's been a huge amount of work done," he explained.

Lyons had lived in Barnsley all his life but had worked elsewhere, most recently as the vice-principal of a further education college in Nottingham. Now, towards the end of his career, he had returned to work in this changed world.

"I worked as a teacher in Darfield between 1975 and 1980 – if the boys wanted to get a job there were four pits within walking distance. They didn't need any qualifications. There was a sewing factory that took every single girl without qualifications who wanted to work. It was a working class area – not particularly poor but nevertheless working class – with low aspirations but with a work ethic. That would have been replicated in virtually every village round here.

"People say there are jobs, and there are, but what's replaced the reasonable levels of income that the pits used to provide, and the sewing factories? Villages were sustained by the mines, corner shops – they've disappeared. What's replaced the reasonable wage levels of the pits is very low-level minimum wage temporary contracts. The choice of employment now is very minimal," he said. "This work's opened my eyes to what's not been replaced."

Whenever I left Barnsley to drive home down the A1, I left with mixed feelings. Unlike London, which had many identities and much that was confusing and alienating about it, Barnsley had coherence and warmth. Yet that coherence seemed in part to have been achieved by absorbing a sense of loss, of absence. The sense of belonging, of identity that came with the mines and the factories, had not gone away with them; not completely. It was still there. Now it was an identity sustained not by the presence of those things, but in a strange way by their absence. Barnsley was a place that used to have pits; a place that used to have factories; a place that used to have a clear reason for existing.

The role of local networks

It was clear, then, that coherence and local pride had to some extent become negative factors for young people in Barnsley. They had grown up with a sense of loss, and with an almost fierce kind of pride in their town and its heritage. They sometimes seemed to have a feeling that other places, other futures, were for other people and not for them. Yet the strength of their communities, their social and family networks, was real.

Barnsley was not the only place where I found local social networks strikingly strong. In Manchester, I was out and about one day when the young man who was showing me around was introduced to a teenager of a similar age who lived a mile or so away from him. Within minutes the two of them had established they had several friends in common, and when we all repaired to someone's mother's house for a cup of tea she was quickly able to add a few more mutual acquaintances to the list. That might sound trivial, but my feeling was that it mattered. In their classic study of life in the East End in the 1950s, *Family and Kinship in East London*, Michael Young and Peter Willmott described these relationships as a kind of glue that held communities together, suggesting the welfare state was taking over the supporting role that had traditionally been played by the wider family:

> When a person has relatives in the borough, as most people do, each of these relatives is a go-between with other people in the district. His brother's friends are his acquaintances, if not his friends; his grandmother's neighbours so well known as to be almost his own. The kindred are, if we understand their function aright, a bridge between the individual and the community … They share the same background. The people they see when they go out for a walk are the people they played with as children.

In Manchester and in Barnsley, it seemed to me, those types of networks still existed and played an important part in people's lives. While they were certainly positive in many respects, they left some young people facing real dilemmas about whether they should leave to pursue educational and career success, or whether they should stay.

TOM

I first met Tom a few days before Barnsley's big cup tie against Chelsea. A big, cheerful, bright lad who loved football, his mates and the occasional good night out in town, he seemed a bit shy at first but was always open and friendly. This time I arrived in Kendray by a different route, up Redhill Avenue, where the houses all had new walls and gates. Coming into this neat, spacious semi with modern décor and a lush garden at the back, it would have been easy to forget

Kendray had until quite recently been known as a sink estate.

Although he was excited about the football – he had a season ticket for home games – Tom was philosophical about the outcome. The key thing, he said, was that Barnsley's team had been a credit to the town. He spoke with a kind of pride and an insight that was genuinely moving.

"If they don't win, they've still done us proud," he said. "It's pride about where you come from, isn't it? It's wanting to be the best, playing Chelsea in the cup. When we go to watch football everybody just joins together. Normally everyone stays in their little villages, but this unites us."

Tom's mum, Karen, had grown up in Kendray, and his dad, Andy, had too. But they had moved out, a couple of miles down the road to Ardsley. Karen said she wouldn't have moved back six or seven years ago, but since the regeneration Kendray felt like a different place.

"They used to call it the Bronx of Barnsley," Tom said. "It was where all the rough kids came from. All my mates in primary school were from Ardsley, but if kids from Kendray came down on the park you'd think: 'The scruffs are here.' They were always causing trouble."

They moved back, eventually, to the house where Andy grew up. His mum and dad bought it from the council in the 1970s, and when they decided to move to a bungalow round the corner, Karen and Andy bought it from them. Andy's dad worked locally, first at Wood's glass factory and then at BXL Plastics in Darton; Andy works at a printer's in Leeds doing 12-hour shifts, four days then four nights.

It soon became clear Tom's parents – Karen in particular – were ambitious for him. His family, having moved from Kendray to find somewhere better but then having moved back as the area improved, were a real tribute to the success of the Kendray regeneration programme. But there was this sense of tension between Tom's love of his family and community and his parents' ambitions for him to grasp opportunities they never had.

"We always thought Tom was special, he was going to achieve," Karen said. "I think I put some of my wishes onto him and then I stepped back off the pressure because I'd done it myself. It was Tom's shot in life, not mine. I always felt I didn't do what I was capable of, just through not having the confidence."

Karen left school at 16, "hating education": "There was an option to go to college at 16 but we were told: 'You're going to be a housewife, why bother? You haven't got what it takes.'"

She worked at Bowater's paper factory and left at 25 when she had Tom. She wanted to be a stay-at-home mum, but after three years she was going stir crazy. She got a part-time job at the Halifax bank agency, and stayed 10 years. Then one day someone came in and said they were starting a women's assertiveness course at Barnsley College. It changed her life.

"They built it up slowly and convinced me that I wasn't stupid. First of all I did a women's programme, and did a taster of psychology and sociology, assertiveness and social skills. And then I moved on to a level two and did sociology and psychology GCSE, and then I went on to an access course. I did an A-level in sociology … then I was, 'Am I going to university? What to do next?'" At that point, Karen was offered a job as a youth worker and decided to take that instead.

"When I'm writing anything I have to concentrate. Tom doesn't have to. With him it's just there. It annoys me, sometimes," she said. "He's got an ability to really fly, but Tom will do what Tom has to do. Just enough to get him through it."

Karen would have loved Tom to have taken A-levels and aimed for university, but he didn't want to leave Barnsley. Instead, prompted by friends who thought an apprenticeship would provide a good, steady trade, he took a plumbing test, in which he gained full marks. Then he started to look for an employer who might take him on and send him to college for a day each week.

"I just got the Yellow Pages out and looked underneath plumbing, and rang everybody from Barnsley and Doncaster," he said. "But they were all just saying, 'We don't want anyone.' I must have rung 50 or 60 different firms. It just knocks you down. I thought: they're just going to say no."

Tom's confidence was soon at rock bottom: "I saw the difference in him," Karen said. "I've seen him go down and down."

With the new college year approaching fast, Tom decided to go for a full-time college course instead: "But I couldn't get on because it was too full. That was in August. So I was just stuck. There's nothing to do for a year."

Apart from a few weeks' casual work at an electronic goods warehouse in the Dearne Valley, Tom had been jobless for nine months by the time I met him. When we met, he was about to start a 26-week bricklaying course with a charity called Independent Training Services, which was replacing the walls and gates in Kendray. It was just to fill in time, he said.

"I went to talk about plumbing, but they were only doing bricklaying. It put me off a bit going there, because I saw all the bad ones there from school, throwing gum at each other. But it'll get me out of the house. It's a new skill, isn't it? I feel better now."

Where in other places I saw dislocation, even anger, Tom had none of that in him. What he did have was a strong belief that this was where he belonged, and that it was where he wanted to stay. Even his struggle to find an apprenticeship had not led him to think about leaving.

"I love where I live," he said. "It's a nice, safe place. I've got a lot of mates – there's always people to talk to. If needs be, everyone will stick together."

Cultures of exclusion

Tom's attachment to the place where he grew up – and to his strong network of family and friends – could certainly be said to have held him back. Yet he talked in very positive terms about those things.

The Teesside researchers who looked at whether young people moved or stayed had come to the conclusion that the lack of mobility they found did tend to keep families together and to strengthen social networks. However, they also said the attitudes and beliefs within those networks reinforced people's sense of economic alienation. So people had good reason not to want to move – because their family and friends gave them good support, and understood the social and economic problems they faced. But by staying put, they clung to the attitude that said there was no real alternative: they made social exclusion normal.

Other commentators had gone further, suggesting that beyond the practical restrictions of life in a poor community lay attitudes, local cultures and assumptions that perpetuated poverty. The former Conservative leader Iain Duncan Smith, for example, had suggested some communities were in effect becoming ghettoised, that there were some areas – in particular social housing estates – which had simply become repositories for society's failures. He published a report on housing estates which argued these estates had become home to collections of dysfunctional families, left behind when the more successful moved on. Was that the case with my subjects? Only partially. Of the eight, two were in owner-occupied accommodation and the rest in rented social housing. Three of the six who lived in social housing were living with a single mother on benefit. One lived with both parents in a council house and had a father in a managerial job, while two were living independently after being forced to leave their family homes.

I would say, though, that in some of the places I visited that sense of belonging spilled over into a kind of defiance – a kind of "them and us" culture that said outsiders, or more particularly those seen as being from the world of officialdom, were not necessarily welcome.

Collyhurst

In Collyhurst, a mile or so north of Manchester city centre, I found much of the same warmth, many of the same strong social ties, that I did in Barnsley. But here there seemed to be an additional edge. Perhaps it had been there in Kendray before the regeneration work – nothing like that had happened yet in Collyhurst. But I was left feeling that even if improvements were made to the local environment here, even if aspirational families like Tom's were encouraged to move in, some residents' negative attitudes would be hard to shake.

Nudging over speed bumps in a police van, Sergeant Stephen Gilbertson, who ran the neighbourhood policing team for Collyhurst, and Cath Keane, the city council's community safety co-ordinator for the area, gave the impression their work was at an embryonic stage. The Collyhurst Village estate had been built, Keane explained, using principles first introduced in the 1920s in Radburn, New Jersey. These estates, with their pedestrian walkways, were meant to be "gardenesque" and "child-friendly", according to a recent speech from an American professor that I found on the web. Gilbertson had other words for it.

"It's like a rabbit warren," he said more than once with a sort of quiet desperation. "If you're pursuing someone, they'll be away and gone before you can ever get near."

Keane tended to use the word "challenging" a lot. "People do need to look after their properties better," she said, as we rounded a bend by a series of derelict railway arches and passed a house with boarded-up front windows and a debris-strewn garden. "It is a challenge because there's so much to do, but we have had a word at that house. We've embarrassed them into cleaning up a bit."

I looked at her in some surprise: did she mean the house was someone's home?

"Oh yes, it's occupied," she said. "There are children living there."

On Thornton Street North, just past a boarded-up pub, Keane pointed to a piece of open land with a skatepark on it. It had become a focus for heroin-users and was due for demolition, though today the only sign of life was a stray dog chewing on something unidentifiable. A couple of streets further on behind St Patrick's Primary School, she suddenly asked Gilbertson to stop. "Look! They've started work! That's brilliant, isn't it?"

In the middle of a fenced-off piece of wasteland, diggers were at work clearing a mess of thorns, trees, brambles and accumulated debris.

"The problem is that the Oldham Road is near here, and stolen vehicles are coming on there. All sorts of things are getting thrown in after they've done a robbery, bikes are razzed across it. If you live there, there's no respite," Keane explained.

Collyhurst, a mile or so north of Manchester city centre, apparently meant "wooded hill", which was odd, as it was mostly flat and had almost no trees, apart from the scrubby bushes we saw being ripped out on the wasteland. Although the people I met were to show me a different, warmer side to the place, it was clear Sergeant Gilbertson and his team faced an uphill struggle. Keane told me Collyhurst had tended to be forgotten because it straddled the boundaries of various police divisions and local authority wards. It was, I thought, easy to ignore for another reason: unlike the more glamorously violent, multicultural neighbourhoods with their headline-grabbing gun-and-knife crime, Collyhurst was largely white and working class, its crime not so much organised as disorganised. Everyone agreed on one thing: people in Collyhurst did not tend to like the police.

"Before I came the police had major problems with anti-social behaviour and criminality," Keane said. "They put up a CCTV camera to try to keep an eye on things. Somebody sawed it down – you have to devote time to that. Whether it was guns, or drugs, I don't know. We replaced it, and the police made arrests. But the police were saying: 'We can't do this on our own.' A new inspector came in; he was describing it as being like working in Beirut. It was crazy.

"For me, south Manchester is green, it's leafy. You come to north and east Manchester and there are areas where it's quite bleak. It's the Radburn effect, it's housing with these connecting walkways, where you don't always get that community feel. For me I think Collyhurst Village does suffer the most, and I think we have a lot of work to do to support the residents' groups."

Gilbertson talked with nostalgia of the days about 10 years ago when he used to work in Ashton-under-Lyne, a solidly respectable working class area.

"I used to like nothing better in Ashton than walking around, smiling and saying 'Hello' to people. Now people look at you like, 'What are you doing?' You try to talk to people, and straight away the defensive barriers go up."

When I first visited, Collyhurst Village was officially the second most deprived area in England – the most deprived was in Liverpool – out of a total of nearly 32,500 districts. Seven out of 10 people of working age were on benefits, almost eight out of 10 school leavers were out of work. Yet the area was just a mile or so from a then booming city, its skyline bristling with cranes amid a rash of soon-to-be unsaleable luxury apartments.

But it struck me, as time went on, that some of the families who lived here must have been here for generations. Looking at the names on the local shops, many of them were Irish. There were at least two Roman Catholic primary schools and at least two Roman Catholic churches within a square mile or so. I guessed some of the area's inhabitants would have been able to trace their local roots back to the mid-nineteenth century, when Friedrich Engels described the area between here and the city centre as "Irish Town", a place where a multitude of poor and desperate refugees from famine had gathered. The deep valley which bordered the east of Collyhurst and then ran south towards Victoria Station was particularly fetid, Engels said, describing the view upstream from a city-centre bridge:

> At the bottom flows the Irk, a narrow, coal-black, foul-smelling stream full of debris and refuse, which it deposits on the right bank. In dry weather a long string of the most disgusting blackish-green slime pools are left standing on this bank, from the depths of which miasmic bubbles of gas constantly arise. Above the bridge are tanneries, bonemills and gasworks, from which all drains and refuse find their way into the Irk, which receives further the contents of all the neighbouring sewers and privies.

The area around Ducie Bridge, where Engels stood while surveying this scene, had been at the centre of the great Manchester cholera epidemic in 1832, which left nearly 700 dead. Collyhurst had gone through several attempts at regeneration since: pictures from the 1970s showed decaying tenement flats with boarded-up windows and with weeds sprouting between their concreted open spaces; recently Urban Splash had built smart blocks of wood-clad flats along the Rochdale Road which were for rent at £450 a month. Yet there was no secondary school, and the names over its one row of shops read as follows:

Convenience Store, Bargain Beer, Hair Salon, Tantastic, Lucky House Chinese Takeaway. Collyhurst had always been poor, it seemed, and it wasn't likely to change much. And maybe, too, its inhabitants had always felt that degree of alienation.

RICKY

"I had Ricky on the living room floor," Sarah told me the first time we met. "They gave my date as February 22nd to 26th, but he didn't arrive till the 8th of March. Then I coughed, and he arrived eight minutes later. He weighed 8.8 pounds." Then she looked at her son and laughed: "Eight, eight, eight. Should have been 666."

Sixteen years later Chris Nolan, an outreach worker from the Rathbone charity, caught Ricky breaking into a car near their maisonette in Collyhurst and brought him into its centre to start a course called Progress to Success. Ricky turned up regularly, if sometimes late, and did indeed progress, on to another course called Entry to Employment.

Sarah, a trim, practical woman in her forties, usually seemed to regard the recurrent dramas and traumas of Ricky's life with a wry humour. Ricky, meanwhile, was pale and had the kind of skin that suggested he did not look after himself, but he had angelic eyes and the most winning cheeky smile. Sometimes as we talked he'd be looking down rather than at me, and I'd ask a question he knew would show him in a bad light. And he'd look up from under long lashes and give me a grin that spoke volumes.

Sarah's older children, now in their twenties, had done fine: her son got an apprenticeship in a joinery firm south of the city, and still worked there as a manager. Her daughter was a supervisor in a sandwich bar. It was after she got divorced and then met Ricky's dad that things started to go wrong.

"When Ricky was three weeks old his dad went away for four months. Then when Ricky was one and a half he got eight years for armed robbery. After that we moved to get away from him."

From Collyhurst, where Ricky was born, they moved west to Beswick, then north to Blackley, then back south to Collyhurst, where they now lived in a three-bedroomed maisonette. The place looked dilapidated from the outside, but inside it was neat and freshly decorated. "We're getting there," Sarah remarked dryly.

After moving to get away from Ricky's dad, they moved again to escape Ricky's troubles. When he was 12 and they lived in Beswick, he got in with a drug dealer who used to employ him as a runner. Then later, his school threw him out, and for a couple of years he stayed at home most days, smoking skunk – a potent form of cannabis. "From my point of view a young person's got to go through something to realise it's wrong," he told me.

The block where Sarah and Ricky lived was just east of the Rochdale Road, but Ricky used to volunteer at the youth centre, which was on the west side of the road on the border between Collyhurst and Collyhurst Village. When we met, he had stopped going because there had been some local trouble between the two areas.

"It was all to do with a lad called David. Some lads from Collyhurst Village were shouting at David's mam and dad when they were walking home from the pub, and aggravating them. David's mam hit one of them with a stick, and so they beat her up really badly. Then David's mates beat up the lads who did that to his mam. They haven't been done for it. There's going to be more trouble. So the people from Collyhurst don't go to the club any more, because the Collyhurst Village people go."

This story struck me as so horrific that I was sure the police must have been involved – later someone showed me a gruesome photo which had been passed around by mobile phone, of a young man with his face mashed and an ear missing. Yet when I asked the local police sergeant, Stephen Gilbertson, about it he told me he was not aware of it ever having been reported.

I questioned Ricky about it too – why didn't David's mum and dad just go to the police when she was beaten up, I wanted to know? He looked at me in a way that said he thought I was a bit simple. "They'd be labelled as grasses, and their windows'd be smashed. They'd have to leave their homes. You might as well just go and live somewhere else," he explained.

Even Sarah, who spent her childhood near here, sometimes received odd comments when she went over to Collyhurst Village. "I went to the advice centre on Southchurch Parade, just the other side of Rochdale Road. And the woman said to me: 'Have you come from the other side?' I said: 'What do you mean?' I grew up over there. And she said: 'People won't come from the other side of the road.'"

For the most part, Ricky had stayed out of trouble.

"The only thing Ricky's done, he was stupid and got drunk and smashed this lady's car up a bit," Sarah said. "I handed him in. He was fined £350. Who's paying it? Me. Out of my benefit."

"I was clever not to get caught," Ricky said. "They were doing stabbings and stuff, and robbing off the streets. But I was never there when they were doing that."

Although Sarah felt at home in Collyhurst, she hated Manchester city centre, a mile or so away: "I hate our town. I've always hated it. If I got to town I go first thing in the morning and get back, because you can't move later on. I wonder where all the people come from."

The East End

Yet while Barnsley had its warmth and pride, and while even teenagers growing up in Collyhurst had a real sense of belonging, the feeling I got from London was quite different. This was the only place where I met young people who were angry about the contrast between their own poverty and the wealth of those living close by. And it was the only place where I felt sometimes that there was fear among them, where the descriptions of the lives they lived were even sometimes tinged with despair.

London, of course, is a very different place from Manchester or Barnsley. There were families living in the East End whose ancestors had been there for generations – and who had experienced just the same loss of traditional industry, with the closure of the docks, that Barnsley had with the loss of the pits. Yet the population of East London has always been one that changed and migrated; one that arrived from elsewhere, settled, prospered and moved on, shifting outwards geographically towards the M25 and upwards socially. The Jews followed the Huguenots and the Bangladeshis followed the Jews. Yet now, it seemed, some communities here were stuck, unable to move on as their predecessors had done. Some white working class families, in particular, seemed left behind. Nearly 40 years had passed since the containerisation of freight began closing the docks, and yet there were still these little pockets of families which seemed almost to be clinging to the hope they might return. Often those families now found themselves living alongside Bangladeshi families who had migrated here in the 1970s or later; and that led to tension.

The Aberfeldy Estate was a case in point. Getting to the Aberfeldy Estate was quite a performance, despite its close proximity to several major roads. So much so that John Baker, community activist and director of the local housing association, thought it best to meet me at Stratford in order to show me around. From there we took the Docklands Light Railway south to Langdon Park, then negotiated a busy road, some Victorian housing and a scrubby playing field before coming face-to-face with the Northern Approach to the Blackwall Tunnel. At this point conversation became impossible as the traffic roared north on its way up to the M11. Baker shouted into my ear that the link road cut the Aberfeldy off "virtually from everywhere". To reach the estate we made our way through a dingy underpass adorned with the usual detritus of old takeaway wrappers, where clouds of tiny flies puffed up from under our feet as we climbed the steps on the other side.

Standing in the centre of the estate, between the church and the neighbourhood centre, we could just see a single row of attractive flat-fronted terraces with little arched windows. For the rest, we were surrounded by a post-war mix of terraces, maisonettes and flats. From the bottom of the estate we could hear yet more traffic on the East India Dock Road, which ran from east to west and which, with the M11 link, formed a fume-laden bracket around the Aberfeldy.

Until the 1860s this area – about a mile east of where Yasmin lived – was largely uninhabited, marshy scrubland onto which the River Lea was allowed to flood. When the East India Dock was being built in the early nineteenth century it was used for stabling horses and housing construction workers, then for a brickworks whose products were used to line the docks. Later housing went up – all third and fourth rate, Baker said – to accommodate the dock workers. Through two World Wars and through many intervening periods of boom and bust, the Aberfeldy never really prospered. By the end of the Second World War two-thirds of its houses had been destroyed or damaged, so the authorities pulled down most of the rest and started again. Things did not really improve. The docks began closing in the 1960s, and people began moving further out of London, and at around the same time the Bangladeshis came, fleeing civil war. That, according to Baker, gave rise to the popular misconception that people were forced out because of the arrival of the Bangladeshis. He gestured along Dee Street, beyond the church. One night in 2003 someone put a firebomb through the window of the Culloden School Bangladeshi Parents' Association, he said. The local paper ran a headline: "Race Hate Arson". The Parents' Association, up in arms, organised a protest march on the town hall.

"People were racing about here saying, 'They did this' and 'They did that to us'," Baker said. "It was all rubbish. In actual fact the deed was done by a couple of old established Poplar ne'er-do-wells with drug habits. They tried to get in and couldn't, so they thought 'F' or 'B' or whatever you say in such circumstances, and they got a can of petrol and set fire to the building."

Baker said the episode exposed a running sore within the community: "I think there was a tension there already, but the question about tension is: Is it tolerable? Is it absorbable? The road to intolerability was this incident."

Inside the Aberfeldy Centre, which opened in 2000, a dozen or so young people had gathered to look at Facebook. A separate group of young men were playing cards while the young women shrieked with excitement over something they'd found on the screen. Katherine, a PhD student and temporary administrative assistant at the centre who had been helping Baker research the community's problems, quietened them down so we could talk at a nearby table. Then Baker produced a diagram, a series of concentric circles with a cross through the middle. At the top he had written "elation" and at the bottom "depression". On the left it said "fantasy" and on the right, "reality". Most people, he said, were somewhere in the middle, but if you were too far off to the edge, particularly if you were in the quarter framed by "fantasy" and "depression", that left you with a view of the world that was unrealistic but also very negative. That was what was happening here, he said.

"A lot of people round here are anchored below those lines. If the qualities of this community were described as if they were an individual and shown to a doctor, that doctor would say it's mild-to-moderate depression." He turns to Katherine: "I did it with you, didn't I? And you said, 'It sounds like depression to me.'" She nodded.

"What happens if everybody's below that line?" he asked. "If everybody in a community is not only oppressed, but abused? People are saying: 'Why aren't you queuing up to get work in Canary Wharf?' It's because there's been too much damage for too long. It's them and us. It's adversarial. Big time. In some psychiatric conditions, people perceive that the enemy is upon them and they will be aggressive to that enemy. If we look at community depression … they're not going to be very nice."

The children of the Bangladeshi community, he said, were much more likely than those of the white community to go to university and to carve a decent future for themselves. The whites, meanwhile, were left lamenting the loss of the local spirit that some could – just – remember.

"The fabric of the local community was held together quite tightly so that everybody behaved towards everybody else. People do say it was a good place to be. They had the feeling that they did things to survive and they survived, and they felt quite cheerful about that," Baker said. "When you come to think what could your son or daughter or grandchild do and the answer's nothing, because there's nothing worth doing, as a result you feel angry and you say there's nothing here because it's gone off, it's gone downhill."

It would be wrong to suggest that the Bangladeshi community was thriving while the white community declined – unemployment rates among both communities were high and both suffered from poor housing and overcrowding. Yet this white community, clinging to a long-lost and at least partly mythical past, was particularly hard to understand.

Further south, at the far tip of the Isle of Dogs, building work had transformed the scenery in recent decades, with luxury flats lining the river frontage; cordylines and yuccas adorning the balconies. On a sunny day in Island Gardens mothers played with their children on the grass under huge plane trees, with a view across the Thames to Greenwich and the Royal Observatory. Yet the scene was deceptive.

Just behind Island Gardens was George Green's School – while just 5 per cent of pupils at Yasmin's school, a couple of miles to the north, were from white British backgrounds, the figure here was 10 times that. Surrounding the school, a street or two back from the river, were blocks of post-war flats and maisonettes where most of its pupils lived. And just down the road was Christ Church, where in a mezzanine office Linda Ruthven runs the Isle of Dogs Youth Employment Brokerage.

"I was born and brought up on the Isle of Dogs," Ruthven told me when I called in for a chat. "I'm an island girl, but my parents moved when I was quite young. Then I moved back with my husband into one of the yuppie developments. It was definitely a 'them and us' situation, it was incredible. You would get the kids coming along the side of the housing, swimming in the docks. And they would climb up onto your property and if you told them off they'd say: 'Go back to where you belong.'

"I've seen a big change. I remember it being a working area, the docks, all the families worked. I can't think of any family that was unemployed, or where you would say they were deprived of anything."

She and the vicar, Father Tom Pyke, enumerated the sources of employment there used to be locally: a paint factory, a pickle factory, MacDougall's flour mill, Kenco coffee. All gone, along with the docks.

Now the big employers in the area were at Canary Wharf, whose towers loomed over the whole of that part of East London. Yet while the employment it offered was almost as close as the docks used to be, it seemed a million miles away.

"I would say the majority of people that work in Canary Wharf don't live locally," Ruthven said. "The manual-type jobs would be for the locals, cleaning and security. But our youngsters wouldn't want cleaning or security jobs. If I said to them, 'We can get you into a cleaning firm ... [she mimed a little double-take] they'd say: 'I don't want that. I want to be the managing director.' No-one's ever said to me that they'd like to train as a chef. They do want to be mechanics, plumbers, electricians, engineers, but unless they have a relative who's taken them on, the only opportunity they have is to go to college, to entry level courses."

At that time – in the summer of 2008 – there was still some construction work going on locally, Ruthven said, but there were few openings for local youngsters: "You won't find an apprentice. I'll say it: it's because they can get cheap labour from abroad. If you go on the internet looking for apprenticeships, the majority of places are looking for A-C grades and the people we work with aren't going to get that."

In fact, "Youth Employment Brokerage" turned out to be something of a misnomer, for it suggested Ruthven's task was merely one of matching up applicants with suitable job offers, while in fact it was nothing of the sort.

"Linda's work is often saying to young people: 'We've arranged for you to have work experience in Bow or Mile End'," Pyke said. "And they go: 'I'm not going off the island, Miss.'"

Ruthven laughed: "They get a nosebleed if they go off the island. They can't understand that they can't get a job working next door. Most parents aren't working. Most of the young people we see come from homes that have been split up ... The first obstacle we have is getting them to start a college course. But they don't want to go off the island, and Tower Hamlets College is in Poplar, which is off the island."

Pyke said: "They do go off, to shop at Bluewater in Kent and Lakeside in Essex. Lakeside, mainly."

"And they'll go to the West End," Ruthven added.

"And Romford."

"And they do shop in Canary Wharf. But if they go in more than two or three at a time the security guards throw them out."

At that time, there was no real shortage of jobs in London. The sandwich bars and coffee shops of Canary Wharf, by themselves, would have mopped up a couple of hundred Isle of Dogs school leavers each year, were they to have been interested and suitably presented. Yet instead they were taking on migrants from Eastern Europe and beyond. There seemed to be a real mismatch here between the aspirations and expectations of local youngsters and the real jobs – or training places – that were available to them. This was not just a question of them or their families clinging to the past. It seemed they had developed the expectations borne of living in a vibrant, fast-moving twenty-first-century city – without having the means to fulfil them.

Back up at the northern end of the Docklands Light Railway, in Stratford, I visited Focus E15, which provided more than 200 self-contained flats for young people. Its manager, Louise Joseph, smart, energetic and direct, took a slightly more optimistic view than Ruthven. There were opportunities out there, she said, particularly as Stratford was transformed in advance of the 2012 Olympics.

"There's going to be more jobs than local people could ever fill," she said. "There'll be hospitality, retail. There's going to be an underground shopping centre bigger than Bluewater. The opportunities are going to be huge. We've already started to look at what areas we can prepare young people to up their skills in."

She admitted, though, that for many the goal was not a steady job on a building site and a wage every week, but show business, glamour and millions: "The vast majority of boys are hooked on this music image – I'm always telling them to keep their options open. Some of them take it on board, I suppose. They probably think I'm old, so I don't know what I'm talking about. There's even a TV channel where you actually pay to have your music video on. Whereas previously you got paid, now you pay them. We've got a couple of residents who have appeared on there."

Some had come out of care, or the armed forces. Most, according to Joseph, felt let down: "Most have left school before 16. Maybe social services has let them down, the education system has let them down, their own families have let them down. Some have been moved from one foster family to another, and they've never actually settled anywhere. Some are young offenders; some have been subjected to physical abuse. It's just huge. We've had asylum seekers who've seen half their families killed."

Traumatic childhoods left young people not just scarred, she said, but lacking in the basic equipment they needed to survive. As we walked around the corner to the block where housing was provided for the centre's residents, I felt London would prove to be very different from the other places I had visited. Here there were opportunities – for those equipped to take them. Yet it seemed some young people here had such disrupted, fractured lives that they would be unable really to focus on such mundane matters as qualifications or jobs.

WILL

I had arranged to meet some Focus residents in the hope of finding one or two suitable subjects, but in the event none of them showed up. So after my meeting with Louise Joseph I wandered into one of the building's public areas in search of recruits. It was busy and noisy, with crowds of young people swirling around, talking to staff. Here, sitting on the edge of a table chatting to his friend Darren, I met Will.

Will, who was 20 then, was a talker, youthfully good looking, tall, pale but not too skinny. Most of his talk was positive, about all the great things he'd done, the things he was going to do.

"I was in *Harry Potter*, you know! Only as an extra. But I want to be an actor. I make my own films."

I asked him what his dream acting job would be.

"My top thing – *Lord of the Rings*. I could play Aragon, but I'm too young."

Darren interjected: "Frodo!" And they both laughed. Will pressed on.

"I went to this casting, with all these casting directors, looking for new talent. It was in the City. It cost me £100, but I raised the money. But it was worth it because my acting went from being best to being better than best. I learned so much. At the end of the day they called four names out of about 500 who were there. And I was number one. I was so proud. They were going to get me parts in theatre, in films, everything. But I lost my phone. Stupid things happen to me."

As we were talking, a young woman who had been talking to the office manager came over: "I'm sorry to interrupt, I'm not listening in to your conversation or nothing but I work for a theatre company. It's called Faith Productions, we're going to be putting on a play at a West End theatre and I'm looking for people to be in it. I used to live here, but I've moved out now. Why don't you come along to an audition? I'll give you my contact details ..."

Will was both engaged and taken aback. It was almost as if he was holding up a hand, going "Whoa!", as if this was all happening too quickly. He leaned forward in his chair again, though.

"What sort of theatre? Physical theatre? What sort of production? What kind of performance? I've done theatre for many years, you know."

The young woman probably wasn't much older but next to him she seemed very grown up, very confident.

"We train up actors. A lot of our young people go on to drama school. We're doing a play based around five young people and the different choices they make when they're young. We'll be looking for young people to take part," she said.

Will was feeling round his neck and looking at Darren. "Where's my USB? I had it round my neck ... it's got my CV on it ... I used to be in productions at Stratford Theatre Royal, you know ..."

After she'd gone, though, he deflated. "The thing with these acting things, I'm finding a lot of them are below me. Not to be rude, but you know ..."

Then a sort of apocalyptic despair welled up and spilled out of him, as if from nowhere.

"I want to do my acting, more than anything, but I know something bad's going to happen," he said. "Everyone feels this. Every year, the world gets worse. It don't get better. Everyone says it's going to get better, but it isn't going to happen, unless there's someone … like Noah. Something like that needs to happen. Since I've lived here, I've seen everything. I've seen people get stabbed; people get shot. I've got a friend who was stopped from jumping off a building. At first I was like, 'Oh my God, where am I?' Now I just carry on walking. I'm cold-hearted."

Will told me he had started out in Ipswich. Family life was never easy – he didn't remember his father, and he had a very difficult relationship with his stepfather, he said – but there were lots of relatives and friends around.

"My Great Nan is like my angel. When bad things happened, we'd go to her house," he said.

When Will was 14 his mum ran away from his stepdad, taking Will and his two younger half-sisters with her. Will's elder sister stayed behind, with her grandmother.

"I hate London but I had to come here, to look after my mum. Because I was the only boy," Will explained. "Then my stepdad came and moved in with my mum. There was loads of dramas. When I arrived my school said I was set for straight A's, but that all went. Then I went to sixth form college to do performing arts. I had to leave three-quarters of the way through the second year. I probably would have killed my stepdad if I hadn't. He's massive, isn't he, Darren?" Darren nodded in agreement.

"So I went to the army and did the training. But something stopped me from properly finishing. They didn't pass me out. I'm a trained soldier, I can shoot and I can march. But I had to leave. There was this one day a couple of weeks before we passed out, and they put this piece of paper in front of me. It was a will. You had to sign to say who'd inherit your stuff if you got killed. And I thought: 'I've got nothing to leave.' There would be nothing for anyone to remember me by, because I didn't have anything."

After he left the army Will got a job at City Airport, where his mum was working. He did passenger handling, calling the flights, tannoy announce-ments, that sort of thing. But he didn't like that, either. Then Darren got him a job in Tesco. But he left because they wouldn't give him paternity leave – legally he would only have been entitled if he had been there 40 weeks before his baby was born. That was a few months before we met.

Will pulled out his phone, flicking through it, then he handed it over to reveal a picture of a tiny baby with thick dark hair. "She was born two weeks ago," he said. "I have to see her. She's just part of me. But me and her mum aren't together. I saw her this morning … It's definitely over this time."

Will seemed to be swinging between momentous decisions, not knowing which direction to take. Should he go back to Ipswich? If he did that, he could see his childhood friends and his great nan again. If he stayed, he could get to know his daughter.

"I hate London. I've messed up myself. I've done my purpose, my mum's got a new boyfriend. But for some reason London has its teeth in me. I would leave, but then there's my baby." He looked emotional. "Yes, there's my baby, but I wonder … is it enough?"

Will had stopped signing on because he had been told he would have to go on a course to help him find a job – he was meant to be there the day we met. But his mum, now working for London Underground, had fixed him up with a test and interview at her workplace. As we were talking, it seemed he was forming a resolve about it.

"We're all born, we all have to die. In between we have to decide what to do, and the choices we make aren't just going to affect us, they're going to affect our children, our families. I'm going to go to the interview," he said with a sort of finality, as if admitting for the first time that he'd been thinking of not going. "It's £600 a week after tax. I could work for a year and save money and invest in my acting." He smiled, a slightly sad smile. "I think my life's got a higher purpose, but I don't know what it is."

So, how much does place matter? To put it bluntly, would the young people I met have been at risk of dropping out if they had been in the same families but in different places? I think they might have been. Many of their parents had problems of their own which prevented them from focusing fully on their children – or even prevented them from bringing them up at all. That said, though, I would argue their life chances could in some cases have been significantly improved by being brought up in different surroundings. Ricky, forced to move with his mother Sarah because of marital breakdown, went into a tailspin that led to drug-taking and educational failure. Sarah blamed the neighbours in one particularly poor part of Manchester for leading her son astray. For the most part these eight youngsters' education had taken place in schools whose results were well below the national average – as was usual in these areas of deprivation. Most of them at some stage or other had lived in substandard housing that was overcrowded or failed in other ways to meet their needs.

More complex questions remained, though. To what extent did the striking lack of geographical mobility I found matter in itself? One council official in Manchester told me she was sure it didn't – kids in the leafy suburbs probably wouldn't take a job in Collyhurst, she suggested. Yet I felt she was wrong for two reasons: first, similarly tight social networks in the suburbs, if they existed, would bring contacts with successful and influential people who could provide a far more attractive leg-up into the labour market than the young people I was meeting had. Second, those wealthier young people would probably be encouraged to leave, at some point, to go to university. Most would then go where the graduate jobs were, while the Collyhurst teenagers and the Isle of Dogs teenagers remained for the most part just where they had started out – in a workless environment surrounded by people with little money and less influence.

This "stuckness", as one head teacher put it, *was* related to the failure of some young people to make a smooth transition into the adult world – but not only because they wouldn't get on a bus to go where the work was. It was, I felt, connected in a more subtle way to longstanding attitudes and beliefs which led them to feel – rightly, in some respects – that they were best off sticking with what they knew.

Chapter 2

Changing chances

The old days

Barnsley's coat of arms is flanked by two figures: a miner on one side and a glassblower on the other, marking out the two main industries which used to sustain the town. Tom's mum, Karen, told me she came from a mining family, while her husband Andy did not. His dad had been in the RAF, she said, and after that he had gone to work in one of the glassworks. That was how things used to go, she explained — most people came either from a mining family or a glassmaking family.

If your dad wasn't a miner, the chances were you wouldn't be one either. If he was a miner, like it or not, you were probably destined to be one too. Everyone had the same experiences, the same recreations.

"When I was a teenager there used to be discos at the working men's clubs, and there could be 15 or 16 buses lined up outside. They were the heart of the community, but they're not now. The Kendray Hotel was really posh when I was young. It's still there but Tom wouldn't go in. I would, because there's still Kendray in me. A lot of the people in there I went to school with."

Karen thought that sense of belonging, of coherence, started to fall apart during the miners' strike in the 1980s. It was a time of bitterness and of violence, she said. When some of her relatives went back to work before the strike ended, that made her own life at the paper factory very hard because some of her workmates' husbands were still on strike. Kendray changed after that: "Now they shut their door, and that's it."

What had also been lost, of course, were the industries which stood so proudly on the town's coat of arms, and the others that went alongside them too. Mining and glassblowing were men's work, but there was women's work, too — sewing, the Slazenger tennis ball factory, the bedding factory, all gone now. In the spring of 2008, just after my first visit to Barnsley, the old Beatson Clark glassworks chimney which had marked Barnsley's skyline for 117 years was blown up with great ceremony. But with those industries something else had gone, it seemed. People didn't feel there was that same sense of belonging, of certainty about life, that there used to be. And that, I thought, was one of the keys to what happened next to the young people of Barnsley. Maybe it was a major clue to what had happened to so many young people across the whole country, as well.

The Dearne

Between Barnsley and Doncaster lay the starkest vista on this changed landscape. The Dearne Valley, which stretched from Wombwell in Barnsley and through part of Rotherham before ending at Conisbrough near Doncaster, was green now, its roadways fringed with young birch and willow and behind them lakes used for fishing or as bird reserves. Dotted across the whole area were office blocks and huge, modern, shed-like warehouses. In one of these a modern office blocks I met Andrew Nettleton from the Rotherham Investment and Development Office. He had to produce an Ordnance Survey map to show me what the area used to be like. The names on the map gave away the place's history: Greasborough, Grimethorpe, Rawmarsh.

Nettleton ran his finger across the map to the place where we were sitting. All this used to be a vast industrial site, he said – a coking plant, a coal byproducts plant, workshops, a coal washing plant, a laboratory. Now it was largely occupied by offices and the Dearne Valley College, which opened in 1996. We drove around the area and he pointed out some of the highlights: a start-up company making jet engines for model aircraft, more than one carpet tile manufacturer, a factory making cardboard boxes, a frozen food warehousing firm. At the Cortonwood Business Park – the site of the pit where the miners' strike started – we pulled in to reflect for a minute between a Royal Mail contact centre and an electrical goods warehouse.

The biggest employers now – and Nettleton said they didn't go out and look for them, they just arrived – were the "contact centres". Ventura – part of Next, which also had a huge distribution centre here, employed about 5,000, most of them young, female and part-time. As we drove around we had passed several, all with huge recruitment banners outside. So, there were jobs here.

Nettleton told me he used to work in the coal industry and so did his dad. Yet he was upbeat about the current situation – finding work had not been too hard for those with skills or qualifications, he said. His dad finished his career as a maintenance engineer for Tesco. Actually, the number of jobs in the Dearne Valley was higher now than it was when it was just coal and steel round here – about 12,000 compared with 9,000 before, he said.

I looked at him in some surprise. The Dearne Valley, according to the official statistics, had some of the highest levels of worklessness and deprivation in the country. Was he saying this was wrong, that the Dearne was in fact working? Not at all: almost a fifth of its adults were drawing disability benefit and less than half were economically active, he said. People didn't want to do the types of jobs that were now on offer, and employers had to cast their nets outside the area for staff.

Clinging to the past

A generation on from the closure of the pits, why were there whole communities where fewer than half the adults were working, even though there were plenty of jobs? Later, talking to Terry Connolly, the chief executive of the training charity with whom Tom was learning bricklaying, I began to think that old sense of cohesion had brought more with it than just jobs. It was the types of jobs, the ways they were offered and organised, that had been in some ways the greatest loss.

Connolly, Chief Executive of Independent Training Services, to give him his proper title, was an energetic man and clearly a networker. I had already heard his name mentioned several times before he slipped a card into my hand at a meeting in Barnsley and suggested I should visit his headquarters in a converted school near the centre of town.

Connolly told me he started his working life, like Karen's dad, at the Barnsley District Coking Company. His stepdad worked there, so it was natural he would be taken on. All he had to do was to go and see Mr Black, the under-manager.

"They allocated five or six jobs a year, to people whose families worked there already," he told me. "I put my suit on for the interview. I walked in and Mr Black looked up at me – he had this big brown floppy hat on – and he said: 'What are you dressed like that for?' I said: 'I wanted to make a good impression.' He said: 'You can't work like that. Well go home and get changed. You've got an hour. You're a trainee manager.' That was my interview. My brother worked there, my two stepbrothers, my stepfather, my uncle, they all worked there. They sent me to Barnsley College to do business studies."

Such nepotism had since come to be frowned upon, of course, but it did have its advantages. With his brother, his two stepbrothers, his stepfather and his uncle all working in the same place, Connolly knew he had to mind his P's and Q's. And there was something else – a sort of built-in support system. They would never have called it mentoring, or work-shadowing, but that was what it was.

"You used to have labourers' mates," Connolly said. "You had gofers for plumbers and electricians. You don't have any of that now – you tell me the last time you saw a driver's mate. You could go to the pit without any qualifications whatsoever. You could go to Star Paper Mills: they'd train you up. You could go to Barnsley College on day-release."

So what had been lost was not just jobs, or even just that sense of certainty that there would be a job waiting at the coking plant or the pit where the rest of the family worked. It was a certain type of job, a job that lasted. A job that was likely to last, to provide full-time hours and full-time pay. Connolly told me he now lived on one of the new housing estates in the Dearne Valley. But he was scathing about the types of companies that had moved there. For most people in Barnsley, these jobs were not a viable option.

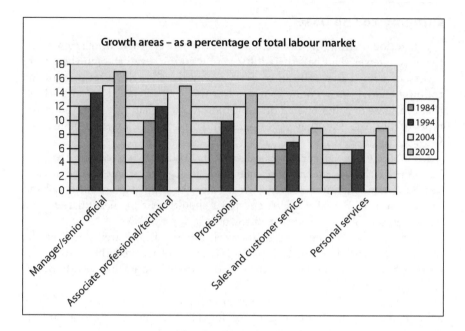

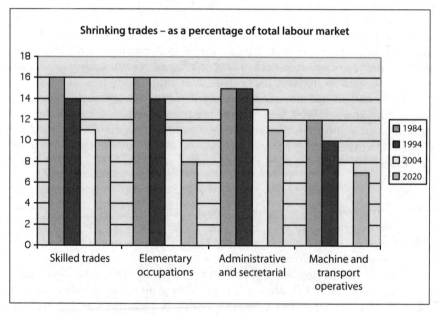

Figure 2 Areas of growth and expansion in the UK.

Source: Leitch Review of Skills, p. 63.

"The call centres prefer part time, so its predominantly female. They work shifts, and after 7 pm if you haven't got a car it's a struggle to get back. You try to get out there by public transport – it's not easy. One of the new distribution centres has advertised in Poland for workers. And it isn't going to employ that many people anyway. There's units of 2,000 and 5,000 square feet, but some of them employ eight people."

In some ways all this made perfect sense. The older generation, brought up to believe it would always have access to unskilled manual jobs as a kind of default option, was finding it hard to adapt to a changed world. It was always hard to see how a former miner in his fifties was going to develop the skills to cold-call people to ask if they would like a store card. But all that was in the past. The pits had been gone 20 years and more, in many areas. A new generation was growing up which quite possibly knew little of what had gone before – surely they must understand that the labour market had changed, that the skills they needed were different from those of their fathers?

Oddly, though, that was not entirely the case. I had been surprised to hear Tom talking about the old days, almost as if he remembered them: "With the miners' strike it brought everyone together. Especially with the football. When we play Nottingham people still shout 'Scab!' at them because they went back to work," he had told me.

The miners' strike had ended six years before Tom was born, and at 17 he was too young even really to remember the pits being open. Did he and his friends talk about the industries their town had lost, I asked? They did, he said: "We talk about the pits, but it's happened. It's done. There's no point worrying about it. It's all changed round here."

I was left wondering whether there was some lingering, psychological effect that all the initiatives, the incentives and the regeneration programmes had failed to crack. Young men like Tom had been born into a world where in some ways the way forward seemed to be quite clear. As he said, the old industries were gone. The new industries were there for all to see, their corporate logos fringing the Dearne Valley skyline. The skills they wanted had been much talked about too. The modern world needed not muscle, but brains. The new generation would need to be proficient in management, technology, sales. More than anything, Tom and his friends needed to be good communicators, they needed to be able to deal with people.

They seemed to live their lives, though, in the shadow of the past. The legacy of the old labour market, I thought, was an almost complete lack of self-determination. In the Dearne Valley, I had heard that levels of self-employment and entrepreneurship were extremely low. Everyone knew the old certainties were gone, yet young people were still growing up with a sort of passive assumption that something would come along. Or perhaps not even that – maybe it was an assumption that even if something didn't come along, it wasn't up to them as individuals to make it. This sounds like a criticism of them, but it isn't. No-one had taught them how to think differently from the way their parents had thought. No-one had taught them they would have to be different, more proactive, more qualified. There seemed to be a sort of glass wall between them and the modern labour market. They could see it, they knew its requirements. Yet somehow their images of themselves, of what they should be, did not match up the reality of the world in which they lived.

CLAIRE AND HER FAMILY

When I arrived at the neat semi where Claire lived with her dad, Mark, and her grandparents, Vic and Pat, she would bound to the door to greet me, puppyish in huge, yellow foam Bart Simpson slippers: "Look!" she'd cry. "I found our house on Google Earth! There's Granddad, cleaning the car!"

Claire, who was 16 and about to leave Wombwell High School near Barnsley when I met her, was the antithesis of how the world tended to see today's teenagers. Full of enthusiasms and eager to please, she had none of the sharp, brittle attitude with which others seemed to mask their vulnerability.

Yet despite the fact that Claire did not fit the stereotypical image of a teenager, her family, more than any of the others I met perhaps, described almost too neatly the story of work over the past half century.

Vic, Claire's granddad, worked in a foundry and a paper mill before he went into the army: "I was a radio operator," he told me. "They say this thing: 'Go and see the world.' But I was glad to get home."

For more than 30 years Vic worked at the Beatson Clark glassworks – the one whose chimney had just been demolished with such great drama. He hadn't felt the need for qualifications before he left school.

"What I've learned I got after I left," he said. "I think there's lots of opportunities now. I think the reliance is on the qualifications too much."

"You went on a lot of courses from work and got qualifications," Mark said.

"They were more manager courses," said Vic. "You can learn more on the job than you can reading it."

Like Vic, Pat left school at 15. She didn't know what she wanted to do, so her mother gave her a choice.

"Right at the last minute, I still hadn't got a job," she told me. "My mum said 'It's either the mill or the laundry.' The laundry was on the doorstep, but everyone that worked there hated it, so I said 'No.' I went to Hinchliffe's, a woollen mill near Huddersfield, as a spinner. My mum worked there – she finished on the Friday and I started on the Monday. So everybody knew me, including the overlooker. I enjoyed every minute. You never had time to be bored. We used to sing all the way to work and sleep all the way home.

"I was a spinner on piecework. You had to start at the bottom, just taking bobbins round. Then it was someone's job to show you the job. We took the wool from the sheep's back to the roll of cloth. In the end I earned more money than you, didn't I, Vic?"

She looked at Claire, playing with an iPod Mark had recently bought for her, her blue top intensifying the colour of her eyes.

"I don't think she would have done it," Pat continued. "They wouldn't do it now, but there weren't much else for us. It wasn't long after the War. If you didn't work, you didn't get any money. I'd been working 12 months, when I was her age."

Neither Vic nor Pat was ever out of work, though Pat gave up when she married and started a family. Their eldest son, Mark's older brother, got an apprenticeship at Beatson Clark and stayed there till they closed their Barnsley plant. Their younger son, Claire's dad Mark, quiet but with a wicked, dry sense of humour, entered the world of work in troubled times.

"It was 1983. The country were in a bit of a state," he said. "Jobs were like gold dust round here. There were several pits near, but the jobs that came up tended to go to the offspring of the men who worked there. It was kept in the family, more or less. If your dad or your uncle worked in the pits you'd have an interview. Quite a few of my friends went down the mines, but they were only employed for about 18 months.

"I'd worked in numerous places, building sites, laying drains. And digging canals. Painting and decorating. A lot of them were schemes, you know. It was hard work but I enjoyed it. I did labouring jobs until I was 22, and then I had my accident."

Claire had told me before I met Mark that he was disabled and unable to work. In their lounge there were some beautiful ornaments and vases Mark had made from wood in a shed in the back garden. Some were turned so exquisitely they looked like Art Nouveau pottery; one had rainbow effects of blurred and muted colours.

When I asked how the accident happened they all laughed, sharing a joke they must have shared many times.

"I got drunk and climbed up a tree," he explained. "But I came down faster. I fell 25 or 30 feet onto concrete. That was before Claire was born." He stopped laughing. "In a way, it probably saved my life. I was an alcoholic. Whilst I were in hospital I realised what an idiot I'd been. I didn't stop drinking, but it opened my eyes. I haven't drunk alcohol now for 13 years."

And so Mark was out of the labour market, perhaps before he had really found a permanent niche in it at all. He had not been able to work since.

Now Claire was about to leave school, with no really clear idea of what she should do next. Her school had sent her to a group run by a charity, for those who were thought to be at risk of dropping out. But as always, she was full of enthusiasm.

"I've put down for drama and music," she said. "But I'm still thinking: 'Shall I go for shop work first, or college first? Or shop work part-time and college part-time?'

"Really, I've been thinking about my future, and I've been doing it in RE because I completed my work so the teacher said: 'You can just day-dream if you want.' So I was thinking: 'What can I do?' Because I was so bored. I day-dreamed, and I saw myself going to a college and walking in."

What did Mark want Claire to do, I asked? Would he prefer college, or would he like her to get a job?

"I'm happy, either way," he said. "If she wants to go to college, she can go to college. But if she wants to get a job, that's fine. I'm a great believer in going out there and contributing. But if she wants a qualification, it's up to her."

I wondered what hopes he had for Claire.

"I don't really expect anything. I wanted her to grow up in a comfortable, safe environment. Really ... how can I explain it? As long as Claire tried her hardest at school I was happy. She weren't going to be Einstein, but if she tried hard, Dad was happy. She gets into trouble for not keeping her bedroom tidy, but its not too bad."

For Vic and Pat, there had been plenty of work, a clear route ahead and no real need for educational qualifications. For Mark, there had been very little indeed – just a recession from which many like him never really recovered. For Claire, at that time, the future seemed unclear. There was still the feeling, despite the first rumblings of economic dyspepsia, that the economy was strong. But what place Claire might have in it, and how she was to find her way into that place, seemed very unclear.

Chapter 3

Aspirations

Sarah, the mother of Ricky who was picked up by the Rathbone charity while robbing a car in Collyhurst, went to the same school as my Granny, Mary Bentley. In the years before the First World War, part of the pleasure of attending Manchester Central High School for Girls was being able to travel the mile or so into town on the electric tram that ran past Granny's house in Ashton New Road, Clayton. But the greatest joy of it was the books.

"I will never forget the thrill in the first week, when my desk was filled with new books – all my own. On the top was Robert Louis Stevenson's *Black Arrow*, which got me into trouble because I couldn't resist reading it right away," Granny wrote later in her autobiography. "My bursary only covered fees, and all those books had to be paid for."

For Granny, whose father was a foreman cooper in a soap works, the high school was a step up in the world. She said her four years there were happy ones, though she feared at first the other girls would look down their noses.

"I had to take sandwiches because I could not afford the hot dinners. However, as time passed I found that it was only myself that felt any inferiority, and my mother made me a gym tunic that could compare quite favourably with the ones the richer girls wore."

At Seymour Road Elementary School she hadn't felt marked out by her family's economic status, particularly – she didn't have a silk dress, as one or two girls did, but on the other hand she didn't smell either.

What Granny's family did have, though, were aspirations – she never described her father as just a barrelmaker, always as a *foreman* cooper. Granny went on to be a teacher, and none of her three siblings stayed in Clayton. Her father had had to leave school when he was 12, but he wanted his children to have the education he missed out on.

"We used to go on Sunday afternoons to Ancoats Brotherhood," she wrote. "The entrance was free and the entertainments consisted of half an hour of music, a talk by some famous person and another half-hour of music. They originated so that the poor people in the slums of Ancoats should have somewhere to go for free entertainment and intellectual stimulus." Sylvia Pankhurst came to talk about her work in London and Bernard Shaw gave a lecture on "The Ideal Citizen".

Sarah was born and bred in Ancoats, though things had changed by then. The brotherhood was long gone, and by the time she attended the Central High School for Girls in the 1970s it had become a standard, non-selective secondary school.

"I hated it," she told me. "I think I kept it up till about the third year and then I just kept skipping.

"It was different then, because when I left school at 16 I went straight into a job," Sarah explained. "It was at Permonides cable factory. I was there for 10 years and I loved it. You know that cable you used to have on a drum? I used to have to feed it on to the reel, my hands used to get really burned. Sometimes the cable was 250 or 500 metres – the Post Office cable was the worst. I used to work with my Mam, she was a supervisor there. I'd walk there with her every morning, and there was always someone to walk home with."

Sarah worked at the cable factory until she married and had her first two children, Ricky's older half-brother and half-sister. When she moved it was not usually because she wanted a nicer place to live or a better-paid job, but because of family problems. After her first marriage broke up she lived in Collyhurst with Ricky's dad, but then she had to move again to get away from his violence and his drinking.

So why was it different for Granny? And why was it different again for Ricky, who certainly did not leave school expecting to follow his father or his mother into a steady job? For one thing, the labour market had changed, and the job Sarah and her mother did no longer existed – not in Ancoats, anyway. The school system had changed, too: grammar schools, it was often said, provided a means of escape for children from working class backgrounds, and certainly Granny's story would support that. But while schools could open doors, it helped a very great deal if their pupils, and their parents, were pushing at those doors already.

"What do I want for Ricky?" Sarah pondered the question for a minute: "I'd like him to achieve something ..."

"Prison," Ricky cut in, with just a hint of one of his cheeky smiles.

"I don't want you in prison, you know that."

"I don't want that either. I've got a mate who's 15 and he's looking at going to jail."

Sarah thought about it some more: "Ricky isn't a bad kid. The police said to me: 'For a Collyhurst lad, he isn't that bad.' Not if he puts his mind to it. He's just lazy. He's got nothing to do."

From Sarah's point of view and from Ricky's, education did not have much to offer.

"If you've got nothing, you can't get nothing," Sarah told me. "You've got to have GCSEs. Or you've got GCSEs, but you've got no experience. Sometimes I wonder what's the point of getting qualifications."

For many families, then, in the old industrial landscape, aspirations were less important. They could have them – and many, like Granny's family, did. But if they didn't, that was fine too. There were jobs, and young people could grow up with certain expectations about what would happen next – for boys, manual work; for girls, different kinds of manual work followed by marriage and motherhood. Now young people had to aspire to live their lives in a different way from their parents if they were to be successful. Yet often they still talked in very similar language to the older generation – in the case of the boys – about doing solid, manual jobs, or – in the case of the girls – of doing something that might suit them until they had children of their own or even as a part-time job after, such as beauty or childcare.

Home and family

It took two attempts before I managed to meet the mother of Yasmin, the girl who used to climb the school gates in Poplar at lunchtime. The first time I arranged to visit at 10:30 one morning, but arrived to find her out and Yasmin still in bed: "We had a family crisis. She had to go to Poplar," she explained blearily.

In Yasmin's home, there was no lack of aspiration – Yasmin had talked before of going to college to do business studies; of starting her own company one day – and when I finally did get to meet her mum, it was clear she supported and encouraged those dreams. Yet that was the problem – they *were* dreams, based on only the vaguest notion of what Yasmin actually needed to do to fulfil them. Her mother, with only a basic education and no English, was in an even worse position than the parents I met in Manchester when it came to making a realistic assessment of the modern labour market.

As we talked in their neat living room a Bangladeshi TV station was running a film, and Yasmin's mum was pottering around with a pile of post, occasionally handing a letter to Yasmin for translation. Yasmin's two little nephews, aged two and three, ran in and out of the room and at one point both started to undress, the littler one following his brother's lead. "*Will* you put your trousers on!" Yasmin exclaimed in mock annoyance. She told me she had recently found a part-time job in Primark. Rathbone had previously placed her with a car hire company but she had found it boring, she said.

I wanted to know about Yasmin's mum's background, and about the aspirations she had for Yasmin. Where did she go to school, and for how long? Did she enjoy it? "She left really young," Yasmin translated. How young? "I don't know. She doesn't remember." I pressed the point: 12? 13? "Yes, something like that." Did she enjoy it? She asked the question, and her mum replied. "Yes, she enjoyed it. Then she was at home until she got married. She came here straight after she got married."

I asked Yasmin about her mum's attitude to her education. "She's always wanted the best for me. When I was in school she wanted me to do well and get the best results, so I could get the best job in the future. She wants better things for me," she said.

I picked up on this: Better? How better? Would she like her life to have been different in some way? She consulted her mother and then said: "She wants me to do well in life and do things she couldn't do." What things, I asked? Would she have liked to have had different opportunities? She smiled a slow smile as Yasmin translated: "If she'd had the opportunity to be where I am, she would have done good at school, got good results and tried to get a job," Yasmin concluded. "If she had done it, she would have gone further. Because she couldn't, she didn't get that chance. But if she could, she would have."

I wondered why Yasmin's mum thought she hadn't really thrived at school. She clearly wanted the best for all her children, and wanted them to do well. So what went wrong? "She thinks it was for the fun of it, because we found school boring. Most of my brothers and my sister did the same," Yasmin explained. I asked how she felt about what that did to her parents. "Mum was very upset. The school would call the house constantly, saying I was truanting. Mum and Dad didn't like it. They tried to stop me, and tried to tell me off. But I still did it more. They would just make me understand and give me advice. But with me it just goes in one ear and comes out the other."

I asked what her mum would like her to be doing in five years' time. Again, the answer was well-meaning but vague: "She wants me to do well in the future, have a good job and make lots of money." We all laughed. What would she do with the money if she had it, I asked? "Probably give half of it to my mum … and she wants me married off," Yasmin concluded. When would that be? After a short consultation Yasmin replied: "As soon as possible." Her mum laughed and nodded as I made motions with my hand: "Away!" No, really – what age would her mum like to see her married? "About 20, 22. Lots of time – make lots of money first."

How that money was to be made by the age of 20 or 22 was not clear – what sort of business Yasmin might start, and how, seemed yet to be considered. Yasmin's mother clearly wanted the best for her, but lacked the means to turn her aspirations into reality.

What do parents expect?

Yasmin, in a sense, had gone out into the world with one arm tied behind her. While other girls from more affluent homes had parents who could push, prod and even carry them if necessary, Yasmin had to make her own way. She went to school, of course. Yet her school, however good it was, could only ever make a marginal difference to her prospects in life.

This might sound a surprising statement – the debate about why children achieved and why they failed had been dominated for so many years by discussion of what happened in schools. Over the previous two decades schools had been forced to open themselves up to scrutiny, to set and meet targets, to face possible closure if they failed to do what the state required of them. An assumption had crept in that schools were where education happened; that therefore the route to higher educational attainment and to success in the labour market was through the education system.

Not so. As a matter of fact, it had never been a secret that schools could only divert children marginally from the paths marked out for them from birth by geography, social class and family. Time after time, studies had shown the pupils whose parents had the most education did best at school. There were obvious, practical benefits to having parents who knew things, of course, because they could offer real, concrete support. But there was something more about the way parents had come to view schools. The heavy focus on teachers, the curriculum, exam grades and the structure of education seemed to have led some parents to feel that learning *was* about schools. Take, for example, a research study by academics at the University of Sunderland. They interviewed 3,000 parents in North East England, in Kentucky and in St Petersburg about their attitudes to education. When they were asked what would help to raise their children's attainment, the Russian parents were four times more likely to say their offspring needed more help at home than they were to say they should have more help at school. The British and the American parents were far more likely – 15 times more likely in fact – to say help from teachers was more important than their own input.

Professor Julian Elliott, who led the study, said when it was released that the emphasis placed on schools in some countries – the UK and America among them – was actually undermining efforts to raise standards. He and his colleagues found the Russian parents were much more likely to push their children to use their free time to study, even though their schools made more demands of them than those in the US and Britain.

"We would suggest that the positive views of parents found in this study are redolent of the 'Lake Wobegon factor', where all the men are strong, the women are good-looking, and all the children are above average," Professor Elliott said. He suggested that educational reforms might have resulted in too great a burden on schools and a corresponding neglect of the role of parents. The recent emphasis upon the school as a self-contained unit wholly responsible for student outcomes was flawed, he said – the home had a vital role to play too.

Other research backed up this view. British youth cohort studies, which followed young people born in 1946, 1958 and 1970, found a striking correlation between the views of young people and their parents, regardless of which social class they were born into. So those from professional backgrounds were likely to agree with their parents that higher education was the best course, while those whose parents were in manual or routine jobs were more likely to agree there was no need for it. There was an interesting corollary, though: young people from all backgrounds tended to think education more important than their parents did, having grown up in a world where qualifications were more vital than they used to be. This changed world, then, was making an impression on the young, but a differential impression, impacting more sharply on those whose families were already open to the notion that a formal education was the key to success.

Yet among the young people I met, this divide was not clear-cut. In multicultural London, particularly, there was a feeling that some young people, even from quite poor families, were being pushed to get the best possible qualifications. In many ways the future looked to them like a middle-class future, in which those with professional, technical or managerial skills would thrive. I asked the Mayor of London's peer outreach team, which was made up of between 20 and 30 young people who worked on research projects and helped with policy development, what support they had from their parents. Almost by definition these were ambitious young people who had seized the opportunity to work for the Mayor, but many of them had not come from affluent homes.

Most said their parents had been ambitious for them, though most also said their parents did not have the resources or experience to offer much in the way of practical advice about education. One young man, Dominic, said the support his mother gave him had been both practical and psychological.

"I was told: 'Anything you want to do; do it.' Mum gave me full support," he told me. "I was into roller skating – I had £200 skates. I was into ice hockey, she used to drive me to Lea Valley twice a week – it took hours. If you've got 10 kids and they're all told 'You're not going to do this', the majority are going to listen to what's being said. They're not going to reach their potential.

"If your mother works three jobs to make sure your sister and you are fed, you can never decide to do nothing with your life, because that's spitting in her face. It's a moral obligation."

It struck me that perhaps Dominic's mother's positive attitude possibly counted for a great deal more than her willingness to buy expensive skates or to drive her son across London. He said her determination to give him whatever he needed carried both inspiration and a sense of duty. That willingness to say "If you want it, do it" must have swept away many obstacles.

Families which had a dynamic parent driving them forward in this way had long since used education as a ladder on which to climb into the middle class. Others, perhaps like Sarah's, had no real reason to do that. She had her family and friends around her, she lived in an area of town where she felt comfortable and in the early part of her working life she had always been able to earn money for the things she wanted. There was nothing wrong with any of that, except that the world changed and Ricky did not have the same chances she had.

In the past, aspiration was for people who wanted it, and the alternatives were often perfectly viable. Now everyone was being told to aspire, yet for many young people the sense that they needed to reach out was not fully formed. They heard this message, from school and often from home too, that education mattered, but no-one was spelling out in clear terms precisely *why* it mattered. What, precisely, was it they were supposed to aspire to? What did they need to do, right now, to achieve it? How would their lives be better as a result? Most did not have any clear idea.

Perhaps families, even communities, had certain trajectories on which they were travelling. A newly perceived set of opportunities, created maybe by migration to a different country or a better area, could act as a sort of spur to greater effort. There was a sense, in some of the families I met, that they were going forwards but were poised on the brink, wondering whether or not to make a leap into the unknown. Karen in Barnsley, fresh from her women's education programme and wondering whether to take that step: "Am I going to university? What to do next?" And her son Tom, put off going to university by the thought it would separate him from his friends. Their trajectory seemed to be pushing them forward, yet there was much to lose too. The sense that moving on would be moving away, too, was a strong one. Others simply weren't going forward at all. It seemed possible whole communities, having seen their economic bedrock crumbling beneath them, felt their trajectories were, and would continue to be, downward ones. And families within those communities, not having had any particular need to go anywhere in the past, had developed a sort of resistance to doing so under pressure.

ASHLEY

"I'd move like a shot," Ashley's mother, Ann, told me. "I've lost my parents, but my husband, Mark, still has his. He's a family man, and so he works away from home but he still lives here."

When I asked what Mark did for a living, Ashley, who was 15 when I met her, chipped in with a cheeky grin: "As little as possible, because he's the manager."

Before I had had time to ask what he was the manager of, Ashley was off, talking about what she'd been doing at school; how she was having a party for her sixteenth birthday.

After a few minutes Ann stopped her, laughing: "Did you say you'd talked to Ashley before? Do you know what you're letting yourself in for?

"At school one of her teachers calls her 'Owl', because her head's never still. It spins. You can be talking to her and she's like this ..." She swivelled her own head around to demonstrate. "We were most worried about her, being like that ..." – Ashley has a facial disfigurement which has flattened her nose – "She had her first operation when she was six months old. We knew she'd have a lot of knocks."

Mark had always lived in Wombwell but had always worked away – he was, it turned out, a quarry manager for McAlpine's, in Somerset.

"He went to price a cottage down there," Ann explained, "but it was £250 a week. We pay £50 for this." The house was a concrete pre-fab council house which looked as if it had had no work done since it was built – which I later found out was during the War. At the top of the road, some of the houses were being renovated and given new fascias but the slow march of progress was yet to reach Ashley's house. A string of greying Christmas lights blew in the wind over a neighbouring front door on the day I first visited in March, giving their end of the street a dismal air.

Ashley lived here mostly with her mum and with her sister Stacey, though Stacey, who was 19 going on 20, spent a lot of time at her boyfriend's. She worked as a cook in an old people's home. Ann ran a catering business too – just a little sideline, she said.

Ann told me she had ambitions that were never fulfilled: "My sister was always really clever – she went into nursing, she's a cardiac sister now in Wakefield. So my parents put her through college, and the money wasn't there for me. I always wanted to be a chef. My dad worked in the pit from 12 years old."

Ann left school at 15 and went to work in a factory, making men's suits. After five years making Arnold Palmer's golfing trousers, she moved to the bedding factory.

"Mark was the same. He left school on a Friday and started work on a Monday. He's always worked and he's gone the hard way to get where he's got. I always said: 'I don't want my kids in the factories.' I wanted better for them. I wanted them to do something. We always said if we could afford it they'd have a better education than we had."

I was slightly surprised by this, as the first time I had met Ashley she told me her dad didn't want her to go to college and had told her to get a job instead. Ann said it was really a matter of Mark wanting to be sure Ashley would work hard and do her best.

"Mark just said no, she's not going to college, because when she's got home-work she's a bit lackadaisical and not buckling down," Ann explained. "He says if she's not going to try she isn't going to try at college. He just doesn't want her to go and waste her time. So long as she shows him she's willing to do it, that's fine."

Ashley was off again, then: "I want to do it, though. I want to do childcare, I've been wanting to do it since I was 10, and I've never changed my mind. But if I can't get into childcare by the time it comes to my college interview I'll go into hair and beauty. My friend went yesterday, to Barnsley College. She went for childcare and they phoned her up the same day to offer her a place. She said all you had to do is go in and they talk to you and say about the course."

When Ashley made up her mind to do something she usually did it, Ann said. But she had been disappointed to hear of others dropping out: "Stacey used to have three friends. One wanted to be a lawyer, one a teacher, and the other wanted to do hair and beauty. But when they went to college they all gave up within six months. They all work at the Ventura call centre now. They were all going to be this, and they were all going to be that.

"I'm really proud of Stacey because out of the four of them she was the one who had to work at it. It didn't come naturally to her, just like with Ashley. The one who was going to be a lawyer, I would have put money on it that she would have done it. It just flowed from her, she didn't have to think and it was there. She gave it all up for money. She started at college and got a little part-time job and that were it. I was gobsmacked.

"I said to Stacey: 'Don't let me down.' She said 'Mum, no. I've put too much into it.' In the third year she said she couldn't wait to get finished. But in the end it was worth it. She got her qualifications. At parents evening they said there were 20 in the class and there were seven who would make it. Stacey was one of those.

"Mark used to be the same with Stacey: 'You're not going to college.' I said: 'They're not ending up in dead-end jobs like I did.'"

Ashley chipped in: "I said: 'Do you want me to have a dead-end job in a fish shop?'"

Ann nodded agreement: "When I see them in the shops looking bored and their faces are dead, I think what a waste of a life. When I was young the money weren't there. It was a shame, but you had to accept it."

Chapter 4

Poverty

When I first met Elvige, through the Mayor of London's office where she had a part-time job, I thought she would not be a good subject for this book. I had decided that while my parameters would be broad – to follow a group of young people who had either dropped out or were thought to be at risk of dropping out – she simply would not fit them. The day we met, Elvige had been taking a practical exam for her drama A-level, and hoped to do well: "I am not a person who gets C's or D's," she told me with a sort of finality that brooked no possibility of slippage.

Yet within half an hour I had decided hers was a story worth telling. Although she struck me as an extraordinarily composed, confident and even charismatic young woman, hers had not been an easy journey. Born in Togo to a single mother who had to drop out of school when she became pregnant, Elvige spent most of her early years with her grandmother. When she was about nine her mother brought her to England to find her father, discovering only after they arrived that he had met someone else.

Of all the young people I met, Elvige was the only one who felt her chances in life had been affected in some way by pure, grinding poverty.

"When we first came here me and my mum were in a one-bedroomed flat in Manor Park," she told me. "It was disgusting. I couldn't speak English, and it was about a year before my mum enrolled me in school. It was a case of my mum doing shifts all day, and I was at home. I remember she worked in Tesco, and I think I remember her working in a café-bar thing."

Sitting at home in East London with the television for company, Elvige grew frustrated. She wanted to be able to watch the Teletubbies, she said, so she learned English by deciphering the little creatures' twitterings.

"I was 10 when we went to the homeless place," Elvige told me as she sipped a cup of Starbucks hot chocolate. "Mum couldn't deal with the rent demands and the landlord wanted us out. We got housed in Kent, in Margate. And from Margate they moved us back to a bed and breakfast in Seven Sisters in London. I finally got enrolled at school there, and then they wanted us to move again. So we moved to Canning Town, but I told my mum I couldn't leave school before the end of year 7."

All this was deeply disrupting to Elvige's education, of course, but she coped. The thing she found harder was the fact that even once she did settle into a new school back in the East End, she had no-one at home to help with her school work.

"My mum didn't learn English as quickly as I did," she said. "So homework and stuff was really hard for me, because she couldn't help me. She wants to live her dream, through me. She's worked really hard. When she enrolled me in school she started applying for college. She got her GCSEs during the day and worked at night."

Indeed, Elvige attributed her success, in part, to the fact that her family hadn't always had it easy: "When you've got parents who go through a hard life, that's one of the strongest motivations that a young person could have. You strive to get out of that position. I have friends who say: 'I'm going on holiday and my mum's going to pay. Do you want to come?' I say: 'If you haven't noticed, my mum's not like the Queen. She can't just produce money.'"

Elvige said her family had all the right words of encouragement, but few practical resources: "When I was little I was mainly with my Grandma, and bless her soul she would say: 'You can achieve what you want to achieve, just make us proud and carry on our family heritage.' But in making sure I was in the proper school? She didn't know how to do that."

Yet Elvige had this sense in her that anything was possible, except failure.

"I can't go to my mum and say I went for a job interview and didn't get the job," she said. "She will look at me with these piercing eyes and make me feel that little. When I came and said I got a job at the Greater London Authority she was jumping up and down. She phoned Africa! If you're oldest you're the one who's going to put your parents in a care home, buy them a house they want, get them a car. I don't know if that's just the African way, but that's the way it is in my family."

Real or relative?

For the most part, though, the young people I met were not obviously suffering from poverty. They were not without decent clothes or school uniforms; they had reasonable housing and plenty to eat. Ricky from Collyhurst was a prime example. His mother, Sarah, told me they were living on a less than £60 a week Job Seekers' Allowance, plus a little she earned by working a couple of hours at the weekend in a bar. Yet their house was always spotless, and Sarah told me she bought meat in bulk to make pies for the freezer.

Certainly several had experienced real hardship at some stage in their lives. The first time I met Will, the aspiring actor, he told me how tough life had been for his family at times: "I remember when Sainsbury's and Tesco had a bread war. And there was a beans war too, and it was 5p to have beans on toast. We lived on beans on toast for a whole year."

Several of these families, I was sure, had money worries. One day when

I visited one of their homes a letter had just arrived from a company that bought up bad credit card debts, and had a reputation for pursuing them very vigorously.

Poverty also narrowed some children's range of experiences. One London head teacher told me: "When we come back after the holidays, a lot of the girls when you ask them what the holidays were like, it isn't like other schools. They haven't been anywhere or done anything very much. Partly that's poverty, isn't it? It isn't as if their parents can afford to fly them off to Spain. A lot of them will look after siblings and help out. We think if we don't provide opportunities to experience things they won't necessarily have them – the Tower of London; even the cinema. Knowing how to talk to adults outside your own home environment is a big issue."

To what extent did these things affect these young people's ability to learn; their ability to thrive at school in the longer term? It would be naïve to say it did not; even on the most basic level of argument – a child who is not well nourished is a child who does not concentrate well at school; a child who gets taken to the zoo may use the experience to develop an interest in the wider world. But on another level it would be hard to argue that genuine, hand-to-mouth poverty was the major factor in causing most of these young people to drop out or to fail to thrive. Where they had missed school or not worked as hard as they should when they were there, it was not a simple, straightforward lack of money that caused that to happen.

Yet there was plenty of evidence pupils from the poorest homes tended to perform badly in exams. While the proportion of pupils in England gaining five good GCSEs rose by eight percentage points to 63 per cent between 2003 and 2008, the proportion of those on free school meals achieving that benchmark was much lower, at just 40 per cent. And better-off pupils made more progress between the ages of seven and 16 than those on free school meals.

The pupils of the twenty-first century in the Western world did not lack shoes to go to school in, but they did worry about money, and they did often feel they needed to go out and earn a living. In some cases this was because of the things they wanted to buy for themselves – Ashley's mum, Ann, felt her older daughter's friends dropped out of school not because they had to but because they were drawn in by the prospect of nice clothes and nights out on the town. According to UK government research, more than four out of 10 pupils who left school at the first opportunity did so because they felt they needed to earn some money. On the other hand, only one in 14 said their parents could not afford for them to stay, suggesting many left because they wanted more money to spend themselves. For those without much money, those whose parents could not afford to slip them the odd 10 or 20 pounds to spend on themselves, staying in education was certainly harder. But the choices they made were more often than not marginal ones, driven by desire rather than by necessity.

One thing was very clear, though. The poorest children, by and large, went on to become the poorest adults. According to evidence from youth cohort studies in the UK, a teenager growing up poor in the 1970s was twice as likely to be poor at 33 as his or her wealthier classmates. For a teenager growing up poor in the 1980s, the chances of poverty in adulthood were relatively even greater – four times that of a teenager from a more affluent background. This issue of social mobility had been hotly debated for many years. Certainly the UK had a poor record – research published by the Sutton Trust found high levels of mobility in Scandinavian countries compared with the UK. It found America, "the land of opportunity", had the lowest mobility of all.

A complex web of factors must have led to this, of course – a lack of understanding of the need for qualifications in the modern world; a lack of aspiration borne of that lack of understanding; a tendency to have parents whose own experiences of education were bad; even a genuine belief, maybe based on experience and observation, that school and work were not the be-all-and-end-all of happiness and human fulfilment. And poverty in the Western world was measured in relative rather than concrete terms, so that no matter how prosperous a society became, poverty could never really disappear. Did it matter? If the young people I met had shoes on their feet and food on their plates, did it matter that they were not as rich as some of their classmates? Actually, it did.

The poverty Elvige experienced was real: her education was disrupted by homelessness when her mother struggled to pay the rent while doing minimum wage jobs. But in her view there was something fundamental about the psychological effects of relative poverty, too.

"You have young people and parents living in run-down council flats. And walking across Canary Wharf, you have all these buildings that are really nice, and it's literally across the road," she told me once. She believed that if the world were a more equal place, fewer young people would turn to crime.

"If you concentrate on cutting poverty out, young people have no excuse for saying: 'This is the reason I sell drugs.' If you take them out of poverty, you make it more obvious that there are opportunities out there for them. Using young people like me who go through a hard time and still come out on top, we can encourage them to do something for themselves."

More than once, my conversations with Will bore this out too. Although he had never been in trouble with the police, he spent a lot of time thinking about how he might make a quick buck. Everyone at the young people's accommodation where he lived was doing the same, he said. When he put his friends' get-rich-quick schemes alongside his other options – work at Tesco, in the airport or even as a tube driver – the real world did not seem very enticing.

There was a sense, in London particularly, that money was all around and yet always just out of reach. A youth worker in Whitechapel, in East London, explained how the firm where Yasmin did her work experience made money. It rented out flashy cars like Ferraris and Porsches virtually by the hour, and young boys – often far too young – would borrow or steal the paperwork so they could parade the streets in one of these cars at Eid or at other festival times. Lots of those boys would be wondering how they could get to drive a car like that every day, he said.

He believed for many young people growing up in London, the gap between the wages they could expect to earn and the lifestyle to which they aspired was just too great. They knew they could never get a Ferrari by going to college to do one of the basic courses for which their handful of GCSEs would qualify them. So they dreamed of finding another way – and that was one of the things that held them back.

"A big car is the biggest thing in life round here," he explained. "An M3 would do. But you're not going to get that very quickly unless you do something stupid. People balance it out: 'What's the crime I could do to make a million, and do the least time for it?' They see the city guys, driving home in their flash cars, they see them every day. Young people see that, and it makes them dream. When that happens you don't want anything else."

Poverty did matter, then, but perhaps not in the way people often assumed it did. It was not so much the lack of money that led young people to drop out, as the proximity of money. Whether that sense of possibility was borne in on them by the flashy cars crunching out of the city along the A13 each night, by the celebrities they could all see on television or in magazines, or just in the unattainable clothes they could stare at in the shop windows, it did hit some of them hard. Only a tiny minority would turn to crime; not many would even dream vaguely of it, as Will did sometimes. Yet for some the ratio of rewards to effort felt very low when it was set alongside all this conspicuous consumption. They were left with this sense that a college certificate in business or the arts would maybe not be a ticket to what they really wanted. Sometimes perhaps it was easier just to fail than it was to succeed, only then to realise your dreams were still just a far-distant mirage.

Chapter 5

School

"I left school with no qualifications, hating education," Tom's mum, Karen, told me the first time we met. "There was an option to go to college at 16, but we were told: 'You're going to be a housewife. Why bother? You haven't got what it takes.'"

On one level it was hard to see what Karen, a bright woman who had gone back to college later – "They built it up slowly and convinced me I wasn't stupid" – had got from her years at secondary school, except a sense that education wasn't for her. There were no certificates to open doors to a better job, no sense either that she had started a journey she could continue. She was marked down for a job in a factory, then motherhood, and for those things a secondary education wasn't really needed.

In recent decades, though, schools had been expected to do much more. Instead of merely looking after young men and women from working class families till they were old enough to go to work, they were now expected to push them through examinations, to guide them through a full academic curriculum and to ensure they hit targets on literacy and numeracy. How much difference did this make? In some respects, it led to improvements – far more young people left school with good GCSEs than previously, for example. But in terms of real *difference* – in terms of education offering young people a future they would not otherwise have had – its results were questionable. Indeed, the research evidence was reasonably clear on this point: most children, in most schools, most of the time, still came out with pretty much the knowledge and the qualifications they were destined to come out with when they went in. That is to say, in terms of social mobility schools did not make a difference to the majority of children in any real sense. The London School of Economics estimated schools could be held responsible for about one-seventh of the causes of educational failure. So if children failed to make a smooth transition into the labour market, that was not for the most part because their schools were doing a terrible job. In most cases they were doing a perfectly good job in handing down the information and the skills they were asked to hand down. The biggest problem they faced was that their pupils did not walk through the door like so many shiny new pencils, all identical and ready to perform precisely the same tasks. They brought baggage, scars, attitudes – not all of them bad or wrong, but different and multifarious. And for the most part, they took those things away with them, along with their GCSE certificates, when they left.

For just about as long as children from poorer backgrounds had gone to school in developed countries, a large proportion of those children had found it pointless. It bore little relation to the world they went home to; they found it hard to connect what they did at school with what they did outside it or what they expected to do in the future. This left the educational establishment with a problem: should they attempt to teach Shakespeare and quadratic equations to all children, knowing full well that many of them would gain little from it? Would the exercise be worthwhile if even a few children from homes without books had their eyes opened at school to the joys of reading, the theatre or algebra? Or would it be better instead to try to teach them skills they would be more likely to need, such as carpentry or childcare? In the world of education the debate had zigzagged back and forth for decades, with those on the academic side arguing it would be a counsel of despair not to even try to engender a love of academic learning, and those on the vocational side pointing out many left school ill-prepared for work.

Recently, this second school of thought had been in the ascendancy, with schools increasingly offering "vocational" courses. Yet the employers to whom I spoke were still not happy. They did not so much want schools to teach young people work skills – though they did – as to give them some notion of the world of work, and what it was about. The owner of a bakery in Barnsley told me he felt there was still a kind of academic "closed shop" operating in which the vocational, despite its increasing popularity in schools, was not really valued. Because all teachers had degrees, he argued, they saw an academic education as a sort of Holy Grail. The other things they did were somehow inferior: "You can be prime minister without a degree, but you can't teach. It's just a closed shop. What it does is it reinforces that view in young people that non-graduate training or non-graduate employment is somehow unclean. Food production is very technical but it has worth, and it has merit, and it has joy. We might be the best bakers in the world, but we are being judged and marked and scored by a system that would reject anything that doesn't conform to these values," he said.

If he was right, it was no wonder so many young people felt school was not really for them. If their parents worked in manual or semi-skilled jobs, and encouraged them to envisage a similar future for themselves, and yet their schools made them feel success was measured in terms of academic success, it was no wonder they became disillusioned; no wonder they dropped out or became disruptive.

Was the baker right? Was this what was happening? Some of the evidence I saw in schools seemed to point that way: there was a tendency to push the less academic youngsters on to external "vocational" courses which sometimes seemed like simple warehousing exercises. Claire, from Barnsley, told me her grades had suffered because she spent one day a week helping at a riding for the disabled group and also missed school regularly to attend sessions for pupils thought to be at risk of dropping out. Among the others in Claire's support group there was one boy who spent a day a week doing mechanics, and another who was on a training course to do gardening work. He said that with one thing and another he didn't really have to go to school much at all. Claire was never in any trouble, but I got the feeling the school might have been rather glad to see the back of some of them. In sending off pupils who failed to thrive academically to do vocational activities elsewhere, schools loosened further their grip on those with whom their relationships were already increasingly shaky. And so those who already found school pointless and boring became even more alienated, even more likely to reject the lessons they were offered when they were there.

Teenagers and the rejection of school

There were many factors of their disillusionment, yet often the stories of these young men were strikingly similar to one another: "The worst thing he's ever said to me," Will's mum, Sheryal, told me, "was: 'Do you know how I feel when you make me go to school?' It made me feel like crying; like the worst mum in the universe. I thought: 'I've made him go to a place where he's terrified.'"

Will, the young man who dreamed of stardom, had been on a long journey by that time.

"He was always full of life and always naughty, but nice naughty," Sheryal said. "Everybody loved him. Teachers loved him, because he had a personality. He was the naughty one getting away with it all. He would do that stupid smile and everyone would forgive him."

When Will was in his early teens, his family moved to London to get away from his stepfather. Soon after that, Sheryal began getting calls from her son's new school to come in and discuss his behaviour. But the real trouble came when they moved again and Will went to yet another school, this time one where he was one of only a few white boys. Not only was he new, he was also different. He did not feel he fitted in, and Sheryal did not feel the school handled the situation well.

"He was beaten black and blue. In class, out of class, in the corridor. Pupils used to hit the teachers. One of the local policemen had loads of stitches on his head from being beaten up outside the school. It was all closed and they wouldn't talk about it because a lot of the violence was Asian on Asian," she said. It was the start of a downhill spiral in Will's educational life: "I had to take him out of school. No-one cared."

Those words "no-one cared" were ones I heard surprisingly often. I had assumed schools were more caring places than they used to be, but that was not how they were seen by most of the boys I met, or their parents. Ricky from Collyhurst had an educational journey that was not dissimilar to Will's, even though they were quite different characters. Ricky was fine at primary school, he said, but things began to go awry after he went to secondary school in north Manchester.

"I think when I went to secondary school I got in with the wrong crowd. I started trying to be a joker in the classroom and then none of the teachers wanted to teach me," he explained.

His mother, Sarah, fished out some of Ricky's old school reports, which bore out what he said. They were a mixed bag: "Ricky must allow other pupils opportunities to learn." "Ricky must be consistent and avoid immature behaviour." "When he wants to, he is enthusiastic."

Some of Ricky's teachers were encouraging. When he was 13, his class tutor wrote: "Ricky is showing ability to make progress across the curriculum. However, erratic behaviour and less than successful attendance are holding him back. Ricky is always pleasant in tutor time. He needs to have greater confidence in his ability."

In year 8, he had no reports either for music or history because the teachers had not lasted the year.

By the age of 14, Ricky was in trouble: "I had a teacher phone me up at 8:30 at night, telling me Ricky was thick," Sarah said. "Instead of asking for help, he was holding everything in. But no-one wanted to know."

At a very late stage Ricky was found to be severely dyslexic. All his B's and D's were the wrong way round. He was given one-to-one support, but then it stopped again.

"From primary school to secondary school, they let him down," Sarah said. "Could I get hold of the head teacher? I used to go up and he would be out. The invisible man, I used to call him."

All the three boys I met regularly fitted this pattern to a greater or lesser extent. Tom said he liked primary school but thought his secondary school was a mess, with peeling paint and with kids who'd been excluded hanging around outside. In Ricky's case and Will's there was almost certainly some acting up because they felt they weren't getting enough attention, and that may have borne some relation to things that were happening in their lives outside school. Phrases such as "Larking about" and "Got in with the wrong crowd" came up time and again. Yet while Ricky struggled because of his dyslexia, neither Will nor Tom should have done. If their schools had been providing what they wanted, or if they had been somehow better equipped to receive what their schools had to offer, they should have sailed through.

To some extent it was inevitable that there would be tension between schools and their pupils, particularly as they reached adolescence and started testing the boundaries of their independence. Yet it did seem with certain pupils, often boys, often white or Afro-Caribbean working class boys, the gulf between their own culture and that of their school was too wide to breach. It was almost as if the language in which they learned was different from the language in which their schools spoke. In his 1977 book *Learning to Labour*, Paul Willis described how the subculture and lingo of white working class boys at school was a sort of prototype for the kind of culture they would experience in the workplace; a way in which they could seek to emulate their fathers. One of his subjects described in some detail the kind of larks his father indulged in with his work mates, and remarked that it sounded a bit like school to him. For many working class boys now, though – Ricky and Will included – there was no father to emulate, certainly not one with a working class job. Their joking about, their playing up with their teachers, seemed a sad echo of what had gone before.

Underachievement

The girls I met tended to react differently to school. While some of them – like Yasmin, climbing the gates at lunchtime – resorted to escape attempts, they seemed less often to have been openly defiant. And while all the boys I met seemed to feel a gulf between their own culture and that of their schools, some of the girls had actually found school quite comfortable and caring. Indeed, it seemed likely that in most schools pupils who felt alienated probably co-existed alongside others who felt nurtured and cared for. While Claire's dad Mark, who left school in the recession of the 1980s, remembered cheerfully how someone burned down Wombwell High School in his day, Claire spoke of the same school, 20 years on, much more warmly. For her, looking back on the schooldays which were coming to an end was almost like looking back to the womb: warm, safe, secure, familiar. Yet it did not seem to me that the school had challenged her, or pushed her much, sending her off instead to support groups and to help with riding for the disabled. Claire had no expectation of passing the magic five good GCSEs on which schools were judged, and I wondered why not. I remembered a teacher in another, more ambitious school once telling me they could get virtually anyone through, if they pushed them and held their hands enough. But in that school, only one pupil in 20 failed to reach the five GCSE benchmark. In Claire's, the figure was more than 50 per cent. Maybe the sheer volume of lower-attaining pupils at Claire's school would have made it impossible for them to offer the necessary level of support. Neither the head teacher nor the deputy at Wombwell High had time to talk to me, so I never got the chance to ask them whether they thought they were ambitious enough for their pupils. Yet other heads to whom I did speak were surprisingly honest about their feeling that maybe they did not push all their children hard enough.

At Central Foundation Girls' School in East London, where Yasmin used to climb over the gates to escape at lunchtime, the head teacher, Dr Anne Hudson, said she feared staff were kind but perhaps sometimes unambitious.

"They have that cuddling and muddling attitude: 'These poor children …'" she told me. "Historically this community hasn't been academically as successful as other communities with economic and social advantages, and I think there has been historically an attitude among teachers who have been here for several decades perhaps not to expect enough in terms of academic achievement. I'm not saying that applies to all teachers; I'm not saying they're not diligent and caring at all, but I think sometimes we don't push as hard as we might do."

The exam results of schools in poorer areas had been improving faster in recent years than those of schools in more affluent areas but many of them started from a low base. Barnsley, for example, had several schools that were being threatened with government intervention because they could not push their GCSE results up above 30 per cent achieving five or more A*-C grades including English and maths. Tom's school had failed to reach that level, and the one Claire and Ashley attended was only just above it. Did that make a big difference? Would Claire, or Ashley, or Will, have done radically better if they had gone to a high-achieving school in a more affluent area? Maybe. Would it have made a big difference to their futures? Maybe, maybe not. The only one of the young people I met who I felt might have made different choices if he had gone to a different school was Tom, who wanted to be a plumber. He told me his friends had played a major part in his decision making. Maybe if he had had different friends, friends who were expecting to do A-levels and go on to university, he might have gone with them. Who knows? But then again, the friends who influenced him most, he said, were not those with whom he was in the top sets at school but the "raggy lads" he hung around with at home.

The brutal truth was that for most schools pupils like Claire, and Ashley, and Ricky were not a priority. They were not among that borderline, target group who could be pushed up from D grades to C grades with a minimum of effort. There were others in their classes for whom a less vigorous shove was needed in order to get over the magic line. The problem for schools was that if they failed to concentrate on the pupils who were the easiest to reach – those who were failing to make the grade but only narrowly – they would be marked down. Maybe this was nothing new. In the 1980s, Tom's mum, Karen, was given the clear impression that her education was not a priority. Today, little had changed. The young people I met often found their lessons increasingly irrelevant to their lives as they grew older and began to gain a sense of who they would be as adults. That often led to a sense of alienation which some, like Ricky, expressed through anger. Many more, like Claire and Ashley, just muddled through without ever troubling anyone's radar. They turned up most days, they didn't cause much trouble. And if some of their classmates sat in the back of the class staring out of the window or flicking through the messages on their mobiles, maybe that was fine for everyone concerned.

Ricky's school

There was no secondary school in Collyhurst, though an academy was being planned. Instead, the Collyhurst children had to travel north to the sprawling outer suburbs, to attend school on a bleak estate of local authority and ex-local authority housing.

The school, which was 50 years old, was showing its age. Its paint was peeling, some of its windows were cracked and it had a general air of decay. On the front door was a sign saying: "This reception area is now a pupil-free zone", and I had to announce myself via an entry phone to get in.

As we talked the door to the head teacher's office was constantly opening and closing. More than once it just flew back as a pupil walked past and shoved it, or the head broke off our conversation to open it to tell pupils in the corridor to quieten down. Several times, though, there was a polite knock from one or more of that year's GCSE students wanting revision packs, which he had told them to collect in person. I found the place simultaneously cheering and depressing – the head's willingness to engage with pupils and knowledge of them as individuals impressive; the level of casual misbehaviour high.

I had told the school I was writing about an ex-pupil who had dropped out, and expected some defensiveness. Actually I found the head – who preferred not to be named – refreshingly honest. Almost as soon as I sat down, he launched into a sort of "mea culpa" about the pressures he was under.

"I'm always conscious: 'Are we doing our very best for every child?' And for lots of reasons, I've got to answer: 'No.' That hurts, because you don't come into this job to give up on kids," he said.

"These kids have lots of problems. But one thing I would never, ever accept is for a member of my staff to say: 'Well, what do you expect from kids like these?'" He stopped, and I prompted him: Had he ever heard a member of staff say that? "When I first joined, I did. But we soon changed that. We've got to get to the community – a lot of this community came to this school in what I call the bad old days, and they are frightened to come back."

I was slightly taken aback by this. Frightened? "Yes," he said, quite firmly. "There is real fear there. There's a fear of the system. I talk to parents a lot, and they are fearful. Our students can't survive unless their parents show some interest. They either have to be very bright and do it by themselves, or they need parental backing. We come across parents who maybe didn't attend school themselves. They may want the children at home, to be carers. They're almost condoning their sons or daughters not being here."

Every year a dozen children left the school with no qualifications at all: "Any child who leaves here with nothing, I know when we turn them on to the job market, they are not going to be very appetising. They're going to go for interviews, and they'll be asked: 'What was your attendance like?' And they'll have to say: 'I never went.' Or: 'What are your hobbies?' And they'll say: 'I watch TV and I go out with my mates.'"

We talked about Ricky: "Low ability, big anger management issues. That's where it goes wrong. We enrolled Ricky in a boxing club as part of coming to school ... but drugs were affecting his personality. They do say in some secondary schools some of the poor behaviour is to mask the fact that they can't read very well. With Ricky, we knew he had poor literacy. I don't think we ever ..."

Was it true Ricky hadn't been tested for dyslexia till he was well into his teens? The school had only eight hours of education psychologist time per year, he said, and they couldn't afford to waste it on pupils who might not turn up for appointments. "If someone's got poor literacy, we'd pick that up straight away. But the way we work would be alien to the way Ricky might think. An awful lot of boys won't be seen having this help. There won't be books at home, there won't be writing, and if you combine that with poor attendance, by the time you get to year 9, I'd say you've lost.

"The government's looking at me saying I must get 30 per cent through 5 A-Cs including English and maths, and they'll let me know when I haven't done it. There's pressure on us in so many ways – and I suppose some groups of students do suffer. The parents want to see the academic achievement ..." He paused, almost as if he wondered whether anyone was listening: "Off the record," he said. "Nobody cares."

He walked to the front of the school with me when I left: "We did some good things for Ricky, you know." He was standing on the step at the front of the school as I walked away, with a look of real sadness on his face. I had the feeling something in him was almost defeated.

Chapter 6

Changing families

In some ways, the educational experiences of young people like Ricky were not so different from those of their parents. Ricky's mother, Sarah, told me she hated school, started skipping lessons in her early teens and left at the earliest opportunity. Her attitude to Ricky's school was largely negative: they never did anything to help him, they weren't there for him when he was struggling. And that surely must have reflected her own – and possibly her parents' – feeling that what she did at school was largely irrelevant to the future she saw for herself.

Like most young women of her generation, Sarah expected to leave school and go straight into a manual job, in which she would continue until she married and had children. And so she did. But just as the world of work was changing, so was the family. While Sarah's parents' marriage had lasted, as the vast majority of marriages did until the divorce rate began to rise in the 1970s, hers did not. So while Ricky's school days may not have been so very different from his mother's school days, his home life while he was growing up was very different. Mostly it was just him and his mum, especially after his older half-brother and half-sister left home. His dad turned up once in a while, but usually that just led to trouble.

In some ways their family's story was that of many white working class families in Britain since the Second World War. Reading some of the classic post-war studies of these communities, it was striking that they barely mentioned family breakdown at all: "In Ashton the family is a group consisting of wife, husband and children," wrote Norman Dennis and his colleagues in their 1950s study of a Yorkshire pit village. "Our starting-point is the family as the centre of the intimate lives and relations of Ashton miners and their wives, a centre where the miners and miners' wives of tomorrow are reared and orientated towards that rather limited world which Ashton offers." In this respect they offered a vision of 1950s Britain that would have warmed the hearts of traditionalists who believed the decline of the family was at the heart of the developed world's social problems. One could almost see the breadwinner of the household whistling each morning as he tucked his sandwiches under his arm and headed for the pit; his rosy-cheeked wife puffing cheerfully as she set about her household tasks. The wife's job, Dennis explained, was to cook, clean and raise children. Her husband's sphere was outside the home, at work and in the pub or the club, his main role in the family the handing over of a reasonable part of his wage packet on a Friday.

Just a year later Michael Young and Peter Willmott published their similar study of life in East London. Again, divorce was simply not mentioned as an issue – indeed, in those post-war days "broken homes" were usually places where a parent had died. They included a table of figures which showed the percentage of people whose homes had been "broken" before they were 15. In the mid-1930s one in five teenagers had suffered such a loss, they said – just one in a hundred because of divorce; the rest through death. In the nineteenth century the death rate was even higher, with three out of ten losing a parent before their mid-teens. Not only did Willmott and Young find families more likely to be made up of husband, wife and children than at any time in history, they also discerned positive changes in attitudes, too: "The husband portrayed by previous social investigation is no longer true to life," they wrote. "In place of the old comes a new kind of companionship between man and woman, reflecting the rise in status of the young wife and children which is one of the great transformations of our time." In the future, they suggested, marriage would be based not on the old division of the husband out in the workplace and the wife at the hearth, but on genuine partnership. In these optimistic post-war times, a sense had begun to creep in that adult life could be based

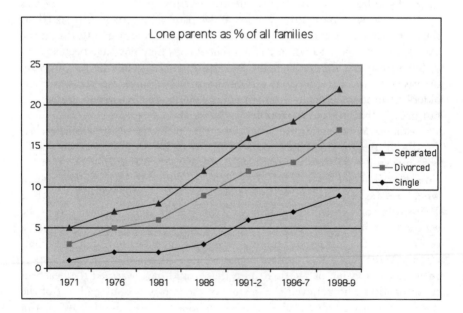

Figure 3 Family changes.
Source: Social trends 30, 2000 edition.

not on economic necessity and the strictures of social norms, but on choice and free will.

Even as late as the 1980s, such studies still reflected the feeling that marriage and children went together and that marriage was, by and large, for life. In a book about young people growing up on the Isle of Sheppey in Kent, published in 1987, Claire Wallace described how some teenage girls aspired to an independent life, maybe working and sharing a flat with friends. But the ideal was still marriage to a man with a job. While high unemployment had led some people to defer marriage – it was important for a husband to be a breadwinner, one respondent said – there was little sign that marriage itself was being rejected, or that divorce was an issue much talked about. Cohabitation was not an end in itself, but a precursor to marriage: "Those couples where the male partner was in a regular job tended to get married, whilst those without jobs continued cohabiting … Young adults did not like to get married unless they could do so properly, with a real wedding and the accoutrements of a real home, and perhaps even their own house."

Yet from the 1970s onwards, the divorce rate rose in Britain. In the latter half of the twentieth century, the number of marriages each year fell by a quarter, while the number of divorces shot up, from around 24,000 a year in the 1950s to 155,000 in 2000. While just one child in 14 lived in a lone-parent family in 1972, one in four did so in 2006. Across the developed world, the trend was similar.

Among the young people I met, the picture was actually rather more pronounced. Out of the eight young people with whom I spent time, just two had parents whose marriage had survived – and one of those had a father who worked away from home. The remaining six mothers had had children by a total of 12 different fathers, and had clocked up 10 major relationship-breakdowns between them. And certainly for many of their offspring this had a serious effect on their wellbeing when they were growing up: Ricky and his mother moved several times to get away from his father; Elvige and her mother left their home and family in Togo in pursuit of a father who had absented himself, and suffered severe financial hardship as a result.

Their stories would to some extent bear out the theses of social commentators such as the former Conservative leader Iain Duncan Smith, who through his Centre for Social Justice had condemned what he saw as a decline in family values over the past half-century.

IAIN DUNCAN SMITH

For Iain Duncan Smith, the key to the problem of worklessness among the young, and in particular among the white working class, was something to which Willmott and Young had nodded back in the 1950s: the notion of choice.

"There's a pretty liberal argument which says the key thing about bringing up a child is that it's a lifestyle choice, that the structure of the family doesn't really matter," he told me over coffee in his House of Commons office, before launching into an almost apocalyptic exposé of what he believed had gone wrong with the family in Western societies.

"All this has led over the last 30 or 40 years to the weakening of the two-parent structure, which led to a growing level of dysfunctional families. It's time we looked at the home – our question at the end of the day is: What kind of family do you go home to?"

In his view, all children needed both biological parents to be present in their homes if they were to develop into emotionally healthy, well-rounded citizens. Boys, he said, often lacked the means to grow into men because they had no father figure in their lives. Girls, on the other hand, never experienced unconditional love from a man that was not connected to sexual attraction.

"Boys basically grow up in a very transient environment and they will then throw their allegiances to father substitute figures such as a gang leader or a drug dealer. These act as alternative family structures which are hugely rooted in criminal activity. Girls become a sort of commodity – in street gangs the value of women is they are often traded between gang members for sexual favours in the sense that this is how you pay your debts. They don't see this as a particular problem."

Had girls stopped wanting marriage and stability and a nuclear family, then?

"I think they do have dreams of marriage but what they're doing is to try to get that relationship, what's on the table is sex. They understand early on that's the reason the man's there. And if it's not on the table the man's not going to be there.

"If there's a lot of dysfunction around you without that male role model, you see nothing else but the same pattern; there's no other check to make you reference something different. The idea of a relationship based on the quality of your understanding and belief in each other is sort of non-existent."

Yet the rosy view that was sometimes perpetrated by those who would have liked to see a return of the "traditional" family was flawed. Those early ethnographers in the coalfields and in East London may have encountered a world in which the nuclear family was the norm, but they certainly did not find one in which its members were happy with their lot. Divorce may have been uncommon up until the 1970s, but unhappy families were not.

"The development of deep and intense personal relationships of an all-round character is highly improbable, and observations confirm the absence of any marriage corresponding to the ideals of romantic love and companionship," Dennis *et al.* wrote in their study of "Ashton" in the Yorkshire coalfields. "Many married couples seem to have no intimate understanding of each other; the only occasions on which they really approach each other is in bed and sexual relations are apparently rarely satisfactory to both partners. Marriages in Ashton are a matter of 'carrying on', pure and simple."

Ashton men, they said, tended to come home from work, wash, eat a meal cooked by their wives, and then go out to the club or the pub. Women's work was in the home, and woe betide those who failed to complete it. The book described an incident in which two couples were sharing a house, and one wife asked the other to cook tea for her husband because she needed to go on a shopping trip. He threw the food on the fire, and when she returned he forced her angrily to cook him another meal. While some of these descriptions of family life may have been one-dimensional, they did serve as a reminder that not all change was bad.

Indeed, in their study on East London, Young and Willmott described the prevailing view of working class family life in terms that might easily have come straight from the mouth of Iain Duncan Smith 50 years later: "Study has been piled upon study of all the things that have gone wrong, of juvenile delinquency and problem families, broken homes and divorce, child neglect and Teddy Boys, which together have created an impression that working-class families are disunited, unsocial and unhappy. And in all this the villain is often the man," they explained.

Young and Willmott found much to be cheerful about in the families they met – a falling birth rate meant women were no longer such slaves to childbirth; better housing meant their homes were healthier and less overcrowded. Yet they were forced to admit they had not been able to include information about men's earnings in their book because husbands so often concealed the amount from their wives. And many of the women confessed that despite the advent of contraception they still felt coerced into having more children than they wanted.

The experience of growing up in a family that was far from perfect was by no means new, then. One day I was in Kendray, visiting Tom – the Barnsley football fan – and his family, when the back door opened and a cheerful face appeared. It was Tom's grandma, Millie, who had lived in this house but had sold it to Tom's parents and moved to a bungalow in the next road. Millie was lively and funny, and looked as if she was in her mid-sixties but must have been a few years older. She was bored, she said, so she thought she'd pop round and see if their black Labrador, Max, needed a walk. Soon I found myself chatting to her about her own early life. Tom's family was possibly the happiest and most stable of all those I had been visiting, so I expected Millie's story to be a positive one. Not so.

"My Dad was killed in the war, when I was six, and my Mam remarried when I was seven," Millie told me. "It was all right when he first came, till he got his feet under the table. But then he used to spend all our money, tossing it in the air and boozing and that. We had a lovely home and he sold all our furniture. We finished up drinking out of jam jars and sleeping on the floor.

"I'd come home and there'd be nothing in the house to eat. The cruelty man (an inspector from the National Society for the Prevention of Cruelty to Children) used to come, and funnily enough there'd be something in the pantry. Mam's husband used to hit me and send me to the shop for cigarettes, then when I came home he'd send me back again. His mother lodged there as well. One time I must have been poorly in bed and I'd been sick and she rubbed my face in it."

In desperation, Millie ran away to her paternal grandmother's house, which was some distance away. Her grandmother sent her back, fearing her mother would be worried about her. On the contrary, her mother was most afraid that her husband would kill Millie if she stayed.

"So I went back to my Grandma's, and I stopped there. I suppose she went to the social," Millie said. "I left school at 15. All that spoiled my li ..."

I stopped taking notes as her voice broke, because I hadn't quite heard what she said. As I looked up, I realised she was crying. Sixty years on, after many decades of marriage and the successful rearing of children and grandchildren, the memories were still raw and painful. Perhaps it was in reaction to this that Millie never let her own children go without, working two cleaning jobs in the mornings and an evening shift in a factory making tins for Swarfega and chocolate biscuits so they could have everything they needed.

For Millie, and also for many of the young people I met, the biggest problem caused by family breakdown was not an absence, but a presence. Usually that unwelcome presence was a violent or drunken stepfather, though in one or two instances I also came across mothers who were violent or unpredictable when drinking. There was no doubt the soaring divorce rate had changed the way many children experienced family life as they grew up, and that was the case for the majority of those I met. Yet I never heard one of them saying they wished their parents had stayed together. Divorce or separation seemed to be merely a fact they understood and accepted. Where they did express regret, or anger, or resentment, it was usually towards an adult who had hurt them. Among the young people I met, having only one parent in the house often seemed to be the least of their problems.

Will, the aspiring actor from London, was a case in point. His mother, Sheryal, told me she married early to escape from a mother with whom she did not get on. Like Millie, she had been largely brought up by her grandmother, but later on her mother decided she wanted her back. When Sheryal met a steel-fixer at the fair and became pregnant by him a few months later, she was delighted – it meant she would get married and leave her mother's house. But it didn't last – Will's father left when Will was tiny and his older sister not much more than a year old.

Will had no memory at all of his biological father. He told me one day, with a real air of wistfulness, that since the birth of his own daughter – she was a couple of weeks old when we first met – he had begun to wonder about her grandfather.

"I've never seen his face. I do want to, obviously. I would get in contact with him, for my daughter, so she's got a granddad," he said. As he thought about it, he seemed to come to a realisation that he needed to know more for himself, too: "I would love to meet him. I only know half of me – you know what I mean? We're a mixture of our parents, and there's a lot of mysteries about me. My mum said I've got the same eyes as him, but that's about it."

Yet if Will had any real resentment towards anyone it was not his father, but his former stepfather, whom he described as a bully.

"I don't trust anyone anymore because of my stepdad. That's when you get hurt most ... I love my mum with all my heart, but I don't trust anyone. We ran away, I left my friends, my childhood friends I grew up with. I moved to look after my mum. We were there for two months and he turned up."

Sheryal believed the problem was jealousy on the part of Will's stepdad, with whom she had two further children. If she put a meal on the table and Will had nearly as much food as him, there would be trouble, she said. Somehow he seemed to resent the fact that Will had his life ahead of him, with all the possibilities that contained: "He wanted to keep him mentally under his thumb. I had more rows with him over the children than anything else, because he'd never let me do anything with them."

Will eventually joined the army to get away from his stepfather, repeating the pattern his mother had set so many years earlier when she too left home at the earliest opportunity. Yet Will soon came back, and eventually his stepfather left. By the time I met him his mother had a new fiancé and another baby on the way – and this time Will got on well with his prospective stepfather. Although by now he had his own place in young people's accommodation, he was often round at his mum's.

All the young people I met, even those whose families had suffered the most traumatic fractures, had strong relationships with at least one of their parents. All had some clear sense of a family network around them, as well – brothers and sisters, half-brothers and half-sisters, aunts and uncles. These were not young people who lacked any sense of their family or of its permanence. Yet it had to be significant that so many of them struggled as teenagers to find their places in the world, and that in particular those who struggled the most were the ones whose family circumstances had been the most difficult while they were growing up.

The trauma of living with an adult who seemed not to care for them, or with whom they clashed, seemed to be a common feature in many of their lives.

Did this cause them to clash with the teachers at school, to lack focus about the direction their lives might take and how they might take hold of their own destinies? Surely it must have done. Many of them felt anger at things that happened in their homes, and although few expressed it in those terms they must have carried that anger into school – when they went to school at all.

In a way, perhaps it was not even those malign presences that caused the most harm, but actually a different kind of absence. The conflicts they experienced drove out so many positive things they might have had in their lives – trips out with the family, the odd holiday or two, even just space in which the subject of their future could come up and be discussed. Some of the parents I met seemed to have had to struggle: to hold their families together, to make ends meet, to find a safe place to be, to settle again afterwards. Maybe there was just no time or energy left, day after day, to keep urging their offspring onwards and upwards. Those who did best seemed to have had a sense from an early age that they not only had the support of their families, but also some clear direction about who they should be and where they should go. Some parents were simply too busy holding everything together to give them that sense.

RACHEL

When I met Rachel at the Rathbone charity's office in Manchester she was about to turn 18. She was pretty with long blonde hair, a butter-wouldn't-melt face and an air that somehow said she'd seen too much, too soon. Later I would find out she had two children, then aged one and two, who were living with their father. Rachel had braved the winter streets of Manchester that February day in shorts. When we met she'd just had an interview for a waitressing job – she'd worked as a waitress when she should have been at school, she said – but it didn't work out: "On the applications when they say: 'Why did you stop going to school?', I think I need to stop putting: 'Pregnant'," she said. "I don't know what else to put, though. I can't put: 'I couldn't be bothered going.'"

Rachel was born in north Manchester, but she had moved around a lot. When she was born her mum already had three sons by other fathers, and another, now 12, had come along later. In the afternoons, she said, her mum liked to sit in the house with some cans and chat to her boyfriend. At the time, she and Rachel hadn't been getting on: "It's like she gets jealous, when she's had a drink. So she has a go at me."

What Rachel remembered most about being little was her mum going off to get drunk, and coming back with "dodgy men". She lived with a boyfriend for a bit, but he used to beat her up. He liked a drink, too. Once she left Rachel's older brother to look after her and went off for about a week. Rachel was about seven or eight then. But then she hadn't had much of a fun life herself: she got married at 17 to get away from her father. He was a drinker, too.

Rachel always got on with her dad, though. Even though her parents split up when she was little she always used to go to see him at weekends, in the flat he shared with her grandma in the leafy south of the city.

"My dad doesn't drink, or anything. He's dead posh," Rachel told me once. I was not sure what to make of this, but when she took me to meet him I could see where she was coming from. He was older than I'd expected for the father of an 18 year-old – Rachel said he was in his early sixties – but tall and good looking, and his accent betrayed a trace of his origins in the south of England. When we arrived he had just sold a car – he made a living by doing them up and selling them on – and greeted us on the back step of his modern block: "You can call me John," he said, though I already knew that wasn't his name.

John told me he had met Rachel's mum on the rebound, after splitting from a girlfriend who was pregnant at the time. He went to court to try to get access to his son, but failed: there was a picture of the boy, aged about two, on the dresser but he said he hadn't seen him for many years. So when Rachel's mum told him she was pregnant a few weeks after their first meeting, he was determined to keep this child.

"The school in north Manchester used to ask why she was so withdrawn," he said. "Her reports used to say she was very good with her own little group of friends, but she was very, very quiet. Extremely quiet. She was the most withdrawn kid in the school."

By the time Rachel was about seven it was clear things couldn't go on as they were: "She started screaming when she had to go home; she wanted to come and live here with me. After a lot of humming and ha-ing, over a couple of weeks I said: 'Right then, you'd better come and live with me.' I thought anything would be an improvement. I thought it was my right and my responsibility to take her into a different environment."

But even though Rachel was happier with her dad and her gran, she had a sort of passivity that never went away.

"When I was that age I used to go to school on my own," John said. "So on the first morning I stuck Rachel out there at the bus stop, and I watched her out of the window. She just stood there, letting the buses go past. I went out and asked her why she didn't put her hand out, and she said: 'Only grown-ups do that.'"

He went over to the dresser and opened a drawer, looking for Rachel's school reports. There was all sorts in there: a contour map she made in geography, beautifully presented with the contours made up out of papier mâché and carefully painted in green; school photographs from year 7 with Rachel looking down and to the side with a little careful smile on her face; a diary of the books she read at primary school, with comments from her teacher: "Rachel is a good reader but she has got to express herself."

John had shooed Rachel and her boyfriend Derek out into the bedroom while we talked, but she wandered in at this point: "I thought you'd burned all those, Dad."

"No, I never did that." He gave her a small, weary smile.

At this point, Rachel's and John's versions of history diverged slightly. John remembered his mother was ill, with dementia, when Rachel was about 13 and he had to make her a priority. He added, though, that he also met a new girlfriend who was hooked on drugs, and that he began spending time with her.

Rachel put it rather more brutally: "His girlfriend's a druggie – he spent all his money on her. When I was about 14 he was going out every night and leaving me on my own, so I started doing a couple of drugs myself. Weed and pills, and coke when we could get it. I'd stay out for weeks and I started wagging school. When I did go to school, I'd get in trouble anyway.

"One time I was in a stolen car with three lads, one of them was my boyfriend. My dad rang me up and said: 'Where are you?' Just then the police sirens started behind us, and he looked out of the window. We were driving past his flat with the police chasing us. We legged it but I was wearing these pink furry boots, and later on they spotted them so I got arrested. Dad nearly put me in care, but he changed his mind. Then he got fined for me not going to school."

John took up the tale: "I had hoodies at the door. They used to come round in groups of 10 or 11. I had my car stolen. They took all my keys away and I had to change the locks. They took my speaker phone out of the bedroom and when I got it back there was a message on it: 'Is that Rachel's dad? I've just had your daughter.' She was 13 at the time. She got to puberty and found a whole new world, away from the more ordered life she had here. It was like she'd gone to a different planet.

"One day I packed her bags and said, 'You're going to go to your mum's.' I said, 'You're getting out of this area because you're dragging in scum. These boys are criminals. They're not bothered about you.' Rachel got back to her mum's, and her mum asked this boy to look after her." He laughed a short, sharp, humourless laugh. "He certainly looked after her."

Attachment and uncertainty

In his classic work on attachment theory, John Bowlby set out to disprove Freud's belief that a child's attachment to his mother was essentially driven by instinct. Freud believed the tendency to cling was a sort of "secondary drive", reinforcing the instinctive need to feed, or even a desire to return to the womb. Bowlby saw things differently – clinging performed a function of control, he said. It helped children keep their parents in check and ensured they provided the things necessary for survival – nature, if you like, versus necessity.

In support of his theory Bowlby described a series of deeply poignant animal experiments in which a newborn lamb was placed not with a sheep but with a dog; or in which a duckling was given a balloon or a box in place of a duck. Lacking the presence of a genuine parent figure, the lamb or the duck would attach itself quite determinedly to the balloon, the box or the dog – even if the dog turned out to be a fierce one. In Bowlby's view, this showed the need to attach was not driven by a clear basic instinct such as the desire for nutrition.

Reading this as I tried to make sense of the emotional difficulties faced by the young people I met, I found myself sceptical. If there was no innate need to attach, or if that attachment was driven by a perceived need, then why would the lamb bother with the dog? Yet slowly I found the image of that duckling, waddling around after a balloon, got under my skin. It seemed to me to say something deeper about the strangeness, the uncertainty, of the world into which many children were born, and the ways in which they tried to make sense of things that failed to fit the accepted view of how things should be.

If growing up is about anything, then it is about learning how the world is, about setting out a sort of framework of things that can usually be relied upon to work in a certain way. For most, those things would include parents who were generally present when required and whose behaviour could largely be predicted; they would include a stable physical environment with which they were familiar, a school, friends and a network of relatives that remained relatively constant. They might also include some reasonably clear idea of the path their lives were likely to take, or some role models they might rely upon as guides. Some of the young people I met had none of those things. For them, the choices they had to make in life were both endless and impossible.

For me the problem was not so much one of nature versus necessity but one of certainty versus uncertainty. Iain Duncan Smith characterised this increased social fluidity as a liberal bent which had taken over in Western societies; the notion that family structure or even the need to work had become a "lifestyle choice". In the past, he seemed to suggest, there was a necessary certainty to the way the world worked: one had to marry to reproduce; one had to work to survive. People had been given more choices, and some people had made the wrong ones. It didn't strike me that most of the parents I met were making anything approaching "lifestyle choices" or indeed any kind of choices. Yes, they made mistakes, often along the lines of marrying someone who turned out to be violent or an alcoholic, but these were not necessarily mistakes their parents would not have made. In a way the major difference was that their parents had no means of undoing their mistakes. Even in the midst of misery or disappointment, there was a stability to these earlier lives. Millie may have had a terrible home life when she was a young girl but she was reasonably sure – unfortunately – that her stepfather would stick around. She made her choice accordingly, and left. Ashley's mother, Ann, felt she missed out because she was forced to leave school at 15 to make Arnold Palmer's golfing trousers when she wanted to go to college, but at least the sewing factory was always there.

But what of those young people now, who cannot be sure what tomorrow will bring? The undeniable result of throwing the old order up in the air – whether that was through the globalisation and casualisation of the labour market or through giving people the freedom to leave unhappy relationships – was that the next generation found it much harder to find a sufficient number of reliable objects to cling to. Even though most of them had at least one strong relationship with a parent, for many a new day might bring a new stepfather, who might be nice or who might be distant, or even violent. It might bring yet another change of address, a new school, a whole set of new friends to be made. It might well bring some drama – a family row, problems with benefits or work, trouble with the landlord. To whom, to what cardboard box or balloon, could they realistically attach themselves, when nothing seemed certain to last? Sometimes it seemed to me they attached themselves to the drama itself, expecting constantly to have some new excitement or upset to keep them occupied.

It was hardly surprising that working towards a goal at school or at college seemed both boring and pointless to many of them, when there were so often more pressing matters demanding attention at home. In any case, they might have added, what was the point of making plans and following them through when the road under your feet seemed so ready to crack apart or to change shape or direction? Perhaps, going back to Bowlby, a child's real need was not for a mother, or even a balloon or a box, but simply for something – anything – reliable; for a personal world in which they could fix certain immovable objects by which to navigate in the future. It seemed almost as if, lacking such firm markers, these young people were constantly having to remake their worlds, unable to make progress because they were left floundering around with basics which others would have had carefully set out for them at a very early stage.

It was hard to unpick what they really felt, if anything, about the uncertainty they experienced while they were little. Rachel's dad's description of how she used to scream when she was made to go home to her mum, maybe to a different house or a different "dodgy man", was one of the few clear descriptions I had. But up until adolescence, whatever they might have felt, they were largely under the control either of a parent or a parent substitute. They did not really have to make their own decisions. Once they hit puberty, though, and started trying to make their own sense of the world, the trouble tended to start.

There was concrete evidence for some of this, but again, it was not conclusive. Perhaps the clearest picture was given in a 2007 UNICEF survey of children's wellbeing in the world's richest countries. Researchers assessed both objective and subjective evidence of young people's sense of wellbeing in health, wealth, education, behaviour, family relationships and general happiness. Those in the United States and the United Kingdom scored significantly worse than those in other developed nations. Why? Was this sense that uncertainty and frequent change led to unhappiness and lack of direction borne out by their evidence? I would say it was.

Although there were significant differences between the lifestyles and values of young people in Britain and the US – those in the US were less likely to drink alcohol and less likely to feel they could expect only low-paid work, for example – the things they had in common also seemed pertinent. In particular, both the UK and the US had very high levels of young people living in single-parent families and in families with a step-parent, and their young were also more likely than those in other wealthy countries to become parents while they were still teenagers. Perhaps also significant was the fact that Britain and the US also had high levels of relative poverty – that is, the gap in wealth between their richest and poorest citizens was particularly wide.

All this could have been coincidence, of course. And while on the one hand it did seem to support the views of those like Duncan Smith, who believed family values – or the lack of them – were at the heart of many teenagers' problems, it also seemed to give weight to the notion that social inequality might also be one of the keys to the issue. Divorce and separation were not exclusive to poorer families, of course, yet much of the uncertainty experienced by the young people I talked to – the frequent moves, the inability to escape violence, the likelihood that a move would lead to a new school in an even more difficult area – was driven at least in part by a lack of resources. Yet there were other pieces of research, too, which underlined the rather uncomfortable notion that family disruption per se did tend to make children more prone to emotional and behavioural problems.

In 2008, the British Office of National Statistics reported on a major survey of young people with emotional difficulties, in which it found that family structure was a significant factor in the onset of such disorders. In particular, children in one-parent families or those who had recently experienced the loss or departure of a parent were more likely than others to suffer in this way. Significantly, they also found certain kinds of change – a parent losing a job, or interestingly even going from being out of work to having a job – were also possible triggers for upset. Those in poorer families, those living in rented accommodation – which in itself meant a greater likelihood of change – and those whose mothers reported having experienced several "stressful life events" such as divorce, accident or illness, involvement with the police or the death of a child were also at higher risk.

Put that way, it seems almost too obvious to mention. Yet this sense of emotional disturbance, of uncertainty and even grief, was one of the things that caused me the greatest surprise when I encountered it among the young people in this book. I suppose this arose from the fact that most of them – certainly those who turned out to be the most emotionally vulnerable – had a sort of crisp, streetwise veneer about them. Yet that veneer was sometimes shockingly easy to crack.

Ricky, from Collyhurst, had the capacity both to display anger and – touchingly, sometimes – his own vulnerability. The second time we met, we sat over cups of tea in the Rathbone centre while Ricky and his mum, Sarah, told me the story of their lives. When we got on to his dad, Ricky, who had leant his head on one arm and almost looked as if he was going to sleep, sat up. Sarah was saying how they'd moved to get away from her violent, alcoholic ex, but that years later he had wanted to see Ricky.

"I thought I'd give him a chance," Ricky said. "He had a nice girlfriend then – Carol – but he messed it up."

"Ricky went on a Sunday, and the next thing I heard this car screeching up outside," Sarah said. "He'd just flung Ricky in the road. Ricky was crying. He'd had a go at Carol and Ricky had fought back. He was 12 then."

At that point, Ricky's troubles began to build up. He wasn't doing well at school, he was smoking weed and robbing people. His grandma was ill, and his mum couldn't cope so he went into care.

"Then one day," Sarah said, "I had the school phoning me up saying they'd found Ricky stuffing his jumper down his throat."

I looked up from my notebook at this point. Stuffing his jumper down his throat?

"I didn't want to live any more," Ricky explained in a flat, almost matter-of-fact tone. "That was when Grandma died."

It was hard sometimes to see where passivity – witness the seven-year-old Rachel, standing hopelessly at the bus stop – ended and anger began. I had wondered, at one point, whether the girls tended to the first and the boys to the latter, but this did not seem reliably to be the case. Rachel's tendency to be easily led, or even to wait to be told what to do, was belied by an occasional act of defiance or an attempt at escape. Like Yasmin, who used to escape to the takeaway because of her aversion to school dinners, Rachel once made her exit from school through the toilet window after a teacher locked her in when she refused to come out through the door.

For most children, the loss of a grandparent would have been a cause of sadness. But for those whose world was constantly changing and for whom little could be relied upon, it could be the trigger for something much worse. Elvige, from London, talked about how she became a bully at school when her grandmother's death – in Togo – coincided with trouble between herself and her stepfather. Will, the aspiring actor, felt the loss of his great grandmother's presence deeply when his family ran away from his stepfather. For many, the web of factors that led to trouble was extremely complex. Paradoxically, uncertainty seemed to be the one constant in the lives of the more troubled young people I met. Often they had, like Bowlby's duck, attached themselves to a single person – usually a grandparent – who seemed prepared always to stick around and never to become so exasperated with them that they gave up on them. The point at which that safety blanket was suddenly pulled away – often through illness or through death – was often the point at which everything began to fall apart.

ROBBIE

I only met Robbie Brown the once. The reasons for that will become clear, but I found our one and only encounter so oddly disturbing that I decided to include it anyway.

As with Rachel, I met Robbie through Julie Ollerhead, a remarkable outreach worker with the Rathbone charity in Manchester. Julie was quite a character, as many of Rathbone's workers were. Her job was to roam the less salubrious areas of town in her tiny and decidedly uncool silver Suzuki car and, upon spotting a group of young people who looked as if they might be "disengaged", to leap out and attempt to engage them. In this way she had come across Robbie, recently out of prison and with a pronounced violent streak, and had decided what he needed most was motherly love. Aged about 50 and with two grown-up sons of her own, she clearly knew what this meant. And it seemed that while he was frequently aggressive and difficult with other adults he would do virtually anything for Julie. She had persuaded his youth-offending officer to let him go out and about with her as her guide and chaperone, and the partnership seemed to be working well. Robbie was just 18 when I met him, but I remember him as someone rather older, hard-eyed and tightly clenched. He had been born in Folkestone but moved to Dover, he said, then on to Doncaster before coming to Manchester: "It was because of my mum. People didn't like her because she was drinking and she had some enemies," he explained. School was "shit"; he stopped going at 15. When his mum was drunk, she was often violent.

"I lived with her till I was 14 or 15 then I just had enough, and I got off. I went over the road to my mate's and stayed there for about six months. I started selling weed, then I thought: 'Fuck it.' I met some bird on the internet and I went to Devon to find her, selling White and Browns – smack and crack.

"When I think about it, it's like it was good while it lasted. Smack and crack, it's like some really dirty drug. All I had to do in the morning was turn my phone on. Sometimes on the weekend we'd buy a car off some crackhead, two of us, and go and bash it up on the country lanes."

After a while he got arrested and ended up inside, which was "sweet", he said. When he came out he came back up here. In Manchester he didn't sell drugs, though – the market was too crowded.

"And there's guns," I added, thinking how easy it would have been for Robbie to fall foul of the city's big drug gangs.

"I had guns, in Devon," he replied coolly.

Could he manage okay on his benefit, without dealing? He smiled, a secret, endearing, smile: "I've got my ways." He had worked, briefly, in a warehouse that sold on fake designer gear, but his youth-offending officer phoned while he was there to ask why he hadn't turned up for a session, and that blew it.

"I don't drink," he said. "Only on special occasions. When I have a drink I get really, really violent. My dad? I remember going to see him when I was six. He beat me up. I didn't speak to him again."

Through the anger and the bravado, Robbie was clearly a bright lad with a clear analysis of what had gone wrong for him. He had even taken four GCSEs – a year early – before giving up on school.

"My mum had a shit dad, and her mum died when she was only young," he told me in explanation of his family problems. "She moved out when she was 16, she got up the duff when she was young. And she got raped. She just had a shit life. She's had a shit upbringing. But you don't bring your kids up even worse than you, do you?"

At this point Julie, who was sitting with us in the kitchenette where the centre's clients spent time having cups of tea and toast, got up from her chair: "You know what I want now? A cuddle." And to my amazement, Robbie just melted into her arms.

"I need a girl to keep me on the straight," he told me then. "Sheree keeps me on the straight and narrow. I'll settle down with her. I've got my own place now. Get a job next." How long had he and Sheree been together, I asked? About six weeks, he said.

As we walked out together into the centre's foyer, we encountered another of the workers with whom Robbie had clashed before. They had words, Robbie called her a "stupid slag" and was duly thrown out by the centre manager, who told us she had barred him. A few minutes later she stuck her head round Julie's door. She had had a call from Connexions – would they be able to take a new lad, Robbie Pemberton? She and Julie exchanged a knowing look. Robbie just wanted to be where Julie was. Shortly afterwards, though, he threatened her, and she phoned me to say she didn't think I should meet him without her there. Although she tried repeatedly to contact him after that, he didn't return her calls.

Chapter 7

Street life

One day Ricky and his outreach worker Chris Nolan took me on a guided tour. Our first stop was to pick up a boy called Mark – another of Chris's charges. He lived a mile or so from Ricky in Miles Platting: a friendly area, Ricky said.

"My uncle lives here. He runs this estate," he explained. "How?" I asked. "People just control it. They control all the kids." I wondered if this meant this uncle was involved with drugs – Ricky had been a runner for a dealer from the age of 11 or 12 – but he said not. His uncle just knew everyone, and if there were problems, he'd sort them out.

Ricky and Mark – who knew each other but only slightly – talked about the local families that "ran" the place. There were big families that you didn't mess with, they explained. It seemed the gangs and allegiances were different, looser, than the drug-based gangs you heard of in the south of the city. Chris pointed out that while Hulme and Moss Side and Whalley Range were largely Afro-Caribbean, this part of north Manchester had been largely white in the past – though that was changing now. Families there went back a long way – it had been largely Irish in the late nineteenth century and still had lots of Irish surnames along with several Catholic schools and churches – and there were wide networks of acquaintance and kinship that stretched between different neighbourhoods.

At 17, Ricky and Mark had grown too old to earn money working for the local dealers: "Men get the little kids off the estate to do it," Ricky explained. "They use the kids. Yeah, you make money, but you're watching your back all the time for the police. And getting robbed by people off the other estates. For the money or for the drugs – both."

We parked up in Miles Platting. It had a similar, "garden village" type design to Collyhurst Village, which I had visited before with the police. Chris and Ricky said they wanted to show me something, and led me round a corner into a pedestrianised area to look at a pink granite memorial, bearing a plaque with lettering in gold. It had two enjoined hands engraved into it, with "Daniel" and "Paul" on them in gold. The script said: "Daniel Dale, aged 18 years. 22-9-82 to 25-7-01. This memorial was laid in memory of a much loved and respected friend whose smile will never be forgotten. Rest in peace. From the whole community." Under the engraved hands it said: "Soul mates."

Ricky told me Daniel Dale was his stepbrother's cousin. Ricky was only about 10 when the older teenager died, but he remembered it very well. Daniel Dale had been due to give evidence at the murder trial of his best friend, Paul Ward. The defendant pleaded guilty but the following day Daniel was shot in the back and killed.

Mark said he was once shot at too, and had bullet holes in his car to prove it. "You can get a gun for £300. It isn't clean – it's been used in other stuff. But if you want to kill someone, you can get a gun."

I asked Mark what he thought about growing up in a place where people used guns so casually and to such terrible effect.

"What do I think about it? That's life, innit? You make sure you're tighter, you get bigger and better things than them. Simple as."

"It isn't going to stop now. You can't do anything about it," Ricky agreed.

"You've got to make sure your car's faster than the person who's chasing you," Mark said. When he was shot at, he found out where the lad's mum lived: "So we did the same thing to him, to his mum's house." Did Mark have a gun? He smiled, coyly. "The next step is if anything comes to my mum's door, it's going straight back to his. It's dog eat dog. It's simple."

As we walked back towards the car from the memorial, we passed two police community support officers: "Look, here's the pricks, man," Mark remarked to Ricky.

Back in Collyhurst, at Ricky's house, they showed me a series of videos they had on their phones. Each represented a different area of town, and had been made to be posted on the internet, a kind of promotional exercise. The Collyhurst one was only about 20 seconds long, and consisted of a shot of a stolen car being spun around and around, with black smoke coming from its exhaust. This was impressive, Ricky explained, because you couldn't rob that kind of car – it looked like a Sierra. You'd need to burgle a house first to steal the keys, he said. The one from Monsall (titled "Monsul") was more professional, with music in the background. It started with a hooded and masked man wielding a handgun, and went on to show a series of scenes – ranging from someone waving a gun about in the street to a gang of youths rolling over a stolen car. Another video – longer, this time – showed two traveller families having a pre-arranged bare-knuckle fight in Collyhurst.

We talked about drugs: heroin was a rich man's drug now, Ricky said. But Mark disagreed. You could get a hit for a fiver, he said. Skunk was £10 for three spliffs' worth, which seemed better value to them. Mark said most nights he would see his "bird", drop her home about midnight and then club together with a group of mates to buy about £40-worth of skunk. They'd stay out till three or so, smoking that.

Ricky said he and his mates didn't drink as much as their parents or grand-parents: "Most of the dads round here became alcoholics, but we just smoke weed. Because of that … I do drink, on the weekend though." If they hung out drinking on the waste ground and the police came, they just told them to get lost, he said.

Afterwards we drove back to Collyhurst Village to find a friend of Ricky's who was due in court the next day. He didn't answer his door or his phone, and we waited for a bit outside his house. After a few minutes Mark started getting edgy. "Let's go, man," he said. "It's hot over here."

Criminal careers?

During that summer Ricky, who was 17, spent less time on the street than he had previously. That was partly because he had been tagged and put under a curfew for breaching a youth-offending order for criminal damage to a car. But I got the feeling he was getting a bit old for it, in any case. He had a steady girlfriend with whom he was spending more time, and although he didn't have money for pubs and clubs he could usually find someone's house to go to. Street life, as Ricky and Mark had pointed out, tended to be for the younger teenager rather than for the disengaged, unemployed 17 or 18 year-old.

My day out in Miles Platting and Collyhurst did raise questions, though. To what extent had Ricky's earlier experiences of casual work for a local drug dealer led to a sort of criminal "career"? Was there a real danger for young people in areas like Collyhurst that they could be drawn in at an early age to the margins of criminality that set a pattern for their later lives? If so, was that one of the key routes by which young people dropped out of the system, if you like, and set out not on a life of work and study but on one of benefits, drugs and petty criminality?

Some academics, notably Rob MacDonald from the University of Teesside, had talked about "leisure careers", and described how involvement in these street-corner societies could be the first step on a kind of ladder that led to involvement in more serious criminal activities and more damaging risk-taking behaviour, such as the use of addictive drugs. MacDonald carried out research in North East England where, he said, heroin had become part of the fabric of society on some estates. He also suggested that "critical moments" in a young person's life – for example being thrown out of home – could lead to a steep downward trajectory, which could lead to more serious problems. Some of that, I thought, could relate to Ricky's situation. Although he said he couldn't afford heroin and regarded "crackheads" as deeply uncool, he was quite dependent on skunk and that had led to problems, including him being kicked out by his mother, Sarah, on occasion. She always took him back, though, and up to now she had continued to provide him with a kind of safety net. Yet for MacDonald, crime and addiction were the results of economic and social exclusion, and not their starting-point, and I would say that was certainly true of Ricky too.

But while all the teenagers I met had either dropped out of education or been to some extent at risk of dropping out, Ricky was the only one who had fitted that pattern. Others – Elvige, escaping her difficult home life; Rachel, hanging out with lads who stole cars – had been part of those street-based scenes at some stage. But all had pretty much grown out of it by the time I met them, without descending into a life of drug dependency or crime.

Anti-social behaviour?

One day I went to meet Claire, the girl from Barnsley whose dad was disabled after getting drunk and falling out of a tree. She was in town when I arrived: "I'm at Rid," she said. "Do you know where that is?" I didn't. It turned out to be a big office block called John Rideal House – home to various bits of official-dom – in whose gardens young people had begun to congregate regularly.

"There's about 200 people there on a Saturday," Claire told me. "My friend took me down there, and I got to know loads of people. Every day now I see people I know from there. They're all from different places ... from Wath ... one's even from London, and he comes to stay with mates here."

I did wonder, briefly, whether this was considered a public order problem, but Claire reassured me that it was all quite above board. The police would come along sometimes for a chat, she said. They'd invited the youngsters there to go on a day trip to Hull, but they hadn't been overly impressed. Later, I checked out the Barnsley police incident reports on the town centre – there was just one mention of police needing to speak to young people at John Rideal House – about rubbish and criminal damage in the area.

There seemed little enough prospect of this activity leading Claire into bad ways. Yet while "Rid" did not seem to be presenting any major problems to the police in Barnsley, the issue of anti-social behaviour by teenagers had been the cause of a great deal of comment and several high-profile political initiatives in recent years. When teenagers hit the headlines it was often through groups or gangs operating on the streets, sometimes criminally but often just socially, as Claire and her friends did.

While Barnsley police did not seem unduly worried about these town centre gatherings, out on estates like Kendray there were complaints about anti-social behaviour: "It's the general stuff that you see in the media," Nikki Norris, a local police officer, told me when I called into the area's newly built police station. "Drinking, smoking, cannabis, the knock-on effects of that. We have a multi-use park a mile or so from here that's been completely destroyed by teenagers. There was a lot of money spent on it, and there's so much graffiti and glass."

Yet when we dug deeper, the description "stuff you see in the media" seemed only partially to describe how things were in Kendray. The deep antipathy the police experienced in Collyhurst was not present there, for the most part. And the type of youth crime Norris, who was attached to the area's city academy, talked about was largely petty stuff, born of boredom rather than of organised wrong-doing. Norris said she knew most of the perpetrators and found it easy to ask them, when necessary, to move on.

In contrast perhaps to some areas of Manchester or London, guns and knives were not a major problem here. Norris said in two years at the school she had never once had to arrest a child for possession of an offensive weapon, and although cannabis use was common she had not come across any younger children working as dealers' runners, as Ricky said he had done in Manchester.

Adults in Kendray certainly felt there was a problem with teenagers hanging around outdoors, and with drugs, but often the police found themselves sympathising with the youngsters.

"Sometimes we'll get calls saying kids are kicking a football about in the park and shouting," another of Norris's colleagues, Julie Mitchell, told me. "But that's what the park is for. I used to run about and make a noise in parks when I was young. We have got to let children be children. Teenagers need to get rid of their energy."

So, to what extent was that media perception the reality for many adults living on estates like Kendray? In areas like Collyhurst and in parts of London, there certainly was a problem – and not just for adults. Will, from East London, was deeply affected by some of his street experiences.

"Since I've lived here I've seen everything," he told me the first time we met. "I've seen people get stabbed, people get shot. At first I was like: 'Oh my God, where am I?' Now I just carry on walking. I know something bad's going to happen."

Yet I would guess Kendray, which for years had a reputation as the worst estate in Barnsley and was certainly not out of the woods when I was visiting, would have been more typical. When we read in the papers about adults on such estates complaining of anti-social behaviour among the young, what we were often reading about was this kind of thing – drinking, making too much noise, generally hanging around. The Kendray police said problems in their area tended to be caused by teenagers aged between about 13 and 15, and that they came and went as each wave grew up and found new pursuits. Anti-social behaviour was a problem – a major problem – for many residents who wished to relax in their houses without being bothered by constant noise, or worse, but it was also, to some extent, part of the normal tension that existed between teenagers and adults.

Was this affecting the life chances of the young people I met? Apart from with Ricky, I could see no evidence of it. Claire would pop along to "Rid" for a chat with her mates after school or college; most of the others I met would have avoided such activities. Will was upset by what he saw, but his problems had other roots. Rachel had been picked up on the street several times for being drunk and disorderly, but in her case – and in Ricky's, too – I would argue that was a symptom, not a cause, of her troubles. And by the time I met her, aged almost 18, she was well past that stage in her life.

I would say anti-social behaviour was for the most part a fairly straightforward public order problem. It caused serious headaches for residents and in some cases the police, but in general it did not signpost any huge moral decline in Western society, or indicate that a large portion of the youth of the developed world were bound for the scrapheap. The vast majority of those involved would grow out of it and be none the worse for the experience. It seemed to me that the way the Kendray police dealt with it – tactfully, and with a certain amount of respect for young people's rights to socialise and burn up energy, but with the option of taking action tucked safely in their back pockets – was as good a way as any I came across.

Rachel made me laugh one day. I asked how many times she'd been arrested, and where: I knew the areas she'd frequented as I'd grown up not far from there myself. Counting on the fingers of one hand, she enumerated the places in which she'd been picked up for being drunk and disorderly: Stockport Precinct, Piccadilly Station ... She couldn't understand why I found this so funny. Eventually I explained I had been drunk and disorderly in every one of those places myself, 30 years or so earlier. Why I was never arrested, I was not sure. Maybe drunk girls did not appear on the police radar in those days. But Rachel's account brought to mind an incident from my own past. I was drifting through Stockport Precinct with a friend one morning at about 2:30 am, both aged 15 and in no hurry to go home. We'd had a drink or two and we were singing and larking about, exchanging a bit of banter with two policemen who were walking along behind us. It didn't occur to us for a minute they might consider us any kind of a problem, and evidently it didn't occur to them, either. Then we came upon a couple of boys of about our age, kicking a tin can about. The policemen were instantly grim-faced. We watched, open-mouthed with shock, as they slammed the lads up against a plate-glass window and ordered them to turn out their pockets. Maybe they knew these kids were a bad lot, but looking back, it did make me think that the problem with teenage street life was as much about the attitudes of adults, and how they changed over time, as it was about the habits of the young. If life had changed, perhaps it had not done so in the way people often assumed it had. Perhaps there were not more young people causing trouble on the streets than there used to be, but fewer. Because parents tended to keep their children indoors and to keep closer tabs than they used to, ferrying them to and from teenage parties and nights out to ensure their safety, the young people who were on the street stood out more. They tended to be the young people whose parents didn't have the time, the inclination or the means of transport to drive them around. To be blunt, they tended to come from the kinds of families who were already regarded, both by the police and their neighbours, as trouble.

Chapter 8

Making choices

Wherever teenagers hung out, whether on the street, at a youth club or at home, they of course spent a lot of time with other teenagers. It was hardly surprising, then, that their friends played a major role when it came to making decisions about the future.

Tom, from Barnsley, admitted he sometimes took the easy option: "I was going to do ICT and somebody told me it wasn't the right thing for me," he said. "This lass told me to do performing arts. I started going to do that and it were proper easy. That was four GCSEs. And the teacher was right nice, and she put me in for the drama group."

Tom's mum would have liked him to consider university, but his friends put him off the idea. "I think I were a bit bothered about moving away from all my mates. Some of my mates at school were in top sets, but my real mates were all raggy lads. They were saying, 'Why do you want to go to university? You want to go into a trade.' They said once you've got your apprenticeship you're set up, and it's loads of money."

Would this have been the case in their parents' day? Probably not, because for most of their parents there had been no real decisions to be made. *Their* parents, virtually all of whom were working, took them in hand and set them down a similar route to the one they had taken, for the most part. Claire's gran, Pat, in Barnsley, told me her mother presented her with two options: the laundry or the woollen mill. As the laundry had a terrible reputation, she chose the mill where her mother had worked, and that was that. Decisions were forced upon the young, largely through economic necessity, and while some – including Pat – said they loved their working lives, others – like Ashley's mum, Ann, who would love to have gone to college – wished they had had other choices. And although Ann guided both her daughters towards a college education in the face of some resistance from her husband, many other parents found themselves blocked when it came to helping their offspring to choose. They simply didn't know what was best. The world had changed, the routes they had taken were gone and the new ones were unfamiliar to them. For most parents this left a kind of vacuum. When I asked what they wanted for their children, they didn't so much express anxiety at the fact they were entering an unfamiliar, changed world, as a sort of fatalism.

"I don't really expect anything," Claire's father, Mark, told me during the late spring of the year she was due to leave school, aged 16. "At Claire's age I didn't have a clue. I just took the first job that came along. I didn't come out of school thinking I want to be a bricklayer. It weren't a case of what do I want to be, it were a case of what can I do?"

Other parents expressed a similarly laid-back attitude. Sheryal, the mother of Will, the aspiring actor from London, said she had been pushed by her mother into a job she hated – working in a pet parlour – and so was reluctant to do the same to her own children: "I've always let them do what they want. I'm a firm believer that you give a child their life, it isn't as if you could have a second life through them. I tend to back off and let them make their own mistakes."

So who was to offer good, well-informed advice to these young people? Clearly, neither their friends nor their parents were fully equipped to do so. Oddly, neither were their schools. In fact in some cases those schools were quite clear that the offering of personalised careers advice was simply not within their remit. When I contacted one school to ask if I could interview its head teacher about the decisions and transitions pupils had to make at 16, I was told quite bluntly that I was phoning the wrong place. I should be talking to the careers service, Connexions, they said, and proceeded to give me the phone number. When I insisted that I was anxious to know the school's perspective on the issue, I was eventually put in touch with a member of staff who had some responsibility, along with other roles, for overseeing careers education.

Employers to whom I spoke often expressed frustration with the hands-off attitude schools took when it came to pupils' job prospects. "A lot of schools round here don't even have dedicated careers people," Sarah Wilkinson, a human resources consultant at Rotherham Investment and Development Organisation, told me. "We've done jobs fairs at schools, but we decided it wasn't the best use of time for us. Mostly what pupils want is to be a beautician, a hairdresser, a plumber or a mechanic. I think there's an ignorance about the world of work and what's out there now."

I could see her point: If schools were not interested in what pupils did after they were 16, assuming they were not staying on to do A-levels, then what were they really doing for them? The stock answer, of course, would be that their job was to tend to the academic side of a young person's needs, leaving others to sort out the future. The standard measure of success or failure, for a school, was the proportion of pupils who gained five good GCSEs at 16. But in many areas, particularly the ones in which I did my research, the majority of pupils failed to reach that benchmark standard. So they were leaving school without reaching the required academic standard, and also without the guidance they needed to go forward from there.

So what had happened? I seemed to remember that when I was at school there was a careers teacher with whom all pupils had a brief interview before they left. His job was to sort academic sheep from vocational goats, directing the sheep into appropriate A-levels for their chosen career path or university course, while suggesting to the goats the types of available work to which they might be suited. This was no longer the case, it transpired. It seemed the careers teacher had somehow got lost during two decades of educational reorganisation during the 1980s and 1990s. By the end of that time, no-one was really quite sure who was responsible for making sure young people had the information they needed to make the best choices. Although schools did continue to have careers teachers, only a third of them had any relevant qualifications.

By the late 1990s, according to a government paper aimed at sorting out the mess, something needed to be done. It said that while most pupils were interviewed at some stage by the careers service, fewer than half felt this helped and many were losing their way. At this stage a decision was made to set up Connexions, a new service that was supposed to guide students between the ages of 14 and 19. Instead of having careers teachers in schools and a separate careers service elsewhere, new Connexions "personal advisers" would be attached to every secondary school.

Connexions

So schools were now perfectly within their rights to say it was not their job to advise young people about career options. That was officially Connexions' job. Yet even among the group of young people I met – all of whom had been at risk – there were some who had never even met a Connexions adviser before they left school.

Tom, who had struggled to find an apprenticeship, pointed out the service operated on a "traffic light" system so those considered most at risk of dropping out received the most attention. Those not thought to be at risk often received nothing at all. For Tom, this meant there was no-one available and qualified to tell him that while plumbing might be a perfectly admirable trade, the opportunities to enter it in his area were severely limited. Thus a young man who should have sailed out of school and into training ended up unemployed.

The reality, according to Connexions staff and other professionals I spoke to, was that much of their time was taken up meeting targets, ensuring young people leaving school were tracked and logged. One youth worker told me she had been talking to a group of teenagers about the choices they were making. Most had been in touch with Connexions, she said, but when she asked who had found that contact useful, not one hand was raised.

"I don't know if it's them or if it's the system," she said. "I got a phone call from the Connexions worker in my area, saying one of the young people I'm working with needed to go to the college. But it was in an evening and they wouldn't work evenings. I know this lad and his confidence is really low, so I asked my line manager if I could take him. But my line manager said I couldn't – it was Connexions' job." More than once, I met people from other, related services who complained that Connexions workers had a very narrow view of their role. At one point I saw an outreach worker who had just picked two unemployed teenagers up off the street, sitting with them in the Connexions office working out whether their dates of birth made them eligible for help, and – worse – whether or not they lived in one of the postcodes that were currently regarded as targets for the service. One of them fitted the criteria; one was rejected because she was supposed to be at school, even though it was clear she had not attended for some time. Yet both were equally vulnerable and both had very similar problems.

There were more fundamental problems with the job Connexions did, though. The first of these was in some respects historical, and pre-dated the setting up of the service. At some point during the 1970s, careers teachers had followed their other school-based colleagues into a culture which said they should focus on the young person, rather than on the jobs market. So instead of advising on what might be available for a teenager of a certain bent, they now tended to ask the young person what they wanted and then offer possible routes they might follow. As a standard work on careers guidance published in 1971 put it: "Ensuring the community's future manpower requirements are satisfied is not the counsellor's job. His responsibility is to his students."

On the face of it, this much more child-centred approach sounded eminently sensible. It was perhaps seen quite idealistically as part of a transition from a society in which sheep were born sheep and stayed sheep – and goats likewise – into one in which there was greater social mobility, and in which each child had a real chance of fulfilling his or her potential rather than simply following an inherited life course. Yet it had major drawbacks. No teenager, it seemed, should ever have his or her ambition thwarted, no matter how implausible that ambition might appear. Nor were the teenagers I met given information that might have led them to reassess their options.

Wombwell High School

At Wombwell High, Claire had been talking to her school's Connexions adviser, Amanda Gannon, about what she should do next. She had told me she might do acting, or she might look for an apprenticeship. But I wanted to know what guidance she had been given. Did her Connexions adviser take her through her options, highlighting the relative probability of her achieving one or other of these goals? She did not.

"What we will say is have your dream, go for it but be realistic," Gannon told me in the school's careers room. Realistic, I wondered? How was it realistic for Claire to believe she might go into acting? Might it not have been better to suggest she join an amateur group first to find out whether she had a talent for the theatre?

"Robbie Williams said his careers adviser told him to go and work in the supermarket. I never want to be that person. I don't think it's fair to turn round to anybody and say: 'You can't do that.' There's always people who will prove you wrong," Gannon told me. "We are realistic but I don't think we can ever say to a young person: 'You're not going to Hollywood.' It isn't a guaranteed job, it might not lead to being a professional actor, because of the nature of the market, but there are other jobs you can look at within that field. And in any case there's no such thing as a job for life any more."

So Claire had applied for a performing arts course at Barnsley College, and was trying to decide what audition piece she should do. Claire's classmate, Ashley, whom I had also visited at home more than once, had a clear goal ahead; Claire did not.

"Ashley has been set on childcare; it's realistic, she's had practical experience and she's aware of what she needs to do," Gannon told me. "Claire is a little bit different; no way is she ready for the job market. I think the performing arts course will look at her for the pre-foundation level that will give her life skills as well."

She was right, in that respect. The college did nudge Claire towards a course called "The Mix" which would allow her to do performing arts plus a taster of another vocational area too. Yet had she been given the best possible guidance? I was not sure. This was not entirely the fault of her advisers – information wasn't given to them, either, about the availability of different types of jobs locally or nationally. If Claire had been told she had about a one in a million chance of making it big in show business, statistically speaking, would she have pursued it, or would she have done something else instead? It was hard to tell. But I left Wombwell High School feeling she should, at the very least, have been given the facts.

Unrealistic choices

Claire, like many of the young people I met, possibly felt she had a wider range of choices laid out in front of her than her parents or grandparents had: "When I was younger I wanted to be a nurse, a firefighter, then I wanted to be a spy," she told me once. Her generation had grown up in a media age, with access not only to youth cultures and fashions, but also to wealthy, famous role models of a similar ages and backgrounds to themselves. Perhaps more significantly, they also had a kind of career path laid out by which they could hope to emulate their heroes. It would be easy to overstate the importance of reality television, but it did seem that, for some, it had an effect. In the past, pop stars were remote figures, glimpsed on airport tarmac and on stage. In general, those who aspired to emulate them could do nothing but hope for a lucky break. Now every cough and spit of their existence was detailed in the media, making them seem simultaneously glamorous and ordinary. More significantly, a potential career path to stardom was laid out on the TV talent shows, giving aspiring stars a perceived route to follow.

Even more immediately, commercial operators had stepped in to exploit those dreams, giving teenagers like Will, from London, the sense that stardom was almost within reach. When we first met he told me he had paid £100 to go to a casting session for new talent, which for reasons that seemed obscure – he lost his phone, couldn't phone them because he lost their number too – came to nothing. The manager of the accommodation where Will lived told me a number of residents had paid to have their music video played on a free-to-air TV station: "Whereas previously you got paid, now you pay them," she said.

There often seemed to be this strange disjuncture, though – a feeling that there were a huge range of options, and yet little or no means of assessing the relative likelihood of actually being able to grasp one or another of them: "I might get into one of these drama groups," Claire from Barnsley told me. "If I can't go into one of them, I might go into an apprenticeship or something." For Claire – as for Will at one point – there was the option of a performing arts course at college. It was impossible for either of them to know whether there was any chance at all that such a course might lead to a career in the arts, because no such information was available. But the presence of the course made the possibility seem real. It seemed to go back to this notion of choice versus certainty, of growing up in a world where there were few clear signposts.

BRIDGING THE GAP – *A MISSED OPPORTUNITY?*

John Graham, a former senior civil servant, spent a couple of years of his life thinking about how the most vulnerable young people could best be helped to get a toehold in the world of work. He was one of the key authors of a 1999 report called *Bridging the Gap*, published by Tony Blair's Social Exclusion Unit, which was meant to set the agenda for the intractable problem of disengaged youth.

"What was needed," Graham told me when I went to see him in his South London office, "was the ethos of the youth service, but with the capacity to connect with young people, to get them onto the tracks that would take them back in."

Graham, who went on to run a criminal justice think tank called the Police Foundation, suggested the government should recruit a small army of advisers to monitor the progress of young people thought to be "at risk". Thus they could be prevented from dropping out, and new placements could be arranged for them if they did. In the vision of Graham and his co-authors, each vulnerable youngster would have had a personal worker who would have stuck with them between the ages of 13 and 19. What emerged was the Connexions service, largely staffed by the workforce of what had been the Careers Service and very tightly focused on targets and unemployment rather than the wider needs of the young. Why, I wanted to know? Graham had a pretty direct answer.

"It was hijacked by David Blunkett," he said. At the time, Blunkett was in charge of the Education Department, and he wanted his Department to lead the change: "The minute he heard we were doing this piece of work he initiated his own study within his own department that led to the setting up of Connexions. He was determined to basically get in there before we could be seen to be dictating to him what policy should be. What happened was a compromise to placate those who said the Careers Service was for young people. Which ignored the very important fact that the population we were dealing with was hugely disadvantaged in terms of access to that service.

"We would have created an organisation that was primarily about meeting the multiple needs of those young people who most needed it. And you could access careers services, mental health services, health services and social services as and when necessary."

So, had his 123-page report had an effect? Had the Connexions service saved teenagers from wasting their lives, or not? When I asked the question there was a long pause.

"There is no tangible evidence to suggest that work has been particularly productive. On the other hand, I would suggest that had that work not been done and efforts hadn't been made to include children and young people as much as one could, then the situation today would be worse than it is now. So you might say that what the government did was to hold the tide."

Later I asked David Blunkett to comment on Graham's assertion that the unloved Connexions service had been the result of a political hijacking led by himself. I found his response refreshingly honest. He virtually confessed something of the sort had indeed taken place: "We certainly did initiate our own review of what should happen in modernising both the youth and careers services, which led to the establishment of Connexions. We were never going to be 'bounced' by any unit at No. 10 – unlike some other Departments. In retrospect, we should not have responded in kind, but offered the opportunity of doing something jointly, which the Social Exclusion Unit had clearly not been prepared to do in these initial stages."

He added, though, that while he had supported the concept of mentoring for young people rather than just careers advice, he had since come to feel the way forward was an even greater emphasis on careers, rather than youth work: "For many of the most deprived youngsters, it is the issue of aspiration, of expectation and of proper guidance that is lacking in terms of their own future."

ELVIGE

Elvige told me she was "not a person who gets C's or D's". Big, bright and full of life, she filled every room she walked into. The story of how she managed to leave school with eight GCSEs, all of them A's or B's, was testament to the strength of her personality.

Elvige's early teens were not easy. Having arrived from Togo aged nine or 10, she missed a year of school through homelessness, poverty and her mother's unfamiliarity with the system, and taught herself English while watching the Teletubbies, alone at home while her mother worked.

Finally settled in a flat in Canning Town, East London, and with a place at the local secondary school, she might have expected life to improve. But her family – she had been mainly with her grandmother in Togo and then with her mother in the first year after she came here – had changed when her mother remarried and had two more children. Elvige's relationship with her stepfather was, to put it mildly, difficult.

"The more it carried on, the more I was losing the person I am today, the person I came to this country as. I was not a nice person," she told me.

At school, Elvige frequently got into fights. After school finished each day, she would hang about on the street or in the park rather than go home. When she was 14 she packed a bag before school one day and ran away, to the home of a friend from North London. The police and social services were called, but she was sent back home.

"I just thought: 'Fuck this.' There were days when I wouldn't even bother going to school. I used to bunk off, go to North London, South London. I really wasn't concentrating and by this time I was starting my GCSEs. In school my behaviour was just erratic. I was climbing the gates to get into the park, smoking, drinking. Doing all this stupid stuff."

Elvige handed the credit for her putting her life back on track to one person: Lisa Marcelle. Lisa was a Connexions adviser, but she was a Connexions adviser with a difference: she was willing to stick her neck out to help a teenager in trouble, even when it was not her job to do so.

"If it wasn't for me meeting Lisa, I wouldn't be here," Elvige told me. "I don't think I would have continued living, let alone continued my education.

"In my school there was one Connexions adviser and you had to book an appointment to see him. It was just to advise on careers, and it wasn't really an informal conversation. I found the Connexions shop from the fact that a group of my friends went in there. There was a computer suite where young people can use the computers and have debates and things like that. The next thing I knew, every day after school everyone was going there."

I asked Elvige to introduce me to Lisa, and as we walked into the Connexions shop together they greeted each like old comrades-in-arms, with a huge hug. Talking to them together, it was obvious they had shared difficult times. Lisa seemed to look at Elvige with a pride that was almost maternal.

Elvige had discovered the Connexions shop not long before she took her GCSEs, and it had provided an alternative to the park. There, young people were encouraged to hang out, use the computers and chat to the advisers about anything they liked. And there she met Lisa.

When she had her last big fight with her stepfather, Elvige called Lisa from her mobile phone to say she was barricaded in the bedroom with her little sister. Lisa kept her talking, helped her to calm down and then stuck with her over the following weeks and months as she did battle with social services and housing departments. Eventually they caved in and gave Elvige a flat to live in.

How was it, then, that Lisa was prepared to give Elvige her mobile number and be there for her any time she needed her, when advisers in other Connexions areas were told this was not their job? East London Connexions had always been different, Lisa told me, though there was now pressure for it to concentrate on targets for reducing the numbers of unemployed 16–18 year-olds.

"Whatever a young person presents themselves with, we have the training to deal with it," she said. "It might be drug misuse, family problems, housing, medical difficulties. In the last couple of years we have been told to focus more on those who are not in education, employment or training. It really bothers me. But to be honest I'm not going to change the way I work. At the end of the day it wouldn't work."

For Lisa, the job was about mentoring, and about continuing to be there even for young people who did not quite fit the right profile or live in the right postcode. Elvige, now 18, continued to see her mentor regularly and also to help out at the Connexions shop herself, as well as doing peer outreach work for the London Mayor's office. Lisa had been through hard times too, she said, and she knew the value of an older guide and protector: "I went through a lot of problems when I was younger as well, and I always had a lot of positive role models. When you're young you think your family just think they know it all. When you get an older person, not in your family, who encourages you, that's another thing."

Chapter 9

Further trouble

And so they moved on, from schools that failed to engage them or that tended to feel they'd coped if they managed to contain them or maybe offered a bit of sympathy and support along the way, into the college system. The lucky ones had a parent or relative qualified to give advice; most did not. The rest, for the most part, clung to what their friends had to say in the absence of informed or targeted guidance from school or the Connexions service.

In the past, going to college was an achievement. Indeed, many of these young people's parents still saw it that way. But like the rest of the world, college had changed. For at least a proportion of its students, the further education system had come to be seen as a sort of fall-back, something they could do if there wasn't any suitable work available. And indeed, governments increasingly saw it that way too. The UK's leaving age was about to rise from 16 to 18, and few other Western countries had leaving ages lower than 16. In the US, 17 or 18 was already the norm, depending on which state you were in. Young people in the UK could not draw the dole till they were 18, but if their household income was below average they could get a small weekly sum – up to £30 at the time of writing – for going to college. The government had guaranteed a place in learning to each school leaver – and in the case of those who were not academic high-flyers, such a place tended to be in a further education college.

When the pits and the steelworks closed in South Yorkshire's Dearne Valley, those responsible for the regeneration of the area thought about building a university. Then they realised that would have been "a bit like having a tower with no ladder up to it", one senior educator told me, so they built the smart, pale brick Dearne Valley College instead. On the day of my first visit, in April, recruitment interviews for the following September were in full flow. There was a constant shushing sound in the reception as the automatic doors opened and closed, allowing in the sound of trickling from the water feature outside along with a procession of teenagers: "Travel and tourism? Into the canteen through the green door and wait there. Someone will be along to fetch you ..."

I was waiting for Karl Lyons, who worked at a referral unit for pupils excluded from school and who also did outreach work in Kendray. He had suggested I come along when he accompanied one of his charges, David, to a college interview. David, 16 and profoundly deaf, hadn't thrived at school. The support he needed hadn't apparently been available, Karl told me, so he had ended up at the referral unit in Barnsley, which was called "The Base". Today he seemed shy, holding back from the throng of prospective students as they pushed their way up the stairs.

David told me he would like to work as a debt collector, but was applying to do a course at Dearne Valley which was supposed to prepare its students for uniformed public services such as the police or fire service. "You learn how to restrain people. It's the same sort of stuff you do in the army," he told me. For higher-level courses such as this one, GCSEs were required, but David wasn't taking any.

After a tour of the college, David was called for his interview with one of the tutors. Karl had primed him well with answers to questions, and with some questions he could ask too. But the tutor looked doubtful about whether he could meet the entrance requirements. His attendance could be a problem too, he said – it had been 70 per cent, but the college would expect better. "To be fair," Karl cut in, "he's one of the best attenders at The Base."

The tutor still looked doubtful: "We don't like turning people away ..." After a while he went away to talk to a more senior colleague, then came back to say they could definitely offer David a place. What it would qualify him to do was not clear to me – he did not have any GCSEs, the army had already rejected him because his deafness could cause danger in a combat situation, and it seemed likely the fire or prison services might well take a similar line. Conversely, a college course would give him two years to mature and to prepare himself for the labour market. Would this be the best use of public money, or the best preparation David could have for life in the labour market? I was unsure.

Later on I put this to the college's principal, Sue Ransom, who had been recommended to me by more than one of my previous interviewees as a leading light on the South Yorkshire educational scene. Were college admissions policies perhaps rather lenient? Would David really be likely to get the job he wanted at the end of his course? Direct, incisive and forthright, Ransom concurred that many of her college's students did not end up doing what they had purportedly been trained for. "There is an argument that 16–18 year-olds should be better advised," she said. "But they are better in learning. Students might come and do beauty here, and end up working in a shop. But they'll sure as hell be well turned out, and they'll be good communicators. There might not be jobs in sport and leisure, but those students will know about teamwork. All of them will get a set of skills."

I asked her for a breakdown of what Dearne Valley College's students would be studying that September. The biggest courses, she said, were public services and health and social care, followed by travel and tourism. The numbers in beauty and in sport would be equal to those in construction, though she expected the economic downturn to bring a drop in applications for building-related courses. Student numbers in engineering, business and catering were much lower; about one-sixth of those on the larger courses such as tourism and beauty.

"Beauty is full to bursting," she said. "Construction is full to bursting, sport is full to bursting. Public services is absolutely booming. But the areas where there are jobs – business, information technology, logistics – there's still capacity in there."

The reason the college was training young people to work in industries that did not need them, she said, was not because there was a shortage of jobs – although in the few months that followed our interview unemployment would start to rise in the area, as it would across the whole country. The main problem, Ransom said, was a mismatch between the types of jobs available and the ambitions of the young: "One of the fastest-growing industries here is logistics and transport. We've been trying to get a logistics course going for three years, but it's just not going. People in schools can't understand what it's about – it's about IT, it's about geography. At the moment we have eight students signed up for September – it isn't enough but I've told them to go with it. We are staying in there, we want to say to young people: 'This is where you could get a job.'"

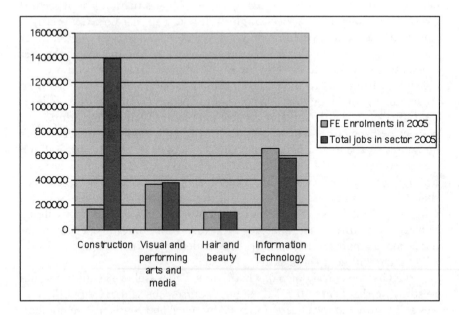

Figure 4 College enrolment and the chances of getting a job.

Source: Annual Business Inquiry/Learning and Skills Council.

Information gaps

Dearne Valley was trying, then, to persuade young people onto some courses that would lead to jobs. But for the most part it was giving them what they wanted, regardless of their actual chances of succeeding. This was not unusual, of course. Indeed, the government had guaranteed places in training or education to all 16 year-olds, and all colleges were expected to play a major role in fulfilling that pledge.

The national figures for college courses in England made interesting reading, though. Each year 160,000 people embarked, for example, on courses in hairdressing. Less than one-tenth of those were trainees taking day-release courses at college. The prospects for the rest looked mediocre, at best: the total number of working hairdressers in England at the time was 145,000 – so there were actually the same number of hairdressers – including trainees – as there were hairdressing students. Likewise with the performing arts. In 2005, 370,000 students embarked on visual and performing arts courses at colleges – slightly more than the total working in the whole entertainment industry, including the staffs of cinemas, radio and television companies, computer games manufacturers and presumably lap dancing clubs as well. The number of actual trainees from those industries who had been sent to college by their employers was 298.

Finding out what actually happened to those performing arts and hairdressing

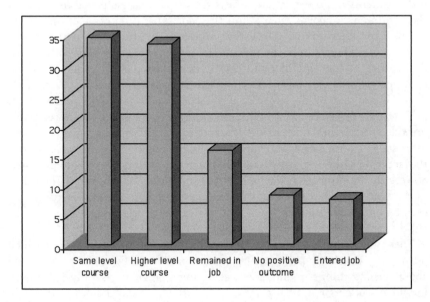

Figure 5 What happens to college leavers?

Source: Freedom of information request to Learning and Skills Council: figures as a percentage of total sample.

students once they finished their courses proved more difficult. My experience, gained over eight months of repeated freedom-of-information requests followed by many long telephone conversations with the Learning and Skills Council, which funded colleges, established that it would be literally impossible for a young person setting out on such a course to find out in advance the chances of getting a job in the area they planned to study. Although the council did ask former students whether they were working, it did not ask what jobs they were doing. It told me – eventually – that it neither filed nor published the information in a form that would make it possible to analyse even whether students on some types of courses were more likely to get jobs than on others.

The council did release information to me, however, on some 100,000 students who completed college courses in 2007. What this showed quite clearly was that only a very small proportion of 16–19 year-olds went from further education colleges into work.

Seven out of 10 who completed a college course, the figures showed, went on to do another course afterwards. Just one in 13 actually got a job – any job – after leaving, and one in 12 became unemployed. For this to be the case in what was supposedly the vocational sharp-end of the British education system seemed, quite frankly, shocking.

For me, the lack of information about what happened to further education students itself told a story. Over the past two decades the public had been bombarded with increasing amounts of information about education and what it did. Parents could see detailed statistics about what happened to pupils at their children's schools – what exams they got; what proportion of them were unemployed after leaving. University students could look at "destinations" data for their courses to find out what the success rates were. For college students, though – nothing. For all the talk about raising skills levels, and about the importance of vocational education, the fact was this remained a Cinderella sector, left to mop up the leftovers of the school and university systems. It cut both ways – no-one was interested, so colleges operated in waters relatively unruffled by the winds of political debate or media interest. Because no-one was interested – politicians would happily line up to say they were interested, but the facts told a different story – no-one much was asking what was happening. So very little information was published, and no-one much complained. But in the process, tens of thousands of young people were let down: drifting, or even being prodded, down roads that would almost certainly turn out to be cul-de-sacs.

There was a simple issue, here, about supply and demand, and about which of the two was driving the further education system. Politicians had talked about turning things around, about changing a previously supply-led system in which students got what they wanted into a demand-led one that would meet the needs of the market. Yet they seemed to want it both ways: they wanted every potential student to have a college place, regardless of ability. They also wanted colleges to turn out students who were ready to meet the particular needs of their local economies. The result was a muddle, and one that did not meet anyone's needs. No-one really wanted a return to the days when young people were channelled into the labour market without any choice or any consideration of their individual aspirations. Teenagers would always have views of their own; given choice, some of them would make bad decisions. Yet the current system seemed to me to be so weighted towards individual choice that it had begun to lose track of hard, economic reality.

DAVID WILLETTS

It is not often politicians say anything surprising, so I was pleasantly taken aback by my meeting with the Shadow Secretary of State for Innovation, Universities and Skills, David Willetts. He had a reputation for ascetic intellectualism – "Two Brains Willetts" – but actually I found him both personable and engaging. We met in his office in the modern Portcullis House, over the road from the House of Commons, where he greeted me cheerfully dressed in a rugby shirt. When I mentioned Claire's Connexions worker in Wombwell near Barnsley, who pointed out that Robbie Williams was advised to work in a supermarket and who said she never wanted to discourage potential talent, I suppose I was expecting a standard conservative harrumph about wishy-washy liberal values. But Willetts sympathised with Claire's adviser:

"In a service economy, soft skills matter. I could well imagine that drama, even if you thought you were going to be an actress and you didn't, could improve your long-term potential by giving you an ability to articulate clearly and things like that," he said.

"The further education argument would be that quite a lot of what they are doing is indirect, rather than direct. And I think there's something in there. I do think getting people to study the rudiments of drama, providing it's done with some rigour, is worthwhile. I think that's true of a lot of subjects. I think once you are in a further education college doing some sort of course, in most cases it's a worthwhile thing to do."

But what about the needs of the economy? Where did he stand on the issue of supply versus demand? Surely he must sympathise, too, with employers who wanted the education system to cater more directly to their needs?

"The truth is, I wrestle with this as a free-market Conservative," he said. "The truth is our system is more individualistic than most. There's less power to direct young people into particular areas of employment. I think that's quite deep in our culture."

His solution was information: "If that college could say: 'Twenty young people did drama last year and five are now working as actresses, and five are unemployed and 10 are at Asda', that might help."

Colleges: What are they for?

I had to confess Willetts and the Dearne Valley College principal Sue Ransom had made me think. Okay, so Claire might not become an actress, any more than she had been likely to fulfil her earlier ambition to be a spy, but what did she actually need? Probably what she needed was a couple more years in a supportive environment where she could grow and develop and mature, and hopefully decide what she wanted next. After all, most university students had that opportunity – why shouldn't she? At the very least, two years at college would be preferable to two years at home doing nothing and feeling worthless.

Willetts was right when he said a large part of what employers wanted was "soft skills", such as the ability to communicate, or simply to turn up on time. And those were skills that could be taught through the medium of almost any course.

Yet it still seemed to me that the further education system was being used as a kind of catch-all solution to society's problems. What was it actually meant to do? On one level the answer was reasonably clear: it was meant to provide work-related education and training, as opposed to the academic education more often provided by schools and universities. Those waters had been increasingly muddied over the years, with universities and schools offering a wider range of vocational courses, and with colleges also catering from the age of 14 for pupils who were disaffected with school. Yet, in reality, colleges had always had to do more than to simply feed suitably qualified students into the labour market.

When it came to catering for 16–18 year-olds, the further education system actually had two key roles. For those who left school with some qualifications and who were capable of rising to a challenge, it needed to provide a clear step forward, a bridge to the next phase of their lives – either an academic route into university or a clearly vocational course that could lead to a job or a recognised training scheme that could meet their needs. But colleges also needed to cater for those who were not ready yet for that; those who needed a more protective environment with adults who could support them as they matured. What struck me as odd was that nobody told them so. It seemed, somehow, like a failure of respect. Surely they were entitled to an honest assessment of their life chances, to be given proper information about the different choices they might make and where they might lead them? For example, Claire might have been told the ratio of drama students to working actors, and encouraged to find out whether she might be one of the tiny proportion with the talent and motivation to make it big by joining an amateur drama group. Ricky might have had spelled out to him the likely consequences of drug dependency and disengagement from the system. They might both very easily have chosen to ignore that advice, but at least they would have been paid the compliment of being treated like young adults who were responsible for their own decisions.

In a field where most of the problems seemed intractable – social change, family fragmentation – this was potentially an easy one to fix. There a seemed to be a straightforward failure of communication and guidance going on. Many of the young people I met told me what they really wanted was a steady job with a good income. If someone had sat down with them and told them about some of the new ways they might earn money – in logistics, for example, which was so undersubscribed at Dearne Valley College – they might well have decided to have a go. Perhaps further education courses should have been covered by health warnings. Perhaps instead of labelling the students "red, amber or green", according to their level of vulnerability and the likelihood of their dropping out, as Connexions did, the courses they chose should have been colour-coded instead. Green for a genuine, employer-led apprenticeship leading to a job; amber for a vocational course leading to an industry-recognised qualification but with no job attached; red for a "soft" vocational course where the likelihood of an opening as even a trainee in a closely related industry was less than 50/50. Those "red" courses could still be promoted as a wonderful route to self-discovery, improved self-esteem and better communication skills. But to let a 16 year-old believe that a performing arts course at a further education college was a reliable route to a career as an actor was quite simply dishonest and wrong.

LORD YOUNG, MINISTER FOR SKILLS AND APPRENTICESHIPS

Lord Young had been in the job of Minister for Skills and Apprenticeships three months when I met him. He confessed, as I pushed across a huge, leather-topped table in a House of Lords meeting room a chart showing just 7 per cent of successful FE students getting a job, that he was not yet up to speed on the more obscure areas of his brief.

"I'm still in my apprenticeship phase as junior minister myself and I'm really getting to grips with the various parts of the system," he said, looking at the graph. "I accept there are improvements that need to be made and you have certainly given me things to think about, but I prefer to look at it as a glass half-full. Some colleges are much better than others, and the challenge is to drive up the standard."

I had rarely met a minister quite so ready to hold up his hands under fire: "I think we would agree," he said when I suggested it wasn't a great idea to enrol more hairdressing students each year than there were hairdressers in the country. "I think you've spotted a gap in the market place. I freely recognise we could do more on that." He looked at his brief, which seemed to consist of notes on a long list of departmental initiatives, and talked about sector skills compacts, which were meant to help employers get their message across to colleges about their training needs. "We might not have totally cracked it, but I think the direction of travel is right. I think you've proved that point. We are going to take that one away."

Could he reassure the many people who felt the Connexions service wasn't meeting the needs of the most vulnerable young people? He explained, correctly, that Connexions was strictly speaking run by the schools department.

"I wish I could give you a comprehensive answer. It's an area I need to look at … From our point of view, what is it we want them to do? We want them to be able to give young people quality information advice and guidance and that's got to be a bare minimum."

At that point the minister's press officer cut in and began talking about integrated employment schemes, and I decided it was not worth pressing the point. I did feel, as the interview wore on, that a man in this job must sometimes wonder if the civil service had a room somewhere stacked high with old-fashioned reels of audio-tape with which to gag him if he ever asked a question. There were 180 different types of apprenticeship framework, all designed by different employers to do different things, he told me almost with a sort of pride, even though the Conservative opposition had criticised this situation as leading to confusion. A quarter of a million apprentices were expected to embark on courses that year, though only a fifth would be on full-blown, traditional apprenticeships of an equivalent standard to A-levels.

When I told him about Claire's dad, never working after falling out of a tree during the recession of the early 1980s, he said he hoped it would be different this time.

"Not wanting to indulge in political point scoring," he said, unconvincingly, "but there was a time when we had mass redundancies, whether in the coal fields or in steel, and where putting people on disability benefit or signing them off was seen as an interim measure. We have to see how we stop creating the next generation of people who don't see themselves linked in to the world of work. There isn't going to be one approach to this, there will be a number of approaches. But we really are trying to ensure that we don't repeat the mistakes of the past."

As I filed out of the meeting room, behind the minister and in front of the press officer, his private secretary and another official from his department, I wondered if he would still be there when the end of the recession hove into view. Skills ministers didn't tend to stay long. I thought perhaps it wasn't considered a good idea to let them get too familiar with the brief. Four months later, Lord Young was moved.

Apprentices

When I visited Tom, from Kendray, in the early summer he seemed to be doing fine. He was busy learning bricklaying with a local training charity and enjoying the work, helping to build new walls and gateposts for the estate where he lived and putting something back into his community. Having been unsuccessful at getting a plumbing apprenticeship – he had rung every firm in South Yorkshire without getting so much as a glimmer of interest – he had decided to try again but also to apply for a college place as a fall-back.

Then I had a call from Tom's mum, Karen, to say all was not well. A renewed ring-around of local plumbing companies had yielded precisely the same result as the last: nothing. Nothing had come of an application to the local council's apprenticeship scheme either – apparently there were hundreds trying for just a few places. Worse still, even his application to learn plumbing at college seemed to have run into the sand. After months of waiting he'd been told the interviews were delayed by an administrative backlog. It was getting harder and harder to persuade Tom to get out of bed in the mornings, Karen said. He couldn't see the point of working full-time as a brickie for a maintenance grant of £30 a week, which was barely more than his mum got when she went on a youth employment scheme a quarter of a century earlier.

"They're just messing us about," Tom told me when I called in to see him a week or so later. "They told us we could get set on, but they're just paying us shit money to labour. I'm not getting messed about for that money."

At that point, I abandoned all pretence at journalistic neutrality and got involved. While some of the young people I had been following had made mistakes, Tom had done pretty well everything right. His only crime had been to assume an apprenticeship was something to which someone like him might realistically aspire. He was in danger of dropping out completely because he felt let down.

I phoned the Construction Industry Training Board (CITB) adviser for the Barnsley area, who could not help much. The only way to get an apprenticeship, it seemed, was to be related to someone who had one to offer. Had Tom thought about refrigeration engineering, he asked?

By now the construction industry, which had been booming when Tom left school the previous year, was going into a nosedive. Even those firms which sometimes took on apprentices weren't doing so, the CITB adviser said. So I phoned Karl Lyons, who had been doing outreach work in Kendray and who seemed well connected, to see if he could help Tom get a college place. He made some phone calls, mentioned there could be bad publicity, and finally things began to happen. Tom had a visit from a Connexions worker, by whom he and Karen were both impressed. He suggested Tom should aim higher than plumbing, and pointed him towards a construction technician's course which was equivalent to three A-levels and could lead to a degree or to on-the-job training for surveying or project management.

Karen was left wondering why no-one had had this conversation with Tom a year earlier: "After he'd been we said: 'Why didn't they do that at school?' Nobody's done it before."

Meanwhile, I was left wondering why it should have been so hard for a bright, capable lad like Tom to find a decent job with proper training. Apprenticeships had been pushed hard by the government in recent years, and the headline figures often quoted by ministers suggested the numbers had been swelled to around a quarter of a million starting each year, from around 50,000 a decade earlier.

I had seen some signs of this elsewhere. When I visited Ricky's old school in north Manchester, there was a notice board in the entrance hall advertising apprenticeships for which leavers were invited to apply. Yet the more I looked at the national statistics, the more confusing they appeared.

In 2005–6, the latest full academic year for which figures were available, there had indeed been 225,000 "starts", or young people embarking upon apprenticeships, and it was hoped that would rise to a quarter of a million. But how many of those were school leavers who had been taken on by employers and who were being sent to college on day-release to learn a recognised trade? Not many, as it turned out.

The first problem was a basic one: What was an apprenticeship? In the past, an apprenticeship involved an employer signing up a young person as a trainee and providing him or her with training that led to qualification as a skilled craftsperson, but not any more. The government inspectorate, Ofsted, had just reported on something called "programme-led apprenticeships", which were college courses with work placements: the participants were in effect not apprentices, but students with no guarantee of a job when they qualified. Were they included in the apprenticeship statistics? When I met the responsible minister, Lord Young, I put the question to him: How many of these quarter of a million new apprentices each year actually had employers? "All of them are employer-linked," Lord Young said. "An apprenticeship cannot be recorded as complete unless there is an employment contract involved."

This seemed clear, yet afterwards I asked the minister's press officer – twice – to confirm it was correct, with no response. Eventually a tiny-print footnote to some official statistics confirmed that actually some "apprentices" were not actually apprentices at all, but students. The statistics did not reveal the numbers on these college-based programmes, but Ofsted did: in 2005, there were 54,000. So only about 175,000 of that 225,000 from 2005–6 were actually employed. In fact a parliamentary committee had already grilled Lord Young on the subject and subsequently lambasted the government for lack of clarity. These "programme-led apprenticeships" should be renamed "pre-apprenticeship training", the Innovation, Universities, Science and Skills Committee concluded, because they emphatically were not apprenticeships.

But still, 175,000 new apprentices each year was an achievement, and a significant improvement on the situation a decade earlier. Or was it? Lord Young had told me with some pride that there were 180 different "frameworks" under which an apprenticeship could be offered, most drawn up by employers. This was clearly going to take some unpicking. How many were going to gain the type of qualification Tom had sought – as a fully accredited electrician, plumber or child minder, for example? Such qualifications were equivalent to A-levels, and were designated "level three". The official statistics showed that of those 175,000 actual employer-led apprenticeships, just 73,000 were at level three. The rest were lower-level qualifications, often not much more than an official stamp on training that already existed within a big retail chain or fast-food outlet. McDonald's, for example, was made an official awarding body for apprenticeships in 2008. It announced it planned to use basic level two programmes to teach its staff literacy and numeracy as well as recognising "job-specific skills acquired through workplace training". While this was surely a valuable exercise, it was not what most adults – those who remembered the apprenticeship programmes of old – would have recognised as an apprenticeship. A level two apprenticeship in childcare, for example, would not qualify participants to work unsupervised with children.

Even 73,000 young people embarking on higher-level, employment-led qualifications each year was a significant increase. Yet the figures revealed one more small glitch: only one-third of those successful apprentices were actually aged 16–18. No more than 4 per cent of those who completed their compulsory education in 2005 – about 12,000 – went on to what most people would consider traditional apprenticeship programmes. Of those, four out of 10 dropped out without completing their training. So about 2.5 per cent of school leavers were actually completing proper, old-fashioned apprenticeships. As the bedrock of the government's plan to provide a good start in life for non-academic teenagers, this looked less than impressive.

There was more bad news, too. Research from the London School of Economics had criticised the way apprenticeships were organised in Britain. Other European governments such as those in Germany, France and the Netherlands exercised much tighter control over their programmes, it found. In Germany the trade unions had fought for young people to have a right to properly transferable training, while in Denmark they had upheld the principle that assessment should be based on objective evidence. British apprenticeships, it concluded, fell short of those in other European countries "on every important measure of good practice".

Some things had happened since the latest research and statistics were compiled: the government had announced it was going to legislate to provide a stronger framework for apprenticeships, though its Bill still gave employers far more control than in other European countries. And, of course, the recession began to bite. As expected, the autumn of 2008 saw a significant drop in the number of new apprentices starting programmes, with school leavers and those applying for higher-level qualifications the worst affected. There was a 13 per cent drop in the number of 16–18 year-olds starting "level three" apprenticeships, provisional statistics revealed.

Even in good times, employers were not taking on well-qualified young men like Tom to train as plumbers, electricians or engineers in sufficient numbers to fulfil the country's future need for skilled labour. So why not? This was the key. Apprenticeships could only work if employers found them a useful means of training skilled staff, and something was demonstrably wrong. On the advice of the Greater Manchester Chamber of Commerce, I visited an engineering company in Openshaw, a mile or so from where Ricky lived in Collyhurst, to talk about this. Thomas Storey Fabrications, which made buckets for diggers, chassis for dumper trucks and the like, had had a prosperous few years. After a management buy-out in the 1990s it had grown from 85 employees to 200 and moved to a huge, new shed-like plant in 2006. "You know how fridges and stuff are known as white goods? Well the stuff we do is known as yellow goods," its human resources and safety manager, Jo Lynch, told me as we looked down on the production lines from an internal window in her office. Thomas Storey had taken on board the government's message about apprenticeships. After a gap of 15 years it had started a new programme for apprentice welders, Lynch said.

"Welding is a trade. There's a lot you need to do. We have a lad who's early thirties and he's the youngest of our old former apprentices. Our general manager was once a Thomas Storey apprentice. And now we have this current batch. We started training them in 2002–3. How many we have varies according to the quality of the recruits we're offered."

Lynch was not taking on apprentices that year, though: "I probably would have looked harder if it hadn't been confounded by the economic climate. But the people I interviewed weren't suitable," she said. Lynch, smart, self-assured and young herself, had some very forthright things to say about the work skills of local school leavers. She was quite clear: if she had had applications from well-qualified, well-turned out school leavers who seemed keen and reliable, she would have taken them on.

"We do have a few apprentices who are shining stars, but I still think there isn't one of our current apprentices who doesn't have a live warning on their file," she said. She paused a moment, checking. "Yes, they all have warnings on their files. All for stupid, childish things. Time and attendance, and in one instance not doing his homework for college. One of them rolled up two hours late this morning – it gets beyond a joke."

So the youth of today just weren't up to the job, then? Not at all. She just did not believe the good ones were finding their way to her door.

"I'm going to be really brutal now. My firm view is that teachers push kids down two routes. If you are bright and academic, you've got something about you, they'll push you towards A-levels. If you're thick but you can lift heavy things they'll push you towards apprenticeships. I think it's an absolute travesty."

When school parties came round and she asked if anyone was considering an apprenticeship, the response was often a mix of derision and horror, she said.

"I was talking to a group of girls about engineering and the opportunities open to them, and I asked if any of them were considering apprenticeships. They laughed as if it was the most ridiculous idea," she said. Yet she believed the firm could offer a really good training to a bright, committed young person. "We specialise in welding apprenticeships. It teaches you to read drawings, it teaches you quality standards, materials, measuring, all these things make you an engineer. I think apprenticeships, if they are done as they are supposed to be, are a fantastic opportunity. I think it's an absolute crying shame teachers haven't been taught that's the case.

"If you're A-level calibre, you're the kind of person I want," she said. "In my view apprenticeships should be the starting point for a career rather than the starting point for a trade. When you're looking for supervisors, your source should be your apprentices. Our operations director started as a Rolls Royce apprentice and now he co-owns the business."

In a recession it was hard to persuade employers to invest in training, but not impossible. After all, apprentices were subsidised and cost far less than a trained adult. If Thomas Storey Fabrications was typical, many more companies might have been prepared to teach apprentices a trade if they were convinced they were not being sold the education system's rejects. It was chicken-and-egg, perhaps. Because the brightest young people were, in many areas, being persuaded to aim for higher education rather than training, employers felt they were wasting their energy if they went out looking for trainees. There was a problem, too, with smaller firms who were reluctant to take on the responsibility. But my experience of talking to employers was that they just did not feel they had much hope of finding the quality of applicant they needed. It seemed there was a conversation that should be going on that wasn't, between young men like Tom and employers like Lynch who needed skilled staff. Would Tom have gone for welding, if it had been offered to him? I think maybe he would have needed some persuading. He would have needed to be convinced that there were genuine career opportunities involved. But the lack of such a dialogue left him feeling let down, marginalised and demotivated.

Dropping out

Of the eight young people with whom I spent most time, four dropped out of further education courses and a further two were thrown out of training schemes. Elvige, from London, came as the biggest surprise – she had always been ambitious and had clear goals. But she was disappointed by her grades in the summer of 2008 – a C and a D in an AS and A-level – and seemed thrown off course by that. This was not how she saw herself. But she was living independently in her own flat, working part-time at the Mayor's office, and perhaps spreading herself thin. She went back to college for a couple of weeks that autumn but then decided to take a year off and go back the following year.

"I still want to go to uni. But I don't want a repetition of last year, where I couldn't concentrate on my classes," she said. "Everybody's always talking gap years, so I said: 'Let me just take a year and get myself financially stable.' I'm just hoping to get some kind of youth work or some kind of admin work. When I finish university I'll look for that dream job of mine," she said.

Not long after, she told me she had been on the phone to the University of East London, and that she was hoping they would give her a place on a youth work degree course, on the basis of her one A-level plus the voluntary and paid work she had been doing with young people in London.

By this time, the economic storm clouds were gathering fast and it seemed likely colleges would see an increase in applications: 17 year-olds could not draw benefit and for those from low-income families college attendance at least guaranteed an allowance of £30 per week. By the same argument the drop-out rates might have been expected to fall, for one of the main reasons students failed to complete their courses was because they had found a job. But even if rising unemployment did lead to a lower drop-out rate, the level would still be too high. About a quarter of all students embarking on further education courses dropped out, and among those on day-release from jobs, the figure was even higher at around four in 10. Among apprentices in the retail trade, the chances of qualifying were less than 50/50.

Despite the enormous efforts made to get some of these young people into college, there tended to be little follow-up once they dropped out again. At Dearne Valley there was a programme for students who had not stuck out their courses, but it had developed almost by accident after they started a scheme for unemployed 16–18 year-olds. "We expected a flood of referrals from Connexions but none came," the co-ordinator, Yvonne Murphy, explained when I called in to meet her little group. "So we went through the database for students who'd dropped out, and invited them to come in for a life skills course three days a week."

The day I visited, there were six students present – two had been doing health and social care, one IT, one sport, one public services and one a basic "Entry to Employment" course.

Two of the girls, Lynsey and Abby, had signed up for health and social care, but it hadn't turned out as they had expected. Lynsey wanted to be a nurse and Abby wanted to be a social worker, and both had been disappointed when it turned out the course would not qualify them for the type of work they wanted to do.

"I only had passes and merits, but I needed distinctions to go on a level three course, which is what I needed to do," Abby said. "It was just to keep you in education for a couple of years, nothing to do with what you want to do."

At school, the story had been similar: "I wanted to do child development at school but they wouldn't let me so I did business studies. After that I said I weren't coming in any more."

"You're what I term 'wallpaper kids'," Murphy told them. "You turn up every day of the year, you try hard, but you don't get much out of it. If you are low-level or a high-flyer, you tend to get the support."

It was clear all these teenagers would have needed far more support to stay the course. When I asked what caused them to drop out, they all chorused: "Stress!" At school, their hands had been held at every step of the way; here they were expected to motivate themselves.

"On my course they never did the work in lessons," Abby said. "You had to do it at home. They kept saying: 'Just do this' and you were getting mixed up with everything. At school they used to take us out of lessons and bring us up to the computer room and say: 'You need to do this now.'"

Abby had a job in a call centre, working from six till nine at night, five nights a week and taking home about £120. "I could work full-time but I wouldn't be able to cope. I would be straight out that door," she confessed.

Some of them had changed their minds several times already about what they wanted, and would doubtless change them several more times before they settled to anything. A few months later I called back into the college to see Yvonne Murphy. She told me Abby had won an apprenticeship with Rotherham Council, doing administrative work. That lasted four weeks. Now she was back at college again, doing tiling.

"She's come and said to me: 'Can I come back, Yvonne? I've always wanted to be a bricklayer.' I said: 'Why don't you go on a taster day of tiling? If you sacrifice 18 months of your life now, you can earn good money.' She's over the moon that she's got a place."

But Murray confessed Abby and her classmates would continue to need more help than they were likely to get: "I would love someone to give these girls a chance to get out there, to hold their hands for six months. Just showing them the social skills and the way it can be done. If they had a good mentor they would blossom."

YASMIN

When I first met Yasmin, she was full of the things she was going to do. "I want to go to Leytonstone College, but as a last resort I'll go to Tower Hamlets College, which is two minutes from my house," she told me when we first met. This would have both advantages and drawbacks: "I know everybody who goes to Tower Hamlets, I know what happens there. All my friends go there. I don't want to feel confined in one place."

There seemed to be a sub-text. "Wherever you go, you get dragged into something," she said, as if anticipating that even in Leytonstone there would be other friends, other distractions like the ones that had pulled her off course at school.

With Yasmin the theme was often one of escape: she didn't want to be tied down, she wanted to travel, see new places, meet new people. Maybe once she finished college she'd go to Australia, see the Great Barrier Reef.

"I'll do A-levels, or business. I'm hoping to open up a business one day – a successful business woman. Hopefully be a manager or something. If I put my mind to something, I could do it. In 10 years' time, like I said, a business of my own. Hopefully be married, and then it starts! The kids come later. You can't bring up kids if you haven't got any money. I'd like to be settled, financially."

She seemed very clear about what she wanted – even if some of it sounded ambitious. And she did start college, in Tower Hamlets rather than Leytonstone, and she did study business. But when I phoned to ask how it was going, a couple of weeks before the Christmas break, it sounded as if things hadn't gone entirely to plan. "I'm on my way to work," she told me. "I've got a Christmas job in Waterstones ... I'll be going back to college in January."

I wondered if she would. At the time, I had the impression Yasmin would go back to college if there was no more work in January, but could easily drop out if a full-time job were offered.

But when I rang again in January, she had neither work nor college. "No, I'm not at college no more ... No, I'm not working either. I'm in Stepney, I'm just eating at the moment ... can you call me back in a bit?" She went off the line, but for a moment or two I could still hear her, chatting to her friends. I had told her I would call to arrange to meet her a few days later, but she wasn't answering her phone that day.

Lost opportunities

Yvonne Murphy had a point, I thought. Huge numbers of young people were dropping out of college courses, mainly because they didn't get the back-up they had at school: Abby, shocked that she was expected to do homework without support or supervision; Yasmin, who had done well on a course run by the Rathbone charity, which gave her lots of support, had floundered when she found herself in a big, impersonal college. I wondered if this was connected in some way with the heavily target-driven nature of schools nowadays. Students like Yasmin and like Abby, who were perhaps what Murphy had described as "wallpaper kids", neither the low-achievers nor high-flyers, would possibly have had constant chivvying from their school teachers in order to try to push them through the magic "five good GCSEs" which the government saw as a benchmark for success. Certainly Yasmin had a great deal of back-up at Rathbone. Yet at college they were expected to sink or swim. It struck me most of these teenagers would not have needed much to keep them in class – a chat with a tutor once a week, perhaps, to ensure they were not falling behind; some follow-up if they started to miss lessons. Neither was in need of intensive supervision, just a little encouragement. Yet for most of those embarking on courses at college there was no such system in place, that I could see. And once they dropped out, in most cases there was no coherent system for ensuring they were offered other options. Officially, Connexions was supposed to find them and offer to help, but that certainly hadn't happened to Murphy's little group. For the most part, it seemed, these drop-outs were on their own. At 17, or thereabouts, they were lost to the system.

Chapter 10

The world of work

About halfway between Barnsley and Wombwell was one of those retail parks you see everywhere: a big Tesco, next to it a DIY store, a carpet retailer and so on. As Claire and I drove past there on our way back from town one day, she remarked that she'd been in all those shops to ask if they had any part-time jobs, without success. She'd also been to the big Meadowhall shopping centre near Sheffield with similar results.

Throughout the year Claire had been weighing the balance between college and a job; and when she thought about jobs she tended to think she might work in a shop. I was surprised she couldn't get work at Tesco. She was cheerful, presentable – if she took out her lip-ring – and keen, and had always been a good attender at school. I could only assume there were quite a few older applicants for shop jobs in South Yorkshire, and that the managers preferred them.

In London, on the other hand, Will had worked briefly in Tesco despite having dropped out of college, the army and a job at the airport. Like the airport, it quickly became too dull for him and he left. Yasmin found part-time work at the clothing store Primark and later a temporary job at Waterstone's book shop. Mostly, though, young people without much in the way of qualifications did not leave school or college, take up a minimum wage job and stay in it. Among the eight young people I met regularly, no-one found a permanent full-time job during the time I knew them. Six tried at some point and one, Rachel, actually got one. It was commission-only sales work and she packed it in after a couple of months.

To me it seemed a sort of collective fantasy, indulged in by the young, by their careers advisers and by their parents too, that it was easy to get such a job. Clearly they were out there – walk into any major burger chain and you would probably be served by someone under the age of 21 – yet I suspected most didn't last long. The government's annual surveys of school leavers showed a rapid decline in post-16 employment. In 2007 just one British school leaver in 20 went to a private-sector job that was not part of a government scheme. It seemed the chances of doing this kind of default thing, the thing Claire talked about as a fall-back if she didn't go to college, were actually quite slim, even when there was plenty of work out there.

When the economy was strong, there was work these young people could do. But it wasn't the kind of work most of them – or their parents – would have aspired to. It tended to be not just routine and low-paid, but also well outside the mainstream economy.

Ricky, from Collyhurst, had a couple of these types of jobs. To his credit, Ricky usually managed to arrive at the Rathbone centre where he was taking a basic-level "'Entry to Employment" course within an hour or so of the 9 am starting time. Most weeks, he did so regularly enough to qualify for his £30 maintenance allowance. The Rathbone staff tried to be stern but they were also fond of him and not likely to throw him out for failing to make it on time more than a few days in a row. His employers were not so indulgent.

I found Ricky's experiences of work instructive. He quite often earned money but he never, to my knowledge, did anything that approximated to actually applying for a job. Nor did he ever receive a wage packet detailing his tax or national insurance. The fact was he had very little chance of accessing what was normally known as the labour market. A trip to the job centre, had he made one, would have been unlikely to have done him much good. He just didn't look the part, really.

Ricky had two jobs during the year or so I spent following his ups and downs. The first involved working at a big, seedy bed and breakfast place on the main road between his home and the city centre – an odd-looking outfit with a car lot at the front. One day on his way home from the centre, Ricky called in to ask if there was any work going, and was told he could help out valeting cars. The owner drove a Porsche and lived in a huge house a few miles further out of town, Ricky said. But no firm deal was ever struck, and it was never clear how much – or even whether – Ricky was going to get paid. Within a few weeks, the deal had gone sour.

"I was going to pack up the course if working was any good," Ricky told me. "But I didn't pack the job in – he sacked me. I was valeting this car and he came out and said I'd done a shit job, so I told him where to go. I didn't want to be treated like an idiot. Anyway, I've got his ring." He showed me a rather tarnished gold-coloured signet ring. "I didn't rob it – he said to sell it, and I could get £50. But it started going green on my finger."

Not long afterwards Ricky was in the pub where his mum did an occasional shift, and two men offered him £20 to deliver some leaflets. Soon he was doing regular work for them, selling CDs and other stuff out of an old railway arch they kept. It was a real Fagin's den, by the sound of it: "They've got TVs, mobiles, they've got wheel rims, £2.50 a pop. I started doing leaflets, but now he's got me selling phones and stuff," Ricky said. "He wants £80 for them, but I try to get £100. And he's got computer games – I can have them for £1 and sell them for a fiver. It's not robbed. He gets them off the crackheads, for money."

I asked how much he was making – he went there most days after he finished at the Rathbone centre – and he said: "Nothing, really. I'm just doing it for a bit so he gives me more work. If he thinks I'm responsible, and he can trust me, he might send me on a job for him."

A few weeks later that came to an unfortunate end, too. Ricky had sold some computer games and hadn't handed over the money, and his employer had decided to administer his own justice.

"He came round here and he dragged me into his car, and he said: 'If you don't get the money I'll have to leather you. I don't want to because your mum's a top lady, but I will.' It was £90. I got it off my friend's granddad."

The matter now settled, Ricky's employer told him he could come back to work helping out with house and shed clearances, but after that it went quiet. At around that time Ricky was in trouble with his first employer, too, after he was accused of being involved in a robbery at the bed and breakfast. Ricky flatly denied it, and the charge was dropped after his accuser disappeared.

In some respects, Ricky was quite capable of working, and wanted to work because he really wanted money. But the reality was no mainstream employer would have been likely to take him on, and if they had he probably wouldn't have lasted long. Instead, Ricky accessed the informal employment market, where life was a little more fluid, where rules and regulations and training opportunities and career development were replaced by a sort of street law.

The employers' view

During the summer of 2008 I interviewed a succession of employers who either had employed one of the young people I met or potentially could have done. Every single one, without exception, said they were suffering major recruitment problems because they could not get staff who would turn up on time, properly dressed, sober and fit for eight hours' labour. At London City Airport, where Will worked for a while, the community relations manager, Elizabeth Hegarty, told me they held recruitment days three times a year at which applicants had to sit a basic entry test with questions such as: "If a flight leaves at 2 pm and arrives at its destination at 4 pm, how long is the flight?" Or: "If you bought five sandwiches on Wednesday and seven on Thursday, how many did you buy altogether?" At the last sitting a third of those who took the test failed it.

"Some of the candidates were nowhere near ready for work. Nowhere near," Hegarty told me. "We had a guy came along in leather trousers and a belt with 'Son of a Bitch' on." Hegarty, a young, smart graduate whose own family had moved out from Bow to Redbridge, confessed it was hard to meet the airport's target that a third of its staff should be from the local borough of Newham.

"A few years ago my chief executive said in a public forum: 'I would love to employ local people but they can't read and write.' 'Crude and rude' was how he put it. I could have killed him, but that's essentially where we fall down.

We have applicants both young and mature who don't have the basic skills required to get a job.

"Sleeping on the job is a big one. You can drive a transit to the end of the field and snooze on the back of the parking stand. We had one guy who left after a week saying he didn't like aeroplanes. With young people attitude is a huge, huge problem. We'd like to bring in young people, but if you have an applicant in front of you who's 40 with two kids and a house to pay for, their maturity is usually much higher than a young person with no responsibilities."

These were good jobs, too. At that time, security and ground staff started on around £18,000, plus overtime. Hegarty confessed the local employment market in Newham might have been stretched by work starting on the Olympic site, but I heard a similar story elsewhere too.

Some of this might be easily dismissed as employers doing what employers do: whingeing about lazy, feckless workers. The ancient Romans apparently used to complain their slaves were always pilfering and tended to disappear off to public entertainments when they were supposed to be working. Of course there was a natural tension between employer and employee – the employer wanting to squeeze every last drop from the worker; the worker wanting to do what was necessary and not too much more. Yet I heard the story so often, in such similar terms, from so many different people that I could not dismiss it. Yes, the majority of young people probably could, by and large, get out of bed in the morning and do simple tasks without too much trouble. But most of them were not applying for jobs during their teens because they had stayed on at school or college.

The employers I heard talking about the hopelessness of their younger recruits were right. There was a minority who, like Ricky, who were not ready for a mainstream job. In truth, some of them never would be. To be brutal, Ricky's drug habit was a major barrier between him and the labour market. Yes, then, Britain – along with much of the rest of the developed world – did have a problem with shiftless, disengaged teenagers. The reasons for their shiftlessness were complex and, for the most part, not of their making. Yet shiftless, to be blunt, they were.

The call centre

The Direct Dialogue call centre was housed in a modern, non-descript office block in the Dearne Valley between Rotherham and Barnsley. Outside, a group of youngish people were hanging around smoking, and I was not sure if I was in the right place. Unlike the larger call centres in the Dearne – the biggest employed thousands, Direct Dialogue just 140 – it did not have a huge banner outside inviting applications for jobs.

Maria Opuni, the company's head of call centres, assured me this was not because she had found an answer to the recruitment problems faced by employers in the area. Despite the fact that some of the highest concentrations of benefit claimants in the country lived within shouting distance, she said she was at her wits' end.

"We got to a stage early last year where we sat down with the board and said if we can't fix this recruitment issue we need to move. That's how serious it got. It was a real baptism of fire, moving to the Dearne Valley."

Opuni had started her career just a few miles away in Rotherham, working at a call centre for one of the major banks. When she and a colleague decided to start their own business in 2005, the Dearne seemed the perfect place. Several call centres were already there and a host company had set up fully equipped buildings, so all they had to do was sign the lease and set to work. But it quickly became apparent the Dearne Valley was not Rotherham. While Opuni's old staff had been largely women with children who wanted flexible hours, here the applicants were much younger, much greener.

"We had so many problems in the early days, with staff who didn't have the bus fare to get to work. Drink problems, drug problems," she said. "You almost have to become a counsellor. My management team has to focus on teaching life skills, rather than just teaching the skills to do the job. We have to help these people to move from school into work, to recognise what working hard is all about, what the benefits are, how to manage their finances and their life."

Opuni, who had always lived in the area, said she had been shocked by what she learned about its youth culture: "It's been a real eye-opener. It really has. You've got to go out every Friday and Saturday and wear the right stuff. That's what your life is. You work, you get your salary, you go out and drink till you're sick. Every weekend.

"About six months ago people were caught dealing drugs in our car park. I spoke to the service management about it and they weren't that fazed. It happens all the time." I was surprised – this was a post-industrial enterprise zone full of offices and warehouses; there were no pubs or clubs here. To whom, I asked. To the staff? She nodded. "And it wasn't just soft drugs like cannabis; it was cocaine and stuff."

Call centres had become the employer of choice for school leavers without qualifications or aspirations, she said. A few did well and progressed up the management ladder, with a team leader earning about the same as a classroom teacher. But many simply failed to fit into the world of work.

"There's a lot less people choosing to leave than being told they have to leave," Opuni said. "People who refuse to sell in the right way; absenteeism is rife. We use the term 'AWOL' a lot. I struggle to get my head round it. People have a contract of employment, and yet when they don't want to come to work they don't even bother to phone. What's that about?" She asked the question with an expression that was genuinely puzzled, almost hurt.

The Dearne Valley had begun its transformation, from derelict steel and coal area to modern light-industrial centre, eight years earlier. So after all this time surely the work culture must have at least begun to re-grow? Opuni didn't even hesitate.

"No," she said, bluntly. "As an employer, there's little you can do to influence people's lives. That's my biggest fear. I don't see how these cycles are being broken."

Opuni struck me as a genuinely caring employer – the conditions at Direct Dialogue seemed far more humane than those some other call centres were reputed to offer. Yet I was not surprised she struggled to recruit good staff – yes, there was clearly a problem with young people who were not equipped to work, but there was something else, too. She had said call centre work had become a natural choice for young people in the area, but I felt it was perhaps more a port of last resort. I never heard anyone aspire to work in a call centre, yet people did talk about taking jobs there, sometimes because the work was part-time and flexible; sometimes because the money wasn't bad and it seemed easier than persisting at college. It struck me that this was part of a pattern – it wasn't that there wasn't work available for young people, but that the types of work available were often the wrong ones. The employers who agreed to speak to me were, by and large, the better ones. But the experience of the young people I met was often that the jobs they could get didn't really offer stability, security or the support they'd need to become useful workers.

Several of my other interviewees, some of whom worked with disaffected youngsters, reinforced this point. It wasn't the loss of the old industries, per se, that had caused the problem, they thought. It was the loss of the old certainties, the expectation of being able to earn a living wage, to go into a job where you'd be supported while you found your feet, and where you could reasonably expect to stay. Certainly it looked as if there was a major mismatch between what today's teenagers had to offer and what today's employers expected them to be able to do.

Workless culture?

One day an employer in Barnsley told me a story that came to mind many times afterwards. This man knew how to tell a good yarn, and as he recounted this particular incident he interspersed his own West Yorkshire tones with a pretty fair imitation of the dialect spoken in the Dearne Valley and thereabouts.

"A couple of years ago," he told me, "one of the staff asked if I'd see this young man. They wanted me to consider sacking him. He was 16 years old and refusing to do anything. His attendance was appalling. He came into my office and stood with his hands in his pockets. He wouldn't sit down.

"I said: 'What's the problem?'

"He said: 'You, at the minute. You think you can bloody tell me what to do.'

"I said: 'What's your ambition?'

"He said: 'To get to 18.'

"I said: 'Why? Have you got some life-threatening illness?'

"He said: 'Don't be bloody clever. Me dad's 38, 'e's never worked. 'E smokes, 'e drinks, we've gorra car. We go on 'oliday every year for two weeks to Cleethorpes.

"'And,' he said, ''E's got one thing ovver thee.'

"I said: 'What's that?'

"And he said: ''E'll not dee o' stress.'"

The implication, the employer explained, was that the lad thought he would go on benefit at 18 and would then be set up for life. I retold this story to several people afterwards, and found their reactions interesting. Talking to experts, academics and even politicians in London and elsewhere, the response was sceptical: this was apocryphal, surely. Or if it was true, it was a rare case and as such was not solid evidence that there was a culture of worklessness out there in the post-industrial areas of Britain. Right-wing politicians, including the former Conservative leader Iain Duncan Smith, argued that such a culture of worklessness had arisen because generations of young people were growing up in families where there had been no work for several generations – which they certainly were. But did those young people really have that sense of almost devil-may-care defiance, the belief that they would – to be blunt – live off the state and laugh at the stupidity of officialdom for allowing them to do so?

Several times, I met employers who thought they did. In Barnsley I went to see John Foster, chairman of the local work and skills board, at his bakery in Mapplewell. Soft white baps were stacked up on Foster's office windowsill as we talked, and a seductive smell wafted up from the factory floor. The company had started out in the Fifties as a transport café but now turned over nearly £10 million and had 230 employees. Foster had little good to say about the local workforce.

"Scum. Dross," he said. "We use those words in our business to refer to people that don't want to work. People in some areas of this country are brought up with, 'I can get so much money for doing nothing, therefore if I work it's only worth the extra to me.' So maybe working is only worth £2 an hour. The rest is benefits. They look at it as an entitlement."

The bakery had recently joined a government scheme under which it pledged to give jobs to the unemployed, but Foster was unimpressed. "The job centre have to send people, and those people have to attend or they'll cut their benefits. One chap was due to come for an interview and he didn't turn up. The next thing, he was trying to smash the place up because he'd had his benefits withdrawn. We sent a few burly chaps out. He was saying: 'You've stopped my benefits.' We said: 'Hang on. We've got a job you can have. You can start now if you want.' He didn't want a job. We found out he'd already got one, cash in hand."

Foster said he resolved the problem by advertising his jobs in Eastern Europe rather than Barnsley.

"About three or four years ago we had one migrant worker who came for a job in the normal way, then another and then another. We realised these people were what we wanted. They turned up for work on time, they weren't trying to skive all the time, didn't have time off, weren't wimps. They weren't looking for a bloody handout all the time. I think it's just a work ethic."

Benefit dependency

However, I never met a young person who said they wanted to live on benefits – or at least, not to me. And nor did their parents. I felt that every single parent I met genuinely wanted the best for his or her children, and that none wanted them to live their lives on the dole. Yet some of those young people had grown up in households without work. Some of them did not see their parents up and about at 8:30 in the morning at all, let alone preparing for work. And I would have to say, if I were being completely honest, that one or two of those parents did not seem to me to be looking all that hard either.

In one home I visited was a mother who told me she had worked regularly in the past but had not been able recently to find a job. Every time I went back, I would hear of how she had applied for a job and been turned down, or how she had been offered something that was unsuitable. She had to turn down a cleaning job because she had vertigo and was unable to work a floor polisher. A night-time job would have cost too much in taxi fares; one shop job was two bus rides away, while she was turned down for another because, she said, she was "the wrong colour". After a while it turned out she did have a part-time job with which she supplemented the money she received in benefits. She was also hoping for a better-paid position she had been half-offered by a friend. This, she told me in an unguarded moment, would allow her to "go legit". Over the course of several months, it failed to materialise. But I do think that if it had been offered, she would have taken it and signed off. It was within walking distance of her home, the hours would have suited her and the money would have been better than she could have got cleaning or working in a supermarket.

Although a benefits officer would, I am sure, have taken a dim view of her situation, I did not think she was laughing up her sleeve at the system. I think the decisions she had to make were marginal ones, and would have been different if anyone else in the household had been bringing in a wage. As pin-money, a minimum wage job would have done fine. But if it meant signing off and losing not only the dole money but also the housing benefit, it would not be worth while. She might, on paper, have had substantially more money: from less than £100 a week in benefits and part-time earnings she could have been bringing home around £200 in wages. Yet she would have to deduct at least £50 in rent and yet more in bus fares, clothing to wear for work and probably other expenses such as drinks and meals. Although she would have been better off, the financial gain would simply not have been enough to make the effort worthwhile. It seemed to me, too, that in the area where she lived there were very few people working, and so there was no shame whatsoever in being on benefit.

That is not to say, though, that being on benefit would have been seen as something desirable or smart – just normal. And this mother, while she sympathised with her children when they fell in and out of jobs complaining of terrible conditions, low pay and unsympathetic employers, was by no means encouraging them to sign on. She wanted them to be happy and settled, and was proud of those among her offspring who had done well for themselves. I think she saw her situation as being the result of a number of factors – traumas, disruptions and childrearing responsibilities had made it difficult her to work for some time, and when she tried to re-enter the labour market it had moved on. And, maybe, she had got used to not working.

Being out of work, for many people, was just part of normal life. As one council official put it: "There isn't an army of people out there in rocking chairs with shawls on going 'Oh my God, I need someone to rescue me.' They're living their lives."

Yet among many of the professionals I met who were actually working on the ground with the young, the story of the boy whose dad would "not dee o' stress" provoked far less scepticism than it did among those whose roles were one step removed.

Karl Lyons, who worked at a centre for excluded pupils but also knocked on doors around Barnsley looking for disengaged youths, told me many young people did not see the point in a minimum wage job when the going rate for "doing a speed camera" was £100. When I expressed bafflement at this – what on earth did "doing a speed camera" mean? He explained that if I looked at the cameras on the main roads around Barnsley, I would see that many of them had been burned out. Motorists who realised they had been clocked would find a local kid and pay them £100 to sling an old tyre around the camera and set fire to it, he explained, thus destroying the film before it could be retrieved.

In his view, this culture had arisen because although there were jobs available, they paid far less than the mines and the glassworks used to pay: "There's a little corridor of used car places at Redbrook – I drive through it into town. At 8:45 these two black African men are always walking there from town – it's two and a half miles. They're employed to wash the cars. They don't seem to miss a day, in all weathers they're there with a big smile on their faces. It's a classic example of the work ethic. The people I'm talking about wouldn't walk two and a half miles for that job. They just wouldn't do it."

WILL

I phoned Will one day in July, and he was on the tube. He was on his way to a job interview, he said. He had applied to be a karate instructor. I wished him good luck, and arranged to meet him the following week near the young people's accommodation where he lived in East London. To be honest, I didn't expect too much. Will often had a job in his sights, but usually the next time I saw him he would say it hadn't turned out to be quite what he expected, or he'd been rejected. When we first met he was applying to be a tube driver, but he narrowly failed the entrance test.

The day we met, in the cafeteria at Morrison's supermarket, Will was not at his best. He'd had a bust-up with the mother of his baby girl, who was now six months old, and had spent the night drowning his sorrows in cheap whisky and wine with some friends. He wondered if he could face coffee, and finally forced down a lemonade and some toast.

How did the interview go, I asked? He told me it hadn't happened. He'd gone all the way out to Essex, but the interviewer wasn't there. "I was going to one of their lessons, but it'd been cancelled. It was just to see what I'm capable of." He was still hoping it would come off. They'd train him up to be a black belt, he said, and pay him £15,000 a year in the meantime.

Had he ever done any karate? No, he said, but he was interested in martial arts and had done a bit of capoeira: "I phoned them up and said I really want the job and I'd be brilliant at it. I convinced them over the phone to give me the job, basically. I love martial arts, to be honest. That would have been a perfect job for me because I want to teach and it would be something I enjoy. Also it would be helping people to defend themselves."

Later I looked up the firm, which seemed to be advertising in several parts of the country. "While working your way through this traineeship you will also earn a good income through our proven marketing and recruitment system", the ad said. The income, so far as I could see, was commission for recruiting new members to the firm's karate clubs. In effect the programme was a pyramid scheme, with successful trainees starting their own companies and then taking on more trainees to do the same job for them. The ad said applicants would need their own car – Will had taken his test the previous week but had failed and didn't know when he would be able to afford to try again. The next time I saw Will he had stopped pursuing it – he'd realised the whole thing was a bit of a con.

Will had kept on the right side of the law but all around him he could see people looking for ways to get rich, few of them legal: "My friend does loads of different scams, selling stuff. He's saying, 'Do you want in?' But I'd never get involved. Today two of my friends are wearing bullet-proof vests and they're transporting – I don't know what. One of them's driving and the other's in the passenger seat. And these are two people you could think were computer technicians! It's £1,500 a day, each."

I asked if he'd work here, in Morrison's. "I wouldn't work in a supermarket," he replied. "I worked in Tesco and it was the most boring thing in the world. Helping people with carrier bags. I'm above that level. I was earning £9.50 an hour at the airport. I'm not going below £8. Money isn't everything to me, I need it but I want to find something that's going to make me happy. But it's really hard to find. I wouldn't go back to college. Simple reason: I'm so impatient. I'm the most impatient person. I don't know – I just can't. I'm not an education kind of person."

I asked if he'd think about looking for work-based training – maybe an apprenticeship? "No. If I want documentation, I know people that can make that for me. I've got a friend who's got PhDs, Masters. He owns a penthouse in Stratford, over the mall. He's about 28. He gave himself GCSEs; he had nothing. He learned computers by himself, then he was charging other people £200 for a qualification. He's got so many NVQs … but he isn't that smart. Anyone can make enough money to buy something, to be honest. Round here, everyone has their own business. You have a front, and behind the scenes you have your money-making opportunities.

"There's scams everywhere. I've met the king of scams – he scammed £7 million; he's Polish or something. He dresses like a bum. He's got this big house outside London. He goes into a library and finds a name and address, buys a house using fake ID with that name, the house isn't paid for and it's sold, the person doesn't exist and the house is gone. It's people like him who make money in this country."

There was a difference, I thought, between the young people I met in London and elsewhere. In London, everything seemed possible and yet unattainable at the same time, and that seemed to pull them back. What was the point of hard work, when there was always this sense that people could get rich by other means? Elsewhere, there was more of a sense that certain things weren't possible at all – and that held young people back, too.

Solutions

But what was to be done? Should governments simply write off the Wills of this world, or sit back in the hope they would work things out for themselves? No-one with any serious handle on the problem believed they should. Even the most hard-hearted pragmatist would have had to admit that could only lead to higher benefit bills and even more overcrowded prisons. And no-one really blamed the employers who said they had tried bringing in unemployed youngsters and the long-term jobless and it hadn't worked in most cases. For many of them, the one or two shining examples of rehabilitative success simply weren't enough of a benefit to their business to make the hassle worthwhile.

The solution, according to several of the people I interviewed, was straight-forward, although the process in some cases certainly would not be. Some young people needed a lot of help, and would not be ready for the labour market in the foreseeable future. A larger group – Will among them, I would have said – probably could hold down a job, but only if there was someone there to provide a strong guiding hand.

In the past, this bigger group was dealt with quite easily. As one training provider had put it: "You used to have labourers' mates on building sites. You don't have them now – you tell me the last time you saw a driver's mate. You had gofers for plumbers and electricians." His point was that the wandering, ill-motivated but fundamentally rescuable youth of the past had somewhere productive to go. Now they didn't. Instead of growing up with the belief they would follow their father or mother into a job, some grew up believing it was normal not to work at all.

Elaine Equeall, who ran the Kendray regeneration initiative, had seen the problem at close quarters. "Going from having a very strong work ethic to not having one in such a short time, you have whole families where nobody gets up for work. There's a blame culture, and also a feeling of exclusion," she said. "Everything's for somebody else, but it's not for me. The stuff out there is for people with education, and I haven't got it. There's no aspiration to want to seek work. I've worked with people in their forties who've said: 'I can't work.' Who've had it drummed into them for so long that they're no good. They haven't got anything to offer."

Yet she did not see the situation as hopeless or intractable. Her own experience had told her even the most entrenched worklessness could be tackled, with the right attitude.

"Against all my better instincts I worked on a mandatory programme in Sheffield," she said. "People were chosen on the basis of benefits and how long they'd been claiming them. The starting point was: 'I can't work.' They maybe didn't attend school, they maybe had one job and maybe a temporary contract here or there, then drifted off on to the Incapacity Benefit, then back on to the Job Seekers' Allowance. But because it was mandatory they had to do something. We would create opportunities. We could broker things, set things up, negotiate with employers, offer them subsidies. The hardest bit was getting people to attend, but it did succeed and people's confidence and self-esteem improved tremendously because they had to do something. They had to get into a routine of getting up in the morning and having a purpose. Because we came all softly-softly and liberal with lots of fluff and 'Let's talk about it' and gave people confidence, we could help people understand the benefit of doing something – and we could take them there in the car. There were people who'd been unemployed for 15 years and we got them back into work. We had a 33 per cent success rate, which was amazing after 15 years."

The programme on which Equeall had worked took place against a background in which low-paid jobs were plentiful, and in today's changed economic climate it would be much easier for the long-term unemployed to cling to the safety blanket of benefits, I felt.

Yet I did see examples, too, of how a positive attitude could turn around a life with surprising ease. The Manchester Chamber of Commerce suggested I should go to visit Anne Wallace at Taylor's Fish and Chips in Woodley, near Stockport. Wallace used to have terrible problems getting people to work for her, they said, until she changed the way she worked. Her family had run the business for decades, but she took it over with a heavy heart.

"I used to drive here in the morning and think: How many hours are there till I can leave again?" Wallace told me in the little café at the back of her shop, as staff bustled around preparing for the lunchtime rush. "We put the place on the market but it didn't sell. We decided to shut the door and walk away because we couldn't sell it. There were already three boarded-up shops on the precinct. As a last desperate measure, my daughter said: 'Why don't you ask the girls what they think?' I said: 'I know what they think: if they cared they'd turn up and not let me down all the time.'"

What the staff told her surprised her: they wanted to get involved, and to help develop the business. Within a couple of years Taylor's was winning awards for training and staff development, and Wallace was talking about starting an "Academy of Fish".

As we talked in the dining room a young girl called Toni was pottering about in the front, putting fruit salad in the salad bar – one of the ideas the "girls" came up with – and giggling with the other workers about some bit of banter she'd had the previous day with a customer.

"I enjoy it," she told me. "I can't say I love it – every job has its down side. But it's the atmosphere I do like. I enjoy serving customers."

A couple of years before that Toni was setting herself up for a life without work, Wallace told me.

"Toni and her sister both work here," she explained. "She has a little boy. She hasn't had the best start. When her sister asked if I'd give her a job, I said: 'I'm not Jobcentre Plus.' But she said: 'She's going nowhere, she's in with a bad crowd, and my mother's going out of her mind.' It was November, two years ago. So I said I'd take her on till Christmas. Now she's done a modern apprenticeship – I could see her running her own business in the future."

It would be harder, I thought, to see how Toni would have found her niche in a world where jobs were in short supply. Would Anne Wallace have taken her on if she had had a queue of older and probably more reliable workers outside her door? Probably not. And if she had not done so, what would the future have held for Toni? Long-term benefits, probably more children, and all of them growing up in yet another household without work. Yet a small gesture, a single supportive employer willing to offer a job on a trial basis, had given her an opportunity that could quite possibly have changed the course of her whole life.

Rachel's job

About six months after I met Rachel, she got a job. She'd tried hard, visiting the job centre and looking in the paper. She'd even had a bit of experience working as a waitress while she should have been at school, but it hadn't helped: "On the applications when they say: 'Why did you stop going to school?', I think I need to stop putting: 'Pregnant'," she'd told me when we first met. But then her outreach worker, Julie, got a call to say she was working in sales.

I arranged to meet Rachel after work one Saturday afternoon, at her employer's office in Manchester, a big old Victorian building with lots of different company names listed by a long row of doorbells. There was no sign of life, so I sat on the wall opposite in the sunshine. Within a few minutes small groups of smartly dressed young people began to gather, all carrying folders or – in one or two cases – briefcases. The men were all wearing suits and ties; the women, smart business clothes. I wondered if they were part of some religious sect or evangelical group, but after a while I wandered over and asked if they knew Rachel. Yes, they said, they did.

A few minutes later someone pointed a little way down the street: "There she is." I hardly recognised her. She was wearing little black shoes, tights and a black-and-white dress that combined a black skirt with a white blouse. Her blonde hair was loose down her back and she seemed different. It was hard to put my finger on why, but afterwards I thought she seemed to walk with more confidence, to hold her head up higher. Her colleagues greeted her with cheers and hugs. As we settled down to talk in a nearby burger bar, an older girl who seemed very polished put her head round the door, then came over and gave Rachel a hug, too. "Rachel is new," she said, "but she's *so* brilliant."

Rachel told me she had answered an ad in the *Manchester Evening News*: "Sales and Marketing. Good pay. Start immediately. No experience necessary."

"I had an interview the same day," she said. "They don't even tell you at the interview what you're going to be doing, because they want you to be open-minded about it. So then the next day I was just watching my leader, Barry. I like him a lot. We do door-to-door all over. You just say, 'Hi, how are you?' If you see something nice you say, 'That's well nice, where d'you get it from?' It's a bit like acting."

Rachel had been recruited as a "charity mugger", canvassing for direct debit donations. She was not employed, and part of her commission would be held back as a "bond" to be paid if she was still there after five months.

"You go through this thing," she said. "Introduction, presentation, a story and then close. Introduction is 'Hello, my name's Rachel, I'm doing a bit of charity work.' Presentation ..." She paused. "I think that's the way your body language is. You've got to use your hands. The story is what's going on." She put on her friendly, doorstep face: "I'm not going to patronise you. You've seen it on TV, thousands of children are dying. It isn't their fault they were born in a world like this.' You have to say words like 'horrific'."

"My first week I only got two direct debits, so I only got paid £50. The week just gone, I got 15. Some people get 12 in one day."

I could see why Rachel seemed so much more confident. For the first time in a long time, perhaps ever, she had done well and won praise. At the end of each day, she said, there was a closing ceremony.

"If you've sold more than you've ever sold before, at the end of the day they put a drum in the middle of the room. You get to bang the drum and everyone else gathers round and they all chant: 'Charity! Charity!' They call it ringing bells. Everyone wants to ring bells."

Rachel was particularly excited because she had been invited to a national rally with 4,000 people from companies in the group: "We get to stay overnight in a five star hotel, and everything." If she continued to do well, she could be allowed to become an "owner" in a year or so. The outfit was one of dozens, if not hundreds, all over the country. The hours were long – the canvassers often worked 10 hours a day and socialised together as well – and she had barely seen her boyfriend Derek or her mum for weeks.

Then Rachel told me she was moving to Wales the next day. "My boss told us last night. She said I was going to get promoted quick. There's going to be about 15 of us living in a house, it'll be like Big Brother. Three people have got cars so we'll go out in groups, all over."

Rachel was delighted with the turn her life had taken. "My dad's happy. He used to do sales himself when he was younger. He says maybe I've got it from him. You've got to have the bug.

"I used to say to Derek: 'I feel like I'm not doing anything, I'm bored out of my head all the time. I'm useless. Sat in a room all day. What kind of life is that?"

In the end, however, it was all too much – living in Wales, Rachel missed her kids, to whom she had access one afternoon a week. After a couple of months, she gave it up and started looking for work in Manchester again. Yet even though the job didn't last, and even though it didn't seem to pay the minimum wage, I had to admit it was good for Rachel. In an odd way, it had given her a glimpse of the real, non-financial benefits of working. It made her feel really good about herself, and that counted for a lot.

Chapter 11

Race matters

The day Elvige took me to meet her mentor, Lisa, she had been speaking about gun-and-knife crime at an event hosted by Boris Johnson. "Your new best friend," Lisa joked, and they both laughed. Elvige was a peer outreach worker for the Mayor's office, and Johnson had recently taken over from Ken Livingstone as Mayor of London.

There had been an MP on the platform, Elvige told us – I think it must have been Dawn Butler, the black, female member for Brent South. She had clearly been impressed by Elvige.

"She said to me that one day I'm going to be this, and I'm going to be that, at Westminster," she told us. "I was like: 'I'm blacker than black! How am I going to go there?'"

It was the first and only time I heard Elvige suggest she felt either her skin colour or her African background were likely to hold her back. Usually our conversations had taken quite a different turn. She had told me she hung out with other black girls at school, mostly from a mixture of West African backgrounds, and that they had tended to be among the more aspirational in the school.

"I had four groups of friends," she said. "There was the Caribbean girls, there was the Somali girls, and there was my best, best friends – we were the mixed ones. I'm from Togo, one was from Ivory Coast, one from Portugal, one from Nigeria. I kind of kept the link between the Jamaicans and the Somalis and the mixed group. They were all quite ambitious."

She also talked sometimes of how her African grandmother would exhort her to do well for her family by saying "Make us proud."

More often it was the white families I met who would talk about race in a negative way. "I'm the wrong colour," one mother told me when explaining why she'd been rejected for a job. Another complained her son had been bullied because he was among a small minority of white children at his school.

For some years the British school system had been witnessing the phenomenon of white children from poorer backgrounds falling ever further behind while those from other ethnic backgrounds – notably Indian and Chinese – raced ahead. Yet the debate about race and education had moved on only slowly.

In 2005 Trevor Phillips, the head of Britain's Equality and Human Rights Commission, had made a plea for new measures to help solve the problem of underachievement by Afro-Caribbean boys. While he acknowledged poverty was an issue – the poorest boys from Caribbean backgrounds actually did slightly better at school than the poorest from white families – he added that those from better-off backgrounds were a long way behind their white peers.

"The main cause of the performance differential is definitely not poverty," he argued, though he was not pleading the cause, either, of those who thought racism to blame. "We have to accept that our historical bleating about racist teachers, class barriers and irrelevant curricula has not moved the performance of these kids one iota. We need new solutions," he said.

I took issue with this on more than one front. First, the statistics on the exam performance of pupils from "better-off backgrounds" were a very blunt instrument because they only covered those not claiming free school meals. If we assumed the black population as a whole was poorer than the white population, then even those black families classed as better off were still on average poorer than their "better-off" white counterparts – so relative poverty could still have been a cause of their less impressive exam results. Those on free school meals, conversely, would mostly have been living at or around the safety-net level of state benefits whether they were black or white, so the economic differential between them would have been only slight. Secondly, Afro-Caribbean boys, both poor and not so poor, had made great strides in the past few years. While the proportion of white boys from wealthier backgrounds who got five

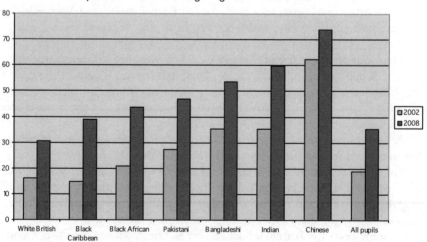

Boys on Free School Meals gaining five A*-Cs at GCSE

Figure 6 Poverty and race.

Source: DCSF statistics. Figures in percentages.

good GCSEs rose by 25 per cent between 2002 and 2008, the proportion of Caribbean boys from supposedly similar backgrounds rose by 75 per cent – the black boys, though still behind, were catching up fast.

As were all the other ethnic minority groups. The figures comparing the exam results of pupils on free school meals from each ethnic group made interesting reading, particularly compared with those from six years earlier. The argument had often been made that educational differences between ethnic groups related to the types of backgrounds people came from – Ugandan Asians, for example, tended to be business people from well-educated families and so their children did well at school in the UK; migrants from Bangladesh, on the other hand, tended to be from poorer, rural families and so did less well. Yet the latest statistics showed a different effect: among the poorest pupils, every single non-white ethnic group now performed better than its white British counterpart, whether male or female. And almost every non-white group, including Afro-Caribbeans – the only exception being Chinese boys, who were way ahead of the field in any case – had improved faster than white British pupils. The poorest white British pupils were now way behind the rest.

So, had the problem of underachievement by ethnic minorities in Britain gone away? Throughout the 1990s in the UK there had been specific government funding for pupils from ethnic minorities, and the government still spent around £200 million per year on "narrowing achievement gaps for black and minority ethnic pupils". There were still reasons for this – for example, helping newly arrived migrants to become proficient in English – but there was a growing question mark over whether such funding should exist at all. Trevor Phillips had acknowledged the issue, saying in a speech in October 2008 that white working class communities, about to be hit hard by recession, might have a strong case for extra help in the near future.

"We may need to do so with the sort of special measures we've previously targeted at ethnic minorities. The name of the game is to tackle inequality, not racial special pleading. We will fail to so do at our peril," he said.

Yet a closer look at the statistics did seem to suggest something else was going on when it came to Afro-Caribbean boys. While they were catching up with their white counterparts at school, the proportion of Afro-Caribbean men aged 18–24 who were drawing benefits remained phenomenally high – nearly 9 per cent, three times the level in the white British population at the time. And as Phillips pointed out in 2005, there were twice as many black men in prison as there were at university.

In 2007, researchers from the London School of Economics looked at the statistics from another angle, focusing on the progress made by different groups of pupils between the ages of 11 and 16. They found Caribbean pupils were the least likely to be what they called "continuing high achievers" in the top 50 per cent at both stages, and the most likely to be "significant descenders" in the top 50 per cent at 11 but in the bottom 10 per cent at 16. The biggest group of "persistent low achievers" in the bottom 10 per cent, both at 11 and at 16, were the white British. The Indians had the greatest chance of improvement – nine-tenths of those in the bottom 10 per cent at age 11 climbed out of that group by age 16, and 13 per cent went from the bottom group to the top group in those five years.

There was something to be said, then, about why some pupils were more likely to underachieve than others. Warwick University produced some interesting research on this point. They questioned pupils in five inner-city schools characterised by poor attendance and underachievement, and found marked differences in attitudes between different ethnic groups. While they too found white British pupils had the lowest aspirations, followed by Caribbeans, they found the reasons for those low aspirations varied. The white pupils' lack of ambition was driven by a lack of belief in their own academic abilities and by low aspiration in their homes, but for the black Caribbean pupils it was more likely to be caused by disaffection and negative peer group pressure.

This seemed to make sense. It seemed to imply that while they were at primary school, pupils from Caribbean families might have had their disaffection mediated, to some extent, by the high ambitions of their parents, while their white peers had less encouragement from home. As they got older and the influence of their peers grew, maybe the Caribbean pupils, particularly the boys, fell victim to negative pressure not to be unfashionably successful.

Certainly the lowest levels of aspiration I encountered were among young people from white working class backgrounds. Elvige was by far the most ambitious and highly motivated, yet she was not alone. Yasmin, whose family came from Bangladesh, lacked focus but was not without ambition, for all that. While even the most able of the white teenagers I met, in their most ambitious moments, would talk about good jobs and decent money, Yasmin talked about enterprise, and entrepreneurship: "I'm hoping to open up a business one day – a successful business woman."

As ever, parental aspirations were vital. Peer group pressure, it seemed, could have either a positive or a negative influence, but in the end parents, as ever, held the strongest cards.

One of the most remarkable and little-told educational success stories in modern Britain is that of the Chinese. Among Chinese pupils in British schools, 85 per cent attained five good GCSEs, against a national average of 67 per cent. Even poverty seemed to make only a relatively minor difference to these pupils, with eight out of 10 still getting five good grades – twice the national average for pupils on free school meals. Why? Was there some lesson the rest of us could learn from this astonishingly successful community? I went to see David Tan, the Chinese Liaison Officer for Westminster Council in London, who told me it was all down to sheer determination, hard work and drive. Class background didn't come into it, he said.

"The Indians who came here had a track record, but we came here with nothing; peasants, working in restaurants, turning raw chicken into fantastic rice and stuff," he said. Tan's father had migrated from China to Malaysia to work in the tin mines: "They came literally with the shirts and singlets they were wearing, and a hoe to work with."

A few decades later, Tan had arrived in Britain with more luggage but no less ambition: "I was sent here by the government of Malaysia to train as a teacher. My son's a lawyer, and my daughter works in an investment bank. I saved and scrimped for my children. Each generation aims to prosper and be better than the last."

"Face is very important to the Chinese ... you know what this means? We used to compete with each other, with the other Chinese people we mixed with. I would tell my children: 'Look at so and so, how come she did better than you?' We made them feel uncomfortable, guilty. Push, push, push. Your daughter's not working? Everyone gets to know and you feel embarrassed. The way I think is, the white British don't feel like that."

RAY LEWIS

Before I went to meet Ray Lewis I looked at the website of his Eastside Young Leaders' Academy and read a description of him from one of the young people who attended it: "Scary", it said. So I was expecting someone quite aggressive and gruff. But Lewis's arrival outside the door of his portable office – about an hour late, for he had been stuck in traffic – was heralded by a cheery cry: "It is I!" He was shorter than I expected, and while there was a definite masculine energy about him he was also affable and forthright.

Lewis, born in Guyana but brought up in London, had been at the centre of a media storm recently. Shortly after being appointed Deputy for Children and Young People by the London Mayor, Boris Johnson, he had had to resign when it emerged that some years earlier the Church of England had barred him from working as a priest – something of which Lewis, who denied any wrongdoing, said he had not been informed. He had continued to run his academy despite the furore, advocating "tough love" for disaffected black boys and putting them through programmes aimed at turning them into achievers. When we met, the first of his recruits had just started university.

Lewis believed straightforward racism did play a part in knocking black boys off course: "We discovered, some of us by accident, that we weren't white. Even though we did our best to align ourselves with white culture rather than African culture it seemed to do little good. I remember a heavily accented Jamaican lady who used to do readings in church – but she never used to be asked for special occasions. If the bishop was coming, you wouldn't have her out the front. The sad thing about it was she believed that herself."

But all that was years ago, surely? Caribbean pupils were catching up fast at school, and those from African backgrounds even faster. Surely there must be something else going on? History played a major part in shaping the psychology of different ethnic groups, he said.

"For Africans there's a real sense of history and community and purpose and culture. They can link their parents and grandparents and great grandparents, and the villages they were from. Caribbeans can't. We accept it when they call us 'slave babies'. The impact of slavery is so deep. We hate ourselves because we're not sure if we're African or Caribbean or Anglo-Saxon or something else."

The lack of positive role models for black youngsters was a problem, he said – there was a tendency to want to be a footballer – but he thought family was crucial, too.

"Where there's a lack of security and a lack of belonging and identity coupled with factors of poverty, I think you often have children who aren't prepared for education or work. Some will try the world of work, but they haven't been prepared. It's a culture shock. Having to get there on time, having to take orders: 'Nobody tells me what to do.'"

Although in many ways life was easier for black boys now than it had been for him growing up, the same problems persisted, he believed.

"My mum was always struggling to get food in our bellies and keep a roof over our heads. She had dreams and visions, but she didn't know how to give us the kind of support we needed and didn't have the resources to get it from other places. All I know about my childhood is about struggle, and I have seen that pattern in other boys we have here. There's certainly not the poverty I experienced, but there's a poverty of expectation and aspiration.

"I think the problem isn't so much the racism we experience from the outside, but the effect of racism upon us on the inside."

Poor white boys

So what happened to the white working class? In particular, what happened to white working class boys? Did they, as David Tan suggested, lose their sense of shame over economic failure, somewhere along the way?

If it were possible to draw a sort of map of the world that marked out all our relative chances of success or failure, perhaps it would look something like a kaleidoscope, split into innumerable tiny shards: the divisions of class, race, gender, family background, experience, innate ability, a myriad of other things. There would be multiple overlaps, of course, little conglomerations of different drivers, some good, some bad. Some of us, though, would have a greater stock of the good, some of the bad. Class, race, gender – in terms of the likelihood that we would succeed at school, all these factors would count as marks for or against us. The poorest pupils would be much less likely to leave school with good exam results than the better off; those of white British origin much less likely than the Chinese, say, and boys much less likely than girls. Somewhere on the darkest, coldest section of the map, certainly where the UK was concerned, would be the white boys from the poorest families. Educationally, poor white boys would be in Siberia.

This had not always been the case, of course. Years ago, boys used to do better than girls in public examinations. But girls crept forward and now they outperformed their male peers at every level, right through to university. They were also significantly more successful in the jobs market. Among those aged under 24 claiming the Job Seekers' Allowance, young men outnumbered young women by a ratio of two to one.

There were many explanations for this. On the educational side, the advent of the GCSE exam, with its heavy emphasis on coursework, was sometimes blamed. Research showed teachers tended to see girls as more compliant and therefore more likely to labour over homework, while boys were thought more likely to hope for a brilliant performance on exam day. The more exam-based O-levels, it was argued, tended to favour the male approach. The predominance of women in teaching was also blamed, though this failed to explain why boys fell behind further at secondary school, where there were more male teachers, than they did at primary school.

The social explanations for the phenomenon seemed to hold water better. Could the problem be, for example, not so much that boys were falling behind as that girls were racing ahead? After all, the exam results of both boys and girls had improved significantly over those years. There was good reason for girls, sensing new opportunities in the workplace as new jobs arose in services, retail and social care, to push harder at school. Boys, on the other hand, suffered from the twin pressures of negative peer group pressure and confusion about whether the changing labour market really had much to offer them.

But why poor white boys? Why should this group struggle so badly? Fifty years ago white working class men had both status and power within their homes. Norman Dennis's story of the 1950s Yorkshire miner who, arriving home to find his wife had asked another woman to cook his tea, threw it on the fire and then forced his errant spouse to cook another one, illustrated the point perfectly. Men were largely absent from the home while either at work or relaxing in the pub or club, but they still exercised some kind of hold, some kind of authority, over the other members of their families. Paul Willis, in his 1970s work *Learning to Labour*, described his working class boys as disaffected from school but also cocky and irreverent, with a confidence born of knowing pretty much what their future place in the world would be. Back in those days this was thought a bad thing – why couldn't more working class boys aspire to middle class jobs? – but later it was possible to look back on the early 1970s almost as a Golden Age for white working class boys.

Willis, chronicling the last days of this fading era, described how these non-conformist boys picked up skills at school which would be useful to them in the larky, male-dominated atmosphere of the workplace. They learned them not through their lessons but through their own anti-school sub-culture:

> In the short to middle term the "lads" experience in the counter-school culture most certainly smoothes their transition into work and produces appetites which manual work satisfies quite well … physical labouring comes to stand for and express, most importantly, a kind of masculinity and also an opposition to authority – at least as it is learned in school. It expresses aggressiveness; a degree of sharpness and wit; an irreverence that cannot be found in words; an obvious kind of solidarity. It provides the wherewithal for adult tastes, and demonstrates a potential mastery over, as well as an immediate attractiveness to, women: a kind of machismo.

The expectation of a niche in one of these masculine, muscle-driven environments had passed on, but what had replaced it? What did today's young men *think* their futures were all about? Of the three I met regularly over the course of my research – all white and broadly working class – only one had any real, thought-out hopes of getting such a traditional working class job. Tom, from Kendray near Barnsley, thought an apprenticeship was the way to go. He soon learned this time-honoured route was no longer available to a young man like him: after ringing every plumbing firm in South Yorkshire, twice, he was ready to give up. The other two young men I met, Will and Ricky, were much more confused. Unlike Tom, whose dad worked in a printer's, neither Will nor Ricky had a father at home who went out to work on a regular basis. Will had no memory of his father at all and loathed his stepfather, while Ricky's stories about his infrequent contacts with his father tended to involve alcohol or violence, or both. Neither had any clear idea of the usefulness of specific qualifications; neither had a clear sense that he should progress from GCSEs to further training to a decent, well-paid job. Will footered around rejecting every offer that came along in the hope that stardom might appear around the next bend, while Ricky descended into drug-taking and a blank uncertainty about what the future might hold.

Broken Britain?

Did Ricky fit the frequently repeated notion of a "broken" society in which some boys grew up without prospects, without strong male role models, without a sense of direction and – for want of a better phrase – without a sense of civic responsibility? Feral youth, if you like, who were reputed to hang around on the streets causing trouble and rarely making plans beyond their next fix of skunk? In some respects, it has to be said that he did. He certainly lacked direction, and seemed unable to focus on the future. Time and again he was picked up and offered help – a place on a voluntary scheme, a course to learn construction skills, a part-time job – but nothing really stuck. Did he have a sense of shame about his own failure? I think perhaps I would put it another way: for him, the criteria by which he might fail were different from the criteria by which others might judge him. Lacking the means to succeed through brilliant exam results or great career success – no-one had ever shown him how to do either of these things, nor suggested he might have the ability – his parameters shrank. For him, success was about being accepted as a part of Collyhurst life, about being "a laugh" with his mates, having a good-looking girlfriend. I think he would have liked some things about his life to have been different, but couldn't see any way to make them different and so instead developed survival strategies that would give him status and credibility in his own small milieu. And did his mother feel a sense of shame, when she related his latest exploits? I think in a way she did – she was protective of her son. She tended to minimise his misdeeds when she could, and to talk about them with a detached humour when she couldn't. She, too, had developed survival strategies.

Ricky was by no means a typical white working class boy. He came from the second most deprived council ward in England, he lived in a workless – or almost workless – household, his relationship with his father was intermittent at best, he dropped out of school without qualifications and at 17 he already had a criminal record. Perhaps Tom, with two working parents, a good clutch of GCSEs and a feeling that a steady job with decent money was a reasonable aspiration, was more typical. But there was something in what David Tan called "face" – what people felt they could or could not live with. If Tan's children had not achieved more than he had, he would have seen that as a source of shame. Most of the white families I met would not have felt the same level of humiliation when describing an out-of-work or drifting child. It would, perhaps, have been cause for sympathy – accompanied perhaps by a little private smugness – from their contemporaries, rather than contempt.

Maybe the young people I met internalised a sense of their position on the social map, some sense of a trajectory on which they felt they were travelling. For white working class boys it must have felt as if everything was going downhill. For some, looking at their parents and their grandparents, it must have been hard to see what they could reasonably hope for, when over the generations steady work had become unsteady and stable families unstable. Girls had the edge in two ways: in the majority of cases, though not all, they had a constantly present female role model in the shape of a mother. She might have been a mother whose life had been hard, but in a way that allowed for a positive trajectory – "I'll get married like my mum, but I'll marry someone better. I'll work hard like my mum, but I'll work at something better." Girls also had the advantage of being able to see their older female peers succeeding at school, getting decent jobs and moving on. For them, there was some sense of shame in not succeeding. For boys, there were plenty of less successful role models – and alternative models of success – to which they could turn for justification if they failed at school.

Perhaps to a degree a successful, upward trajectory had to be one driven by positive change and opportunity. Map the paths recently travelled by different groups within British society and those on the steepest upward course would be those for whom there was a feeling of unfolding opportunity. Many would be the children of migrants who were told, as Elvige was, that their families expected them to "make us proud". There was no doubt some quite deprived groups in British society had been able to use education as a route into the middle class, yet white working class males had not generally been among them in recent years. My best explanation was that after generations of knock-backs they and their families had come to accept that the opportunities which might be out there in this changed world were not for them. Success only became easier than failure for those who had a weight of expectation and aspiration behind them, and they didn't.

One of the things that most surprised me about the young men I interviewed was the way they tended to be quick to reveal their own vulnerability. Far from displaying the stereotypical, testosterone-driven behaviour of the young lion wondering when his day would come, they were often prone to expressing despair. The violent former drug dealer Robbie, clinging to his six-week relationship as if it were for life and needing a motherly hug; Ricky blurting out the pain he'd felt when his grandma was dying. I rarely saw anything that came close to that cocksure, puffed-up, exhibitionist maleness that Willis described in the 1970s. If I had to describe the less successful young men I met, I would not do so in words that described aggression, or rebellion, or a rejection of the adult world. I think I would say they were like so much left luggage, not wanted on the voyage ahead.

WILL

Sometimes, people can confound your direst predictions. About eight months after I first met Will, the aspiring actor from London, he was still out of work and still hoping fame and fortune would come along to relieve him of the tedious prospect of low-paid, nine-to-five work. I have to admit I didn't rate his chances. For a start, he wasn't really doing much. No auditions, no brushing up of his talents in a local drama group or the like. Then, as she had done before, his mum stepped in. Will turned 21 that autumn, and for a special present she put his name forward for a gladiator-style TV gameshow called *Total Wipeout*. And he was picked. There was no pay but there was a £10,000 prize plus a free trip to Buenos Aires, where the filming was to take place.

So I turned to BBC1 one wintry Saturday teatime in January to see Will, billed as "a boxer from London", looking mock-fierce and dancing on the spot as he aimed jabs at the camera. Then he was off, falling off huge bouncy balls into water in the South American sunshine; clambering along a wall from which mechanical fists kept shooting out to push him off. He did well, too – he came third, which qualified him comfortably for the next round.

Then it all came to a swift, ignominious end. Despite having done so well Will had taken a knock to the knee, and at the end of the episode the commentator, Richard Hammond from *Top Gear*, announced that the show's doctor had retired him on health grounds. And so Will's 15 minutes of fame – or maybe two minutes – were over.

Throughout all my meetings with Will, there was an undercurrent, buried beneath all the chat and bravado, of something gone astray. The first time we met it had welled out of him, a sort of apocalyptic despair.

"I want to do my acting, more than anything, but I know something bad's going to happen," he told me. "Everyone feels this. Every year, the world gets worse. It don't get better. Everyone says it's going to get better, but it isn't going to happen, unless there's someone … like Noah. Something like that needs to happen. Since I've lived here, I've seen everything. I've seen people get stabbed; people get shot. I've got a friend who was stopped from jumping off a building. At first I was like, 'Oh my God, where am I?' Now I just carry on walking. I'm cold-hearted."

Will was far from cold-hearted. He would have cheerful, optimistic times but then would quickly lapse back to this feeling that the world was on a downhill slide. Later, overcome by love for his little girl and a feeling that he was going to have to protect her, he told me what he would do if he suddenly became wealthy.

"If I had money I would buy some land and build a house underground," he said. Where would it be? He thought about it for a minute. "In the centre of England, Northamptonshire maybe – far from the sea because of climate change. A hundred metres down, with lead-lined walls. Nuclear-proof. It's just a matter of time before something happens. If you go online there's all these predictions – the year 2012 keeps coming up. I've got four years to save my baby. I just want my baby to be happy. I want her to have things I never had. I want her dad to be there."

Will expressed the sentiment in clearer and more poignant terms than any of the other young men I met. Yet there was something in him that I saw several times elsewhere too. Something that said "Missing in Action", perhaps. Or "Lost at Sea".

Chapter 12

The difference for girls

"It's definitely over this time," Will told me once after a break-up with his baby girl's mother, Chantelle. "She's changed her relationship status on Facebook, so it's official." Will's Facebook page had undergone a corresponding change, from "in a relationship" to "single". A few weeks later they were "in a relationship" again, then briefly "in a complicated relationship". Then peace broke out and they were once again restored to their full, uncomplicated status.

But in truth, it was complicated. Will was not able to play the role he would have liked, as both family man and economic provider. There was never any doubt that he loved his little girl and wanted to be a major part of her life. Yet it was her mother who had a job, not Will. At that point she was on maternity leave, but she expected to go back to the airport where they both used to work.

"Without her my life's going to be much more difficult," he said during their split. "I'm old-fashioned. I believe men should provide … But the girls round here, I think they expect too much. They indirectly take, and they indirectly give. There's no traditional 50/50."

What did he mean by that? I asked – what did they take; what did they give?

"Chantelle buys me stuff, and feeds me, and she provides for me. That's what she's given to me. What she's taken is priceless though. It's being there. With her previous babyfather, he was never there. He was never on the scene. I've never even met him. I think that's really weird."

Chantelle had been more successful in the labour market than Will. By walking away from his job while she held on to hers, he reversed the roles both of them, perhaps, would have liked to play. For years, the media rhetoric had been all about this: women had been on the same upward trajectory as recent migrant groups, grasping opportunities that were never offered to their grandmothers. Much of the chat about young men, and young white men in particular, had been along these lines. And there was something in it. Working class men like Will were certainly growing up in a world where their traditional roles had all but vanished; young women, conversely, had found new opportunities and a place for their skills in a growing service sector.

Yet Will and Chantelle had the same jobs, at one point. Their relative success and failure were not, as far as I could see, down so much to Chantelle having better qualifications or more ambition, but to her being prepared to accept what Will was not. While he could not settle to a job he thought dull, unworthy of him, she knuckled down and got on with it. It could be interpreted, perhaps, not as a lack of ambition on Will's part, but an excess of it – unfocused though it might have been. A feeling on his part, maybe, that this was not a suitable job for a man, and on hers that it would do if it allowed her to keep a roof over her head and to buy things for her children.

In a way, then, the problem they had was Will's reluctance to relinquish what he saw as his traditional role. He wanted to be a good father, and he was. Yet he saw that as a sort of gift he gave, something taken away from him even, because it wasn't really meant to be his primary role. He couldn't grit his teeth and get on with a low-paid job, because that wouldn't enable him to provide in the way he felt he should.

Yet unbeknown to either Will or Chantelle, who had better things to worry about, change was in the air. As recently as 2005, academics from the London School of Economics had declared the gender gap in qualifications was widening, but by 2008 that had begun to change. While the proportion of girls getting five good GCSEs rose by 20 per cent between 2002 and 2008, the proportion of boys rose by almost 30 per cent. While some non-white pupils gained ground on their white classmates – Caribbeans and Africans pushed up their scores by around 50 per cent – in every group, the boys gained on the girls.

There was some evidence this was beginning to push through into the jobs market, too. In October 2008, as recession began to bite, there were 71,000 young women aged under 24 on the unemployed register, compared to 156,000 young men. But the increase since October 2005 was very slightly higher for women – 25 per cent, compared to 24 per cent for men. At the very least the figures suggested female-oriented service-sector jobs had held up no better in the darkening economic climate than more male-dominated sectors. The main message of the figures was still to highlight the massively different positions of young women and young men in relation to the labour market, though. Young men were much more likely than young women – by a ratio of more than two to one – to be unemployed.

So in general young women were doing just fine – weren't they? It depended which way you looked at it. Because although young women were much less likely than young men to be unemployed, they were actually more likely, by the age of 24, to be living on benefits. The difference was that for them life on benefits more often meant life as a jobless single mother. In 2005 – the last year for which figures were available – there were 160,000 young women under the age of 24 claiming lone-parent support. Add those to the number claiming the Job Seekers' Allowance, and young women on benefits outnumbered young men by a ratio of four to three.

Motherhood and careers

This looked to me like terrible news for young women. It seemed that instead of succeeding in the labour market, those without qualifications were mirroring the pattern set by their male peers by falling out of jobs and onto benefits. The only difference, it seemed, was that young women were restricting still further their future chances by taking on the responsibilities of motherhood before they had gained any decent work experience. What would there be for them, in the future, but more benefits, alternating with low-paid and probably part-time work?

Not everyone saw it this way. When I visited a group of young mothers at the Sunnybank Children's Centre in Barnsley, some of them seemed very content with their lot. Michelle, aged 20 with long blonde hair, a confident air, a three year-old and a new baby, told me she had not been overly concerned to find herself pregnant at 16.

"I definitely wanted kids. I didn't really plan out when, but it was just there in my future. I was thinking a bit further ahead than that, though. I was with someone I thought I would stay with – young and foolish, I think it's called," she said.

What did her parents have to say? I wondered. Not much, she said.

"It had already happened. It was just 'congratulations', really. My mum doesn't dictate; she never has done. She just says it's my life," she explained.

Four years on, and with another baby – planned, this time – with a new partner who was a bus driver, she was delighted by the course of events. "We're debating on a third. I don't regret anything I've done. If I'd changed anything I wouldn't have the life I have now, and I wouldn't want to change it," she said.

Michelle had not been an academic high-flyer at school, and had been sent off to college before she was 16 on one of those courses meant for pupils who might otherwise drop out. She had worked – in a bar and at a supermarket – and hoped to do so again. Perhaps, for her, things had worked out okay.

But for others it was not so simple. Andrea, 22 and pale with dark rings under her eyes and a 14-month-old boy who sat motionless on the carpet as we talked, said she had suffered badly from post-natal depression.

"I had two miscarriages," she said. "The third time, we didn't talk about it, it just happened. We were both pleased, but by the end of the pregnancy we were bickering, because of my hormones. We'd been together on and off for four years. We're not together at the moment but he still lives with me, until he finds somewhere else. He doesn't work at the moment," she said. This was not how she had thought her life would be.

"Since I've been little I've always been the same. I used to walk round the house with a towel round my head for a veil, playing at being a bride. So I am a little bit disappointed at how things turned out. It's a lot harder than what I thought it would be."

This was the nub of the issue, I thought. Young women like Andrea, who began training as a hairdresser when she left school but dropped out, and like Michelle, probably always thought the purpose of their lives was more about family and motherhood than about having a career. They probably thought about their lives in ways not dissimilar to their mothers and even their grandmothers – early motherhood had always been largely the preserve of the working class. Young people whose parents did unskilled manual jobs were 10 times more likely than those with professional parents to become teenage parents.

But the problem for me was that while the likelihood that those from the poorest backgrounds would become parents early had not changed, a great deal else had.

New opportunities were now opening up that Andrea's and Michelle's mothers and grandmothers probably did not have. Should they have chosen it, a place at college to learn a trade or to qualify for a better-paid job would have been open to them. But they didn't. They went the same way as most of their mothers' and grandmothers' generations of working class women, into early motherhood.

For them, though, it wasn't only the world of work that had changed. The family had changed, too. While their grandmothers might realistically have expected to marry early and – whatever the ups and downs – to stay married, they certainly could not. Not only were they missing out on the opportunities the modern labour market had to offer, but they could no longer expect what their grandmothers took for granted – the prospect that motherhood would also mean marriage to a man with a job.

In the last 20 years of the twentieth century, the teenage pregnancy rate in Britain dropped significantly, from 54,000 children born each year to 42,000. Yet the proportion of children born to single parents rose significantly. In 1978, two-thirds of the children of teenage parents were born within marriage; by 1996, just one in eight. Of course the past was not all good – too often, unwanted pregnancies led to unhappy marriages – yet it did have the benefit of certainty. It meant more children had two parents around, and usually at least one of them – the male one – had a job.

Were these young women missing out, then? Or were they actually availing themselves of an opportunity not open to their male peers – the opportunity to escape an unsatisfactory labour market into more fulfilling motherhood? I was mildly surprised when one of my interviewees – the head of a think tank – told me he thought girls got the better end of the deal.

"It's a very important difference between young men and young women that young women are able to establish a strong sense of identity by becoming a mother. Young men aren't able to do that in the same way," he told me. "That's broken down, particularly for the group who used work as a mechanism for establishing identity through masculinity. For me, it's the young men who are most disadvantaged."

What mattered, though, was not who suffered most but whether opportunities were being lost. Will's mother told me she escaped from a miserable home life and a low-paid job in a clothes shop into early pregnancy and marriage, and who could blame her? The opportunity wasn't there for her to go to college to get a qualification that would have stood her in good stead when her marriage broke up a couple of years and two children later. Claire's grandmother made a very sensible decision, likewise, when she gave up her 6 am starts at the woollen mill for a husband with a steady job, home ownership and full-time motherhood.

Those who argued motherhood was a fulfilment of a woman's destiny did have a point, which was endorsed by the young women I met at the Sunnybank Children's Centre. They weren't going anywhere in the jobs market; they'd already dropped out of college. None of them would have been prepared to say they regretted becoming mothers, and given the choices they had – low-paid, unsatisfactory work versus parenthood – theirs were not unreasonable. By and large, they were coping well and doing a good job for their children. But would anyone advise a young woman under the age of 20 who had dropped out of education that her best way forward would be to find an equally unqualified young man and get pregnant? I don't think so. Would their children benefit if their mothers were a few years older, more settled in their relationships and perhaps better equipped to cope economically if those relationships broke down? Of course they would.

The young women at the Sunnybank Children's Centre were, by and large, those who were coping. One of the workers there told me she had knocked on dozens of doors with a local outreach worker but only a handful of the young mothers they approached were prepared to join their young mums' group. Karl Lyons, the outreach worker who accompanied her, gave me an eye-opening description of the houses they visited together.

"A minority were living in the family home and being supported by mum and dad," he told me. "There were a very minimal number of young men. And each house you went into had almost identical environmental issues: broken-down fences, gardens festooned with beer cans and rubbish, toys everywhere. The door bearing the scars of being kicked in, or a window boarded up. Inevitably, one or more dogs roaming freely. The young mother smoking, unhygienic kitchen, the child being given its food in an inappropriate place. It appeared they used pregnancy not particularly to gain housing but to escape from their parental home. Very few seemed to regret getting pregnant. They would have liked a better house, of course."

So changes in the family had a disproportionately adverse effect on women, because they could no longer reliably expect access to a male breadwinner while they brought up their children. Changes in the labour market had a disproportionately adverse effect on men, because they could no longer expect a traditional male job which would enable them to support a family. Both, perhaps, continued to cling to a world that no longer existed. Both had continued to make what might have been described as traditional choices – but with modern consequences.

RACHEL

Rachel's dad, John, was in bed when she rang with the news.

"She said: 'Dad, I've got something to tell you'," he related.

"I said: 'You're pregnant.'

"She said: 'How did you know?'

"I said: 'I just know. It's the only thing.' I said: 'I think you should have an abortion.'

"She said: 'I'm having it.' She was in love, and all this stuff. With this *waster*." He almost spat out the word.

Rachel was 15 at the time. Just three months earlier John had washed his hands of her binge-drinking, her drug-taking, her joyriding in stolen cars, her failure to go to school that landed him in court. He had sent her back to her mother who, he said, had asked the "waster" to look after her.

"It was an accident, really," Rachel told me. "No-one ever talked to me about what there was to stop you getting pregnant. I bet if someone came to talk to you in class when you had your friends there, you'd take it in. We never talked about it – you just got your condoms from Stockport Clinic. I thought, 'Oh, it won't happen.' But it did. Stupid."

After she gave birth to Louise there was "a conversation" at the hospital about contraception, but she said she didn't really take it in. A month later she was pregnant again. By the time Bradley was born Rachel had just turned 17 and was living with her boyfriend in a flat in Salford, but he wasn't helping much.

"He'd sell stuff out of the flat. His stack that his mum bought for him for £400, he sold that for £20 for weed. He had mobiles and stuff, saying he'd lost them. He'd text his mum for money, pretending it was me asking for a tenner when it wasn't. I think I had post-natal depression – I'd go round to his sister's and break down and just cry. Everyone in Stockport was going out, having a good time, and I was sat in a flat in Salford with two kids; my boyfriend going out smoking weed. I said I'd leave. He said I wouldn't go. So I just did. He bought me flowers and everything, but I left him."

She left the children, too. After about three weeks he delivered them round to her mum's. "But I'd lost interest in them. I'd leave them with my mum and just walk out. At night I'd get them to sleep and go out, then I'd stay for two weeks and not come back. I just thought: 'If he can go out, so can I.'"

Things at home became fraught. One day the housing officer turned up and found Rachel's brother battering her head against the wall because she'd gone out with a friend.

After that the kids' dad took them again; then his parents had them for a while. Rachel couldn't quite decide what to do for the best. She wanted a life of her own, she wanted to be young. Yet she couldn't face the prospect of having them adopted and maybe never seeing them again.

"They all hate me, my mum, my brothers. It's just normal for mums to look after their children. I do feel I should be the one to look after them. I still have them on weekends and stuff. When Louise calls me Rachel it does my head in. She should call me Mum."

There was no happy ending in sight for Rachel or for her children. At the time of writing, they had gone into care and she was trying to get them back. Sometimes, at 19, she would say she had grown up; she was ready for motherhood. But she never seemed quite sure. There was so much she wanted – a job, some fun with her friends – nothing different from what most teenagers would have wanted.

"I wish I could change everything," she said. "I'd go to school. I wouldn't mind being a bit naughty, because it's fun. But I would have gone. And not had the kids. My mate got pregnant, but she had an abortion. She knows. She's seen me. I would tell anyone not to do what I did."

Chapter 13

Reaching out

Cruising through Hulme in Julie Ollerhead's tiny silver Suzuki on a summer day with the windows wound down and little furry dice swaying in the breeze, it was hard to remember this used to be an area notorious for drugs and crime. Hulme was knocked down and rebuilt in the 1990s and today, with the sun shining, there was none of the old air of menace that used to hang about the place. Julie, who did outreach work for the Rathbone charity, had a new helper called Jack – she had been forced to give up on the previous one, Robbie, when he threatened her and then stopped returning her calls. So today Jack was in the front passenger seat, fiddling with the stereo. Julie had put on a CD of a band called the Lancashire Hotpots, but Jack was not impressed. "Well we're not having your Boom-Boom music anyway," she said good-naturedly as she slung the disc in the glove compartment. Jack retaliated by removing the head from the gearstick. "Look what 'e's done! 'E's 'ad me gearstick!" she retorted. She didn't stop the car, though, but just took it from him, smiling, and screwed it back on again.

Despite Julie's nonchalant air, she was under pressure. The Rathbone charity for which she worked had been funded by Manchester City Council to find 90 disengaged 16–18 year-olds over a 10-month period. But it had taken months to recruit and train Julie and her team of three and by then it was January and not a good time to find young people hanging about on the streets. So, as the spring and early summer had progressed, there had been muttering about missed targets. Now the team must find 12 teenagers in the next fortnight or their jobs were on the line.

It sounded straightforward, but it wasn't. Each young person had to have been born within two precise dates, to live within a particular postcode area and to be out of touch with the Connexions service. In addition to finding them, the team had to bring them to Connexions for an interview and to register them on a website. A certain proportion had to be given life-skills training. And Julie's modus operandi tended not to fit in with city council targets. There was no target, for example, for sitting still while an aspiring hairdresser put Julie's hair up with a pencil and a paperclip, any more than there had been a target for keeping Robbie, a drug dealer with a violent streak, out of prison. Yet the hairdresser was offered a college place on the strength of a website shot of Julie's hair, and even Robbie had been calmed, for a time, by her ministrations.

As we rounded a corner by some shops Julie spotted a couple of girls. "Over there!" she cried. Jack was phlegmatic: "No. Keep driving. I've seen them on this estate before." But Julie's car came to a jerky halt and she bounded off across the road, followed at a more sedate pace by Jack. I hung back for a minute, not wanting to cramp her style, and by the time I joined them she was in full flow. The younger one was 16 but still officially at school, which made her ineligible for Julie's attentions. Nikki, her sister, was 18 but on further questioning turned out to be within the prescribed dates. She kept doubling up with laughter, which slowed the conversation down. "I've got ADHD so I'm always laughing," she said. "And she's been on the weed," her sister added. They were on their way to town so Julie gave them her number and said they could call if they wanted a lift back. Within the hour her phone beeped: it was a text. "Eh up," she said. "We could have a start-to-finish here."

As we drove Nikki to Connexions, Julie grilled her for information and she soon revealed her best friend Sandra was also out of work. Yes, Nikki would like a lift round to her house because she was having a birthday party for her son, who was one year old today – Nikki was his godmother. So an appointment was made for a Connexions interview the next day and off we went again, to a new estate of little terraces in Longsight where several adults were standing in the sunshine with cans of Stella. Inside we declined spam barm cakes but accepted a cup of tea from Sandra's dad, Eammon, who had silver hair curling on his collar and his Stella still in his hand. Sandra was bullied at school, he said, and his wife had mental health problems, so a lot fell to him.

"I've had to cook and keep the house clean and educate everybody, but I've failed. My home is nice, but ..." Julie filled in the gap by complimenting him on how well he kept the house, even though in fact it was dark, carpetless, damp-smelling and not particularly clean. "We've had everyone in here," he went on. "Social Services, Education Welfare. We don't get to know you, and then you're gone. You're moving to Salford, you're going to work with these children somewhere else." Julie did her best to reassure him that she wasn't going anywhere.

She turned to Nikki's friend Sandra, who had wandered in trailing a mucky-faced one year-old. She looked impossibly young to be a mother with puppy fat and a wide, innocent face. "I know as a mum that you're in employment 24 hours a day. It's great you've got the support of your family. But how do you feel yourself about going back to school?"

"No. Never," Sandra said flatly.

Julie tried a different tack. "If you had somewhere to go once a week, to meet other mums or go for a day out, would you take that opportunity?"

"I don't do groups," Sandra said. "Do I, Dad?"

"All I'm asking you to do is to go into Connexions."

"I don't do Connexions," Sandra replied with finality.

"I was going to say I'd pick you up and be with you at Connexions, and I'd bring you home. If you never went again, it wouldn't matter."

"I don't do Connexions," Sandra repeated.

Julie was running out of gambits.

"Can I ask you why?"

"It's boring."

We got up to leave.

"Me and Nikki are going to the park tomorrow," Julie offered casually as Eammon showed us to the door. "Do you fancy coming, Sandra?" Miraculously, Sandra relented: "Yes, okay."

Long-term problems, short-term solutions

The next time I saw Julie she had six weeks left to work. One of her team had already left; the rest were looking for new jobs.

This sense of impermanence was something I met repeatedly during my research. I would phone someone to arrange an interview, and they would respond: "Well you'd better come soon, because I'm leaving at the end of the month." Or I would be given someone's name and when I phoned them a month later they would be gone.

I found it hard to imagine an area of public service where continuity and the ability to build long-term relationships were more vital, and yet almost every project I saw that worked was run by the voluntary sector and funded by short-term grants. Even though Manchester City Council had not deemed Julie's programme a success, it quickly found funding from a slightly different budget heading to start another, similar project with Rathbone. By then Julie had gone elsewhere and a new team presumably had to be recruited and trained.

From Julie's point of view, it was impossible simply to stick within the narrow parameters of the job.

"I have to meet young people, take them into Connexions and say goodbye. I just can't do that," she said. "But I said to them: 'If you want 90 heads of cattle I'll go and get them for you. I've been taking them in at a rate of eight a week recently."

While we were talking her phone rang. It was Nikki. She was getting her own flat: could Julie help her move in? Of course she could. Julie showed me a text from Nikki on her phone, sent after she'd told her she was leaving:

> Itz sad that ur leavin n I cnt believe it bt I also cnt thanx u as much as i wishd 4 wat u ave dne 4 me i wil reli miss u julie thanx u so much ur the onli 1 thatz eva believd in me n gve me the tym ov day! Thanx u so much nikki

But the real surprise came when I asked about Nikki's friend Sandra. Had

Julie been able to entice her out of her parents' flat? I had doubted whether the proposed trip to the park would have come off.

It had taken a few weeks to get a result, Julie confessed, but it had been worth it. She had eventually persuaded Sandra to come to the Rathbone centre and then to Connexions. Now her parents brought her to the centre every day and she was planning to start a childcare course at college.

"Out of all the people I've worked with, Sandra for me has got to be one of the biggest achievements," Julie said. "Jack – I love that guy. He's passed his GCSEs, and he's going to college to do catering. But Sandra ... she was adamant she didn't want to do anything, she said her life was being at home with her kid. If you saw her now! She's still got some weight, but there's a softer side to her. She wears a little bit of eye shadow. Her hair's clean. She ties it back in a ponytail, so you can see her eyes. You can see her shoulders going back."

I wondered how Sandra's father, who had doubted Julie would be around for his daughter for more than a few months, would react when he heard she was leaving. Yet another do-gooder who drifted into and then out of his family's life, each reinforcing his conviction that no-one cared enough to stay around.

Manchester, unlike either of the other places I visited regularly, had an official whose job was to try to reduce the number of young people who were NEET ("Not in Education, Employment or Training"), as they were officially termed. Strictly speaking, Sarah Ross worked not for the council but for an arms-length body, but she oversaw the city's attempts to re-engage the young and had been involved in the decision to fund the Rathbone project. So I thought she would be a good person to whom to put this point: while projects that spent public money did need to be accountable, might they not sometimes become less effective if they were buried under bureaucracy? I wanted to know why it was not possible simply to give young people the individual help they needed, on an ongoing basis. In response I received such an extraordinary flood of bureaucratese that I was left wondering whether there was any point continuing.

"My role is about sitting in the middle and looking at how we can co-ordinate the whole range of services, organisations, agendas, strategies and policies," she said. "To ensure that not only do we reduce NEET, but hopefully we position NEET within achieving economic wellbeing. It's a broader definition of NEET which is about ensuring young people achieve economic wellbeing. Positioning is about these three barriers: educational development, economic development and community cohesion. Previously NEET was seen as a Connexions issue because it was their target, but there might also be a Local Public Service Agreement target around NEET. But it isn't a pure education issue – it's an education and a community and an economic issue. It enables you to pull down other resources and funding streams – it gives you more power to your elbow as soon as you align it to the wellness agenda."

Baffled, I pressed on. Why was it necessary to give these projects such tight targets? Could there not be some flexibility for the voluntary sector just to do what it did best – to form relationships that worked, and to use those relationships to steer young people into positive choices about their futures? Again, the answer was less than enlightening.

"We realised that the voluntary sector had these great skills, but rather than just funding them for those skills we would have a particular aim, to move that young person from NEET to EET," she said. ("EET", by contrast with "NEET", meant a young person who *was* actively engaged in work, training or education.) "Actually, how realistic is that, within 12 weeks? And don't we have a statutory service whose job it is to move them from NEET to EET? This just doesn't make sense. So we drew up a set of common outcomes across the city when it came to funding. So in the recent funding round, we said to voluntary organisations we want you to get people to the point where they're ready to come into Connexions and have a guidance interview, and Connexions can take it from there. That's quite significant because what it enabled us to do was to use the strengths of the voluntary sector."

My impression was she meant that 12 weeks was not long enough to support a young person from unemployment into work or training, so the voluntary sector was given the job of finding them, while Connexions – a government agency – was there to pick them up and move them forward. There was, to me, an obvious flaw in this argument: with just one exception – Elvige's mentor in London, Lisa Marcelle, who was prepared to go beyond her remit to help – I had never heard of a Connexions worker taking a young person to the park, or shifting their furniture when they moved house. I had never heard a young person in Manchester talk about a Connexions worker as someone they could turn to in time of stress. Surely *that* was what the voluntary sector did well? The limitations of the Connexions service were not Ross's responsibility, though local authorities did have the power to pick the most suitable people to run them.

The Rathbone project had been through a "one-off funding stream", she said, and there had been no intention to continue it. And while she recognised such "engagement" work was necessary she believed it was best for outreach workers of this type to hand young people on to Connexions as soon as possible, rather than working with them.

"My view is there comes a point where you have to progress that young person," she told me. "It isn't always healthy for that young person to only maintain a relationship with one adult. Once they get to a point where they do go to college or a training programme, part of the process for them is learning to build relationships with other adults."

To have come from the warmth of Julie's relationships with the young people she met to the aridity of this council-speak struck me as profoundly depressing. She did have a point: that the voluntary sector's strength is in winning the confidence of young people and persuading them to come in off the streets, as it were. And she was right, too, that the statutory Connexions service was supposed to then help them to find the right way forward. But my experience was that it just didn't work like that. Real people, real vulnerable people who had had little in their lives that lasted and who had rarely met an adult who believed in them, didn't necessarily react well to being "progressed". What they needed, perhaps more than anything, was some continuity and some stability in their lives. Several times, I was privileged to witness a young person whose life had genuinely been turned around by a strong relationship with an adult who had believed in them, and who had stuck with them. Elvige and Lisa were prime examples, and Sandra potentially was another – though Julie's disappearance was unlikely to encourage her to persist with her college plans.

This was nothing new. People who worked with young people had made the point time and time again, to no avail. The words of one contributor to a recent inquiry into engaging teenagers rang very true: "Many do not have a critical friend. Many do not have people to inspire them, apart from Wayne Rooney, media stars or people on the estate who make loads of money by dealing. They have to feel that the system has a place for them. If that does not happen, we will not make any headway."

OUTREACH IN BARNSLEY

"Don't worry about the carpets," said Debbie, a trim, pretty woman in her late thirties or early forties, as she opened the door to her family's stone bungalow. "They're all about to be changed."

I had accompanied Karl Lyons, an outreach worker in Barnsley, to see Debbie's daughter Kelly, who had not been to school for some time. If I was surprised to find myself in such well-appointed surroundings – the house was beautifully decorated with rural views, my first impression of Kelly was even more perplexing. Small and slight, she was wearing what I assumed was a stiff blonde wig with a layered helmet giving way to a straight cascade over her shoulders and down her back. Its heavy fringe was cut at an angle so it hid one eye. What little I could see of her face was obscured by thick black eye liner, too much blusher and pink lipstick. I had the impression she was wearing the wig and the make-up like a protective shield.

Kelly, who was 15, said she had stopped going to school because she was bullied: "I was picked on because the boys preferred me to the other girls. One time they grabbed me in the corridor and tried to scrub my make-up off. But the teachers didn't do much. The head used to walk into school and out with me, and then later on I had lessons on my own."

The family had other problems too. They had been forced to move nine times in three years, Debbie told us, partly as a result of trouble with neighbours and partly because they needed specially adapted accommodation "for my husband's problems". The current house was privately rented and had five bedrooms and three bathrooms to accommodate the couple and four children; the bills paid by benefits. I did not ask what those "problems" were, and when later on Debbie's husband wandered in for a chat I was still none the wiser.

It was Kelly's GCSE year, and although Karl had told me she was quite bright there was little prospect of her taking exams. He had helped her get a place to do hairdressing at Barnsley College, but she was having second thoughts. Maybe she would do public services instead, she said, though she looked an unlikely candidate for a course that involved outdoor pursuits. Karl was unruffled: "There's no harm in applying," he said. "You can always make a decision later." No, Kelly decided, she'd stick with hairdressing after all. She gave the impression she was rowing back from doing anything at all, possibly out of sheer terror. Karl had almost to drag her to the hairdressing interview, she said, but it was okay once she got there.

Karl seemed philosophical about the interview. He had spent more than an hour talking through Kelly's options with her that day, only to come away with the situation unchanged. Anyone doing this job had to be endowed either with an almost saintly serenity or with complete detachment, I thought.

In Karl's view, those pupils who were likely to drop out could be identified much earlier: "You could do it in year 7, from family patterns, attitude and attainment. But until you make it something that's measurable and that schools are accountable for, it won't happen. If you start an at-risk list and begin to chip away at these attitudes early on, by the time you get to year 11 that list will have shrunk," he said. It would cost money, but not as much as it cost to have one ex-pupil in 10 drop out.

Karl had been working on some research into teenage pregnancies in the area. These too could be predicted, he said: young girls who were poor school attenders, who had mental health issues or whose own mothers had given birth young were more likely to become teenage mothers themselves.

A few months later I met up again with Karl, and I asked how Kelly was doing. She never went to college, he told me.

Conclusions

After a year following the lives of this little group of young people, certain incidents, certain phrases, stuck in the mind. Ricky, lifting his eyes from the table as his mother described how he tried to push his jumper down his throat at school one day and saying quite simply, without any particular emotion: "I didn't want to live any more. That was when Grandma died." The young man who, when asked why his only ambition was to live on benefits, responded by telling his Yorkshire training scheme boss about his workless father: "And 'e's got one thing ovver thee – 'e'll not dee o' stress." The head teacher who, leaning towards me almost conspiratorially, confessed: "Off the record, nobody cares."

This last, delivered in a tone that suggested the head did care but felt as if he was throwing his small voice into a hurricane, was particularly perplexing. Nobody? His point was that governments were too busy worrying about raising standards for the majority, about hitting those targets that were hittable and thereby keeping the output of the statistical mill moving in the right direction, to worry about the marginal and the hard-to-help. A slogan often used by British ministers in the late1990s came to mind: the many, not the few. It was meant, of course, to convey the idea that the voice of the ordinary, hard-working majority should be heard above that of the overprivileged minority. But every nation has its underprivileged minority, too.

What struck me was that, actually, it wasn't only the government that was looking the other way: many of the families I met were doing the same, in a sense. As one of my professional interviewees put it: "There isn't an army of people out there in rocking chairs with shawls on going: 'Oh my God, I need someone to rescue me.' They're living their lives." For the most part, the people I met were doing just that: getting along, muddling through, coping. Only occasionally did anyone express despair over a workless life, and those who did were usually professionals rather than the marginalised or the unemployed.

Maybe, then, we had all been worrying about nothing? If politicians in their speeches would rather focus the upbeat on policy areas where they could claim great progress, and if those languishing on benefits or education allowances without clear plans weren't shouting about it either, one option would be to leave them to it. The black economy would absorb some of them, some of the time – Ricky, trotting round Collyhurst flogging suspect DVDs, or the youth of Barnsley offering a going rate of a ton to "do" a speed camera. The benefits system would continue to carry them as it had before, in some cases for decades despite endless headlines about welfare-to-work schemes and threats to abolish the "golden back". But of course it wasn't that simple. Even if neither the state nor the families concerned really wanted to care, they had to. Oddly, a decade of economic growth had thrown the workless into sharp relief against a background of unfilled jobs, skill shortages and economic migration. It was not in times of crisis that the marginalised stood out most, but in times of prosperity. The danger, as the gathering clouds began to deposit their load across Europe and the US, was not so much that they would start marching, Jarrow-style, upon their state administrations, but that they would just fade away, the forgotten rump at the back of the dole queue, hopelessly lost among a crowd of much more presentable, better-qualified applicants.

While the economic sun still shone, this group of outsiders inside society had stood out painfully. Action had to be taken. And as the economic boom in the Western world came to an end, the policy initiatives drawn up in times of prosperity and aimed at reaching this embarrassing minority reached their peak. If the UK administration did not care, it was making a pretty good fist of looking as if it did. Everywhere I went, I saw activity. Voluntary sector organisations paid to trawl the streets or knock on doors day after day to winkle out

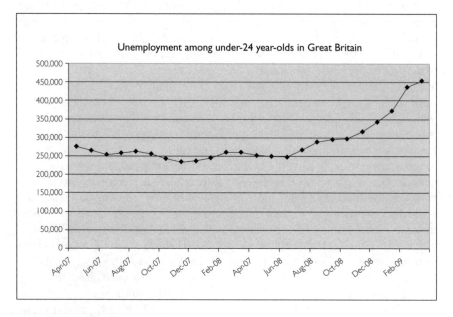

Figure 7 Rising joblessness.

Source: Nomis data: Claimant count.

sleepy, out-of-work teenagers and drag them to a centre to be taught literacy, or life skills. Public sector organisations frantically counting bodies every autumn to try to put the best gloss on the activities of the previous summer's school leavers. Vocational training companies paid to push young people through programmes and present them with certificates that said they were safe to lift heavy weights. Lord Young, the Minister for Skills and Apprenticeships, talked about the mistakes made in the recession of the early 1980s, when a whole generation were left to rot without formal qualifications, and he was right. It sometimes seemed the teenagers I met suffered not a dearth of lifelines, but an excess. The inescapable, frustrating and rather uncomfortable fact was that some of them were extremely hard to help.

Why, then? If some young people did not welcome with open arms the attempts of officialdom to give them a kick-start, why not? The bigger picture was that some communities, some parts of communities, had not adapted well to change. The middle class, always better suited to the types of job which required clean finger nails, was bound to slip more easily into a world dominated by services, office work and sales. Girls, perhaps given additional motivation by post-war equal opportunities legislation, found it relatively easy to locate their place in this changing labour market. Ethnic minorities, often seeing education as a key to opportunity, had begun to creep up the exam league tables in relation to their white classmates – which left, for the most part, white working class boys rudderless on a hostile sea.

That is to oversimplify, of course. While labour market change had favoured presentable, well-qualified young women with communication skills, some young women from the most marginalised communities still lacked those skills. While the brightest young people from ethnic minorities took good advantage of the education system, there were plenty who were not equipped to do so. And the labour market was not the only major piece of the social land-scape that changed irrevocably in the half-century after the Second World War. Increasing fluidity in families, instability even, disproportionately affected young women who more and more often found themselves facing motherhood without a reliable partner or a household income.

Yet in many ways it was the young, white, working class men who seemed most stuck. When I spoke to young mothers and their support workers in Barnsley about motherhood, most of them said they grew up knowing the world had changed and it wasn't all going to be hearts and flowers. When I spoke to young white working class men, they tended to see the world of work in quite a traditional way, to say they thought the best way forward would be to get some sort of skilled job. A graph in the 1996 *Leitch Review of Skills*, which set the UK government's agenda for the next 15 years, told the story more poignantly than words. A vertical line for the status quo, and on the plus side of it a row of bars indicating where demand for skills would grow: Management, Professional, Technical, Personal Services, Sales. And on the minus side: Administrative, Skilled Trades, Machine Operatives, Elementary.

The gap between perception and reality seemed huge. There had always been young men who were underqualified, unfocused and lacking in a sense of direction, but in the past the labour market used to mop them up somehow, by and large. Today's labour market could not do that, and it was easy to see why.

It was hardly surprising that young men whose fathers had never moved on after their skilled trades disappeared 20 years ago should be at a loss about their own futures. Yet what was striking was the way they continued to evaluate their status and self-esteem by reference to a world – the world of masculine, muscle-driven work – that was shrinking fast. In such a situation it was surely incumbent on the state to fill the gap, to try to move these outdated mental pictures of the world from where they were to where they needed to be. That simply had not happened. Quite the reverse, in fact. The education system had spent years coming to terms – slowly – with the need to provide its less academic charges with some skills that might be useful in the workplace. Yet it had not spent nearly so much time, it seemed, coming to terms with what the workplace might actually look like in the future. New programmes for boys who didn't shine at school tended to be dominated by construction trades, or manufacturing, or engineering, while what most of those young men really needed were personal and communication skills. They needed to be taught that a job in an office, in a shop or on the phone could be for them. It would not be fair to say schools never tried. One careers teacher talked of her frustration at the impossibility of getting what she termed "the construction lads" to consider other, potentially more fruitful avenues. Yet the line of least resistance was too often taken, and those who were supposed to be older and wiser allowed themselves to be led by the young and uninitiated along routes that led nowhere. The advantage, for their teachers and college tutors, was that the ends of those cul-de-sacs were outside their bailiwicks. If, to be blunt, a lad with an indifferent school record was safely shepherded through a vocational course and into college, that spelled success for his school. If the same lad was ushered through a college course and out of the door at the end with a certificate, that was a positive result for the college. If the lad then turned up at the dole office on the following Monday morning, it was nobody's business but his own.

The education system needed to start to get to grips with what employers really needed. Schools needed to focus much harder on the "soft" skills so often lacked by 16 year-old males. Colleges needed to offer courses which qualified them to do jobs that actually existed. Perhaps there needed to be a little more stick; a little less carrot. Despite years of endless talk about the "skills gap" and about how education was not meeting the needs of the modern labour market; despite repeated claims that colleges were about to become "demand-led" by employers rather than "supply-led" by aspiring actors and beauticians, very little seemed to be happening about it. I was pulled up short by David Willetts, a free market Conservative politician, when he defended the right of a girl who had never done acting to take a publicly funded performing arts course. He had a point: if she had lacked the ability to communicate clearly and confidently, it might have helped her a lot. But perhaps she needed to be told the course was more likely to get her a job in a call centre than on the stage. Perhaps she would have grown disillusioned and dropped out if she'd been told that; but maybe she would have chosen a course that could have earned her a decent amount of money, if someone had taken the trouble to tell her what sort of course that might be. The carrot, for many young people contemplating a couple of years at college, was not a decent wage at the end of the line but £30 a week in maintenance allowances right now. With no benefits available and – increasingly in these times – no jobs either, even that quite meagre income was a serious draw. But no-one, neither they nor their teachers nor their college tutors, was focusing on any prize much further down the road than that.

Employers, too, needed to play a part. Most of the ones who were prepared to talk to me had already heard that message, and even they would have been reluctant to commit to taking a quota of school leavers, because in their view they too often weren't up to it. But if the world of work continued to sit on the sidelines, wringing its hands and bemoaning the failings of the young, nothing would change. As one of my interviewees put it, what was needed was a reinvention of the brickie's labourer, or the driver's mate. Older employees needed to be asked to help younger ones along with a steadying hand on the shoulder; possibly also the occasional metaphorical kick up the backside. That was how it used to be done, and although the modern world would have different requirements, the concept could easily be reworked.

The most heartening turnarounds I saw – certainly those that lasted – were the ones that happened because a young person who was floundering found a reliable adult who believed in them. Someone like Elvige's Connexions worker Lisa Marcelle, who, it would not be an exaggeration to say, saved her from potential disaster. Instead of spiralling into truancy, family disintegration and homelessness, Elvige was, by the time I met her, a confident young adult living an independent life. She did not believe that would have been the case if she had never met Lisa. Sometimes I doubted it – she had something about her that seemed to say she believed in herself – and sometimes she still faltered, not doing as well as she hoped at college; dropping out for a year – but at the age of 18 she still had Lisa to turn to when things got rough. So many times I heard people say mentoring, usually by an older person outside the immediate family, was the key to helping young people who had lost their sense of direction, or who maybe had never found one in the first place. Quite a small change could make a huge difference – another example was the girl who dropped out, had a baby young, got in with the wrong crowd, then got offered a job in her local chip shop – where the owner was much more interested in people than she was in frying fish. For years, Toni had been trouble. Almost overnight, she saw herself differently – and so did everyone else. She admitted quite frankly she didn't see working in a chip shop as the most wonderful job in the world, but she was quite clear it had been the making of her. One of the older staff had become her "Auntie Brenda"; she often did a bit of shopping for another who was getting on a bit. Perhaps the labour market needed not just the young, but also the old?

Certainly it needed the young, though, for it was in no-one's interests to allow another generation to drift by without really engaging, overtaken as the economy improved by a new batch of college leavers, or by a new set of willing 40 year-olds from Lithuania or Romania. Yet those whose grip on the mainstream world was most precarious needed mentors who understood them, to whom they could relate: "Chris is [my role model] because he was bad in the past and now he's good," one young man told an inquiry run by Rathbone on 14–19 year-olds. "Chris. Chris got us off the streets. He got us started on something." Julie Ollerhead, who drove around Manchester with 17 year-old Jack as her guide, looking for disengaged youth to the sound of the Lancashire Hotpots, had been abandoned on the St Helen's Town Hall steps at the age of six and subsequently brought up by her grandparents. She thought having been a single parent to two sons was more relevant experience; I thought Jack, who was in foster care, would perhaps feel she could see how his life was. She'd been there too, she didn't feel she'd been held back by it; she believed in her charges with a passion that allowed her to give them a severe talking to, when necessary; she was always, always at the end of a phone.

If there could be an army of Julies, Chrises and Lisas and Auntie Brendas out there, the problems of the young would be much diminished. But these would be just practical solutions to the most easily reachable parts of the problem. The underlying issues, the shifting tectonic plates of social change, would not be so easily fixable. The world had changed since the grandparents of these young people first went to work. It was no longer so easy for a young man to leave school and find an unskilled job from which, if he were bright and keen, he could progress. It was no longer so easy for a young woman growing up on a council estate to dream – not realistically, at least – of a long marriage and children with a man who went off to work every morning and brought at least part of his wages home every week. And quite frankly, there was a lot about those changes that few people would mourn. The old world was a more predictable world, but it was also a constrained world, in which the young had fewer choices and put up with what they got. One had only to glance at the social studies from Yorkshire and East London in the early post-war period to discover the work was often dirty, unhealthy and even dangerous, and the long marriages often very far from perfect.

Yet there was no getting away from the fact that for the young the loss of certainty, the loss of stability at home and the loss of a clear path ahead – even a pretty unprofitable path – was serious. This was where the wider debate needed to take place. What could be done, in this world, now – the world where half of all marriages ended in divorce and where no-one got a job for life – to offer the young some sense of hope, some belief that all would be well?

For the key to success, of course, is the belief that it will come. We should make no bones about the fact that most of these young people had the odds stacked against them. There would always be some people for whom that was the case. And the route to success against the odds was fight, not flight. To adapt to failure is to accept it and too often that was what the young people I met were being taught to do. That comment about how people weren't sitting in their chairs waiting for help came to mind often: on the surface it seemed a good thing that they were adapting, making do, getting on with their lives, that they didn't spend their days constantly asking what they had to do to get out, to find some better way to live. The world would be a very uncomfortable place if all those young people rebelled against their lot: schools complained, as it was, that too many hit out and were impossible to control. Yet perhaps in some ways those with that bit of rebellion in them – some of them, at least – were the ones who had the most chance of coming through. The ones who accepted failure would always bump along the bottom.

There it was, then. Perhaps there wasn't much the rest of the world could do about it. Yet there were some things. They might not be comfortable things, or straightforward things, but there were marginal attitudinal shifts that could start to make a difference. The head teachers I interviewed admitted candidly they knew expectations in their schools were too low. One of them used the phrase "cuddling and muddling", the belief there wasn't much to be done for "these poor children". The old belief that they were good for nothing and needed kicking into shape had given way to a more caring response that still did them few favours. They were still seen as being good for nothing, but now their teachers didn't all think it was their own fault.

Perhaps the seeds of the solution to all this lay not in the family, nor in the school system, nor in the colleges, nor even in the work place, but in all of them; in all of us. How was it that as a society we learned to accept failure so willingly? What was surprising about the young people I met – some born into households without work, some to parents who were absent, or drunk or violent, some attending schools where they were chivvied along without any great ambition, pushed on into colleges and programmes that were sometimes not much more than warehouses? What was surprising was not that they failed. Of course they failed. Their whole lives had pointed and prodded them towards failure. What was surprising was that they coped, somehow, with that failure. What was astonishing was that some of them *didn't* fail. And the key to not failing, it seemed to me, was self-belief. Elvige, brought from Africa at 10 with no English, missing whole years of school, forced to endure a fractured and fractious family life, had it in spades, from where I still know not. Yet it carried her through, and it would do so in the future too. Somehow as a nation it seemed we had lost the collective capacity to do what she did. We had lost the inclination to seek out the positive, to think things could get better and to think they would continue to do so.

Recent travails aside, the story of the post-war era had in many respects been one of success: decade after decade of economic growth, of increasing home ownership, of improved healthcare and educational standards, an ever-increasing proportion of the population attending university. There was much to celebrate. And yet we seemed to have ground to a halt when it came to acknowledging the possibility of social progress for the poorest, the most marginalised. It would be facile to say there was no "them" and "us" any more – "It's adversarial – big time", a community worker on an East London estate told me. Yet somehow we seemed all to have united in this belief that nothing could change for the better. It might seem perverse to make a plea for optimism during a period of economic gloom. Yet the key to a solution, at least for the young, was in us all. If they were born to parents who told them they could do anything; if they went to schools where the staff assumed their futures were bright, and to colleges where they were offered real chances to achieve; if they met employers who saw their potential rather than their shortcomings; if they believed in themselves, then – and only then – real, lasting, positive change would start to happen.

Footnote – outcomes

Ashley and Claire, the two girls from Wombwell near Barnsley, had been picked out at school as being at risk of dropping out when they left. Actually, I never thought there was much chance of Ashley doing that. Even though she was on her school's special needs register she had a sort of fierce determination I thought would carry her through, and she told me she had always wanted to work with children. Her dad had his doubts about the benefits of college, but her mum was keen. Claire was less certain what she wanted, but she liked school and had rarely been in trouble. In the end, both of them took the standard route into college courses.

A month after Ashley started at Barnsley College on a level one childcare course, I went down there one lunch time and met her in the reception of her building. It was her afternoon off, and she was dressed in red polo shirt and black trousers, in preparation for an afternoon shift at work. As well as going to college, she had also found herself a part-time job in the children's play area at a local mining heritage centre.

In a café down the road which turned out to be owned by her friend's uncle, she tucked into a huge plate of chicken curry and updated me on the past couple of months – she'd spent the summer in Somerset, where her dad worked, and had only come back in time for college.

She was vague about her GCSE results: "I did ..." she pulled a face, "crap." I prompted her: What subjects did she take? She looked blank. English and maths, I suggested? She nodded. "English and maths. And health and social. I got two U's and two G's." What did she get the G's in? She shook her head. "I don't know."

"So, I'm entry level childcare," she continued cheerfully, pulling a chip from the enormous pile on her plate: "Just a really, really small portion", she had told her friend's uncle when we arrived. "It should take me two years to get qualified, and if I want I can stay on. I don't think so, though – I don't know yet. I might do. After that, I would be level two."

If Ashley wanted to work unsupervised with children she would need to get to level three, which would take three years. Despite some doubts – the work was classroom-based and sometimes boring, she said – she seemed optimistic.

"There's about eight in the group, and they're all nice. We have millions of teachers. Next year, we get to work with children."

The big news from Ashley, though, was that her older sister, recently engaged, was expecting a baby. Ashley was thrilled – not least because she was going to be a godmother. She was off, then, on one of her long, enthusiastic storytellings: "I've never seen my dad so pleased. And I'm going to be a bridesmaid when they get married, but that won't be for a bit, now. I wanted them to do it at Christmas so it'd be a white wedding, in the snow. But they're going to get married in the summer. We've already got a cot, and she's picked a pram. My dad said he'd pay for it. I don't care if it's a boy or a girl. I just want it to be all right, you know? I know I shouldn't say it, but I just want it to be okay. I think it'll be a boy, though. With a girl, you lean forwards, and with a boy, you lean backwards. She's leaning backwards. Not in a nasty way, but I hope it'll be a boy."

Claire, too, seemed full of confidence when I met up with her the following day. Walking up the main road towards me from "Rid", the bit of green space where she hung out with her friends after college, she looked older. At home, she was usually in Bart Simpson slippers but today she had black skinny jeans, a lip-ring and a t-shirt with skulls on it in different colours – the cool effect only slightly modified by a SpongeBob SquarePants badge and the fact that she'd just spilled candle wax down her jeans while doing drama.

In the end Claire did not go on the performing arts course she applied for, but she was enrolled instead on a taster course called The Mix, which allowed her to do both arts and media and another subject. When I'd last seen her she had been planning to do animal care, but in the end she went for catering instead.

Back at her house, her dad Mark greeted her cheerfully. He didn't see so much of her these days, he said. "I do like to see you now and again," he said to Claire. "We have a laugh. You've been coming home and having a shower, then going to bed."

I asked about her GCSE results. "G, G, G, U, U, G," she intoned, mock-solemn.

"It was a little disappointing," Mark said. "It could have been a bit better, couldn't it?" Claire nodded.

Mark thought the course a good thing: "It gives you a taste of various things, but then after 12 months you can pick one. At your age, I didn't have a clue."

Not all Claire's friends had found their feet.

"Jacob White is doing construction at Sheffield College. Jimmy isn't going to college, though."

"What's he doing?" Mark asked.

"Just lazing around the house."

"He must have rich parents."

Even though she'd told me she didn't fancy catering, Claire was really enjoying the course and had decided she'd like to train as a chef. She had brought home quiche, Eccles cakes, pizzas and sticky toffee pudding, and though the toffee apple muffins went out for the birds, most of them were good. Claire was planning a meal for her grandparents' wedding anniversary: "Maybe a nice stew, or something."

"I've had a couple of disasters, like nearly setting the college kitchen on fire. I left a tea-towel near the oven. The chef was shouting at me because I didn't wash this plate right …" She tailed off for a minute. "I love being told what to do."

Mark laughed. "I wouldn't say that. You like being *shown* what to do."

Claire didn't come back at him. "We have to do it *now*. We have half an hour to prepare one big meal. If I can go to a second year of catering and cooking, I'll be a qualified chef after two or three years. I actually want to be a chef. At the beginning of the lesson I'm right bubbly, but when we get down to cooking I'm really focused."

So for Claire and for Ashley things had turned out fine. Both were still well short of their seventeenth birthdays, though, and what the future might hold for them was anyone's guess. There seemed a good prospect, though, that both would gain useful qualifications and maybe find jobs in their chosen fields.

The end of my research did not mark the end of anyone's story, of course. In some ways, little had changed for most since I first met them. The Barnsley cohort were the most successful, but perhaps I could have predicted that. Tom, who had struggled to find a plumbing apprenticeship, went to college a year late to do a building technician's course, and when I last spoke to his mum Karen he was doing well and enjoying the work. Karen, who had now almost completed the first year of a degree in youth work, was delighted that Tom was seriously considering following her example and going to university. He had previously rejected such a move because he felt it would take him away from his friends, but a combination of success at college and the deepening recession had led him to feel three more years in education might be the best way forward.

In London Will ended the year much as he started it, still hoping for stardom. After the excitement of his trip to Argentina to film a television programme, he resumed his old life with his daughter and his "complicated" relationship. The last time I spoke to him he was back at his old further education college in East London, doing a short-term media course and hoping to break into film-making.

Elvige, who had dropped out of sixth form college, was hoping her work experience would win her a place on a youth studies degree course. She was working hard at the Mayor's office and saving for a trip back to Togo, which she had not visited since she left at the age of 10. Yasmin, who seemed to be finding her feet when she started a business studies course at college, had dropped out and wasn't working.

In Manchester, Rachel was out of work again. After a spell as a charity mugger in Wales, she did manage briefly to get a job in a bar. But that only lasted a week or so, and after that she found herself back on benefits. She was still trying to get custody of her children, and was hopeful she might be allowed to bring them back to live with her in a few more months. Ricky completed a brief construction skills course and was given a file of certificates bearing his surname but a different first name, saying he could work on a building site. By that time the name on the certificates was largely academic, for most of the sites in his area had either stopped work or weren't recruiting. In the spring of 2009 he set his sights on a job fixing windscreens, with a company where a relative worked. They gave him some hope they would take him on – but said that would not happen until business picked up. So a major milestone for Ricky when he turned 18 was signing on for the first time at the dole office.

Had they achieved what they would have liked to have achieved, during the year? Not really. Ashley had fulfilled her ambition to do childcare; Claire when I first met her wanted either a job or a place at college to do performing arts. Tom would have liked an apprenticeship, but none was available. Ricky and Rachel wanted to get jobs and earn money – and both of them did earn money, but only briefly and not through what most people would see as "proper" employment. Will, too, would have said he wanted a good job with good money – but none of the jobs available were what he wanted. Elvige would have liked to have done better at college, but with luck she would achieve her dream of going to university regardless. Yasmin wanted to succeed at college so she could start her own business, but the last time I spoke to her, her future looked uncertain.

Bibliography

Albemarle, D., Countess of (1960) *The Albemarle Report on the Youth Service*. London: HMSO.

Bailey, G. (2006) *Re-engaging Young People: an evaluation of the neighbourhood support fund*. York: Joseph Rowntree Foundation.

Bentley, M. (1985) *Born 1896: childhood in Clayton and working in Manchester and Cheshire*. Manchester: Neil Richardson.

Blanden, J., Gregg, P. and Machin, S. (2005) *Intergenerational Mobility in Europe and North America*. London: Sutton Trust.

Bowlby, J. (1969). *Attachment and Loss (vol. 1) Attachment*. London: Hogarth Press.

Bowlby, J. (1973) *Attachment and Loss (vol. 2) Separation: anxiety and anger*. London: Hogarth Press.

Bowlby, J. (1980) *Attachment and Loss (vol. 3) Loss: sadness and depression*. London: Hogarth Press.

Bynner, J., Ferri, E. and Shepherd, P. (1997) *Twenty-Something in the 1990s: getting on, getting by, getting nowhere*. London: Ashgate.

Bynner, J. and Parsons, S. (2002) "Social exclusion and the transition from school to work: the case of young people not in education, employment or training (NEET)". *Journal of Vocational Behaviour* 60: 289–309.

Cassen, R. and Kingdon, G. (2007) *Tackling Low Educational Achievement*. London School of Economics and York: Joseph Rowntree Foundation.

Castells, M. (1996) *The Rise of the Network Society*. Oxford: Blackwell.

Centre for Social Justice (2007) *Breakthough Britain*. London: The Conservative Party.

Clements, A., Fletcher, D. and Parry-Langdon, N. (2008) *Three Years On: survey of the development and emotional wellbeing of children and young people*. London: Office for National Statistics.

Coles, B., Britton. L. and Hicks, L. (2004) *Inter-agency work and the Connexions Service: Joseph Rowntree Foundation findings*. York: Joseph Rowntree Foundation.

Coles, B., Hutton, S., Bradshaw, J., Craig, G., Godfrey, C. and Johnson J. (2002) *Estimating the Costs of Being Not in Education, Employment or Training at Age 16–18*. Sheffield: Department for Education and Skills.

Dennis, N., Henriques, F. and Slaughter, C. (1956, 1969) *Coal is Our Life: an analysis of a Yorkshire mining village*. London: Eyre and Spottiswoode. [2nd edn 1969 – London: Tavistock].

Department of Children, Schools and Families (2006). *Social mobility: narrowing social class attainment gaps*. London: DCSF.

Department of Children, Schools and Families (2002, 2008) "GCSE results by ethnicity and free school meals". Available online at: http://www.dcsf.gov.uk/rsgateway/DB/SFR/s000822/

SFR322008-allKS4noNITables.xls#'Table A1'!A1 and http://www.dcsf.gov.uk/rsgateway/
DB/SFR/s000448/tables49-52-rev.xls (accessed 8 June 2009).

Department of Children, Schools and Families (2009) *Breaking the Link between Disadvantage and
Low Attainment – Everyone's Business.* London: DCSF. Available online at http://publications.
teachernet.gov.uk/eOrderingDownload/00357-2009.pdf (accessed 23 March 2009).

Elliott, J. G., Hufton, N., Illushin L., and Willis, W. (2001) "'The kids are doing all right':
differences in parental satisfaction, expectation, and attribution in St Petersburg, Sunderland,
and Kentucky". *Cambridge Journal of Education* 31(2): 179–204.

Engels, F. (1926) *The Condition of the Working Class in England in 1844.* London: Allen and
Unwin.

Evans, J., Meyer, D., Pinney, A. and Robinson, B. (2009) *Second Chances: re-engaging young people
in education and training.* London: Barnardo's.

Ferri, E., Bynner, J. and Wadsworth, M. (2003) *Changing Britain, Changing Lives: three generations
at the turn of the century.* London: Institute of Education, University of London.

Foote Whyte, W. F. (1943) *Street Corner Society: the social structure of an Italian slum.* Chicago:
University of Chicago Press.

Frosh, S., Phoenix, A., and Pattman, R. (2002) *Young Masculinities: understanding boys in contem-
porary society.* London: Palgrave.

Furlong, A. (2006) "Education and the reproduction of class-based inequalities", in Inglis, D.
and Bone, J. (eds), *Social Stratification.* London: Routledge.

Furlong, A. (2006) "Not a very NEET solution: representing problematic labour market transitions among early school leavers". *Work, Employment and Society* 20: 553–69.

Furlong, A. and Cartmel, F. (2004) *Vulnerable Young Men in Fragile Labour Markets: employment,
unemployment and the search for long-term security.* York: York Publishing.

Furlong, A. and Guidikova, I. (2001) *Transitions of Youth Citizenship in Europe: culture, subculture
and identity.* Strasbourg: Council of Europe.

Gordon, I. (1996) "Family structure, educational achievement and the inner city". *Urban Studies*
33: 407–24.

Hayes, J. and Hopson, B. (1971) *Careers Guidance.* London: Heinemann.

Hoggarth, L. and Payne, M. (2005) "Evidence based or evidence buried? – how far have the
implications of the national impact study of the work of Connexions with young people at
risk informed the Green Paper?". *Youth and Policy* 90: 43–58.

Hoggarth, L. and Smith, D. (2004) *Understanding the Impact of Connexions on Young People at Risk.*
Nottingham: Department for Education and Skills research report 607.

Jephcott, A. P. (1942) *Girls Growing Up.* London: Faber & Faber.

Jephcott, A. P. (1948) *Rising Twenty.* London: Faber & Faber.

Jephcott, A. P. (1954) *Some Young People: a study of adolescent boys and girls.* London: George Allen
and Unwin.

Learning and Skills Council (2007) "Further education and work-based learning statistics
(2005–6)". Available online at: http://readingroom.lsc.gov.uk/lsc/National/nat-keyfactsfee
nrolmentsbyareaoflearning-da-200506-26july2007.zip and http://readingroom.lsc.gov.uk/
lsc/National/nat-keyfactswbllearnernumbersbyareaoflearning-da-200506-26july2007.zip
(accessed 22 March 2009).

Leitch Review of Skills (2006) *Prosperity for All in the Global Economy: world class skills.* London:
HM Treasury. Available online at: http://webarchive.nationalarchives.gov.uk/+/http://www.
hm-treasury.gov.uk/d/leitch_finalreport051206.pdf (accessed 11 August 2009).

MacDonald, R. and Marsh, J. (2001) "Disconnected youth?". *Journal of Youth Studies* 4(4):
373–91.

MacDonald, R. and Marsh, J. (2002) "Crossing the Rubicon: youth transitions, poverty, drugs and social exclusion". *International Journal of Drug Policy* 13: 27–38.

MacDonald, R. and Marsh, J. (2005) *Disconnected Youth? Growing up in Britain's Poor Neighbourhoods*. Basingstoke: Palgrave.

MacDonald, R. and Shildrick, T. (2007) "Biographies of exclusion: poor work, poor education and poor transitions". *International Journal of Lifelong Learning* 26(5): 589–604.

MacDonald, R. and Shildrick, T. (2007) "Street corner society: leisure careers, youth (sub)culture and social exclusion". *Leisure Studies* 26(3): 339–55.

MacDonald, R., Shildrick, T., Webster, C. and Simpson, D. (2005) "Growing up in poor neighbourhoods: the significance of class and place in the extended transitions of 'socially excluded' young adults". *Sociology*, 39(5): 873–91.

McRae, H. (1994) "Too young and too precious to waste". *Independent*, 12 May.

McRobbie, A. (1990) *Feminism and Youth Culture*. London: Palgrave MacMillan.

Mungham, G. and Pearson, G. (eds) (1976) *Working Class Youth Culture*. London: Routledge and Kegan Paul.

Office of National Statistics (2005) *Annual Business Inquiry*. Available online at: http://www.statistics.gov.uk/abi/ (accessed 23 March 2009).

Ofsted (2008) *The Impact of Programme-led Apprenticeships*. Available online at: http://www.ofsted.gov.uk/Ofsted-home/Publications-and-research/Browse-all-by/Education/Youth-services-and-careers/Impact-of-programme-led-apprenticeships (accessed 23 March 2009).

Phillips, T. (2005) "Running faster into the same brick wall". *Guardian*, 31 May.

Prince's Trust (2007) *The Cost of Exclusion: counting the cost of youth disadvantage in the UK*. London: Prince's Trust.

Rennison, J., Maguire, S., Middleton, S. and Ashworth, K. (2006) *Young People Not in Education, Employment or Training: evidence from the Education Maintenance Allowance pilots database*. Department for Education and Skills Research Report 628.

Rosenthal, R. and Jacobson, L.(1968) *Pygmalion in the Classroom: teacher expectation and pupils' intellectual development*. New York: Irvington.

Self, A. and Zealey, L. (eds) (2007) *Social Trends 37, 2007 Edition*. London: Office for National Statistics.

Shildrick, T. and MacDonald, R. (2006) "In defence of subculture: young people, leisure and social divisions". *Journal of Youth Studies* 9(2): 125–40.

Social Exclusion Unit (1997) *National Strategy for Neighbourhood Renewal*. Report of Policy Action Team 12: Young People. London: Social Exclusion Unit, The Cabinet Office.

Social Exclusion Unit (1999) *Bridging the Gap: new opportunities for 16–18 year-olds not in education, employment or training*. London: Social Exclusion Unit, The Cabinet Office.

Steedman, H. (2001) *Benchmarking Apprenticeship: UK and Continental Europe compared*. London: Centre for Economic Performance.

Strand, S. and Winston, J. (2008) *Educational Aspirations in Inner City Schools*. Available online at: http://www2.warwick.ac.uk/fac/soc/cedar/staff/stevestrand/strandwinston_inpress.pdf (accessed 24 March 2009).

Strathdee, R. (2005) *Social Exclusion and the Remaking of Social Networks*. London: Ashgate.

Sweeting, H. and West, P. (1996) *The Relationship between Family Life and Young People's Lifestyles*. York: Joseph Rowntree Foundation Social Policy Research Findings.

Williamson, H. (2004) *The Milltown Boys Revisited*. Oxford: Berg.

Willis, P. (1977) *Learning to Labour: how working class kids get working class jobs*. Farnborough, Hants: Saxon House.

Yates, S. and Payne, M. (2006) "Not So NEET? A critique of the use of 'NEET' in setting targets for interventions with young people". *Journal of Youth Studies* 9: 329–44.

Young, M. and Willmott, P. (1957) *Family and Kinship in East London*. London: Routledge and Kegan Paul.